The Upside-Down
Kingdom

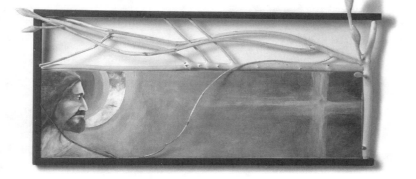

The Upside-Down
Kingdom

25th ANNIVERSARY EDITION

Donald B. Kraybill

Herald
Press

Scottdale, Pennsylvania
Waterloo, Ontario

Library of Congress Cataloging in Publication Data
Kraybill, Donald B.
  The upside-down kingdom / Donald B. Kraybill.—25th anniversary ed.
    p. cm.
  Includes bibliographical references and indexes.
  ISBN 0-8361-9236-2 (pbk. : alk. paper)
  1. Kingdom of God. 2. Bible. N.T. Gospels—Criticism, interpretation,
etc. 3. Sociology, Biblical. 4. Sociology, Christian (Mennonite)
5. Christian life—Mennonite authors. I. Title.
  BT94.K7 2003
  231.7'2—dc21   2003006054

All author royalties from this book are contributed to a nonprofit foundation for distribution to charitable causes.

Scripture quotations are from the *New Revised Standard Version* of the Bible,
copyright © 1989, by the Division of Christian Education of the National
Council of Churches of Christ in the USA, and used by permission.

THE UPSIDE-DOWN KINGDOM
Copyright © 1978, 1990, 2003 by Herald Press, Scottdale, Pa. 15683
    Published 1978. Revised editions 1990, 2003.
    Published simultaneously in Canada by Herald Press,
    Waterloo, Ont. N2L 6H7. All rights reserved
Library of Congress Catalog Card Number: 2003006054
International Standard Book Number: 0-8361-9236-2
Printed in the United States of America
Cover and Book Design by Merrill R. Miller
Cover Art by Paul Grout
Editorial Services by Michael A. King, Cascadia Publishing House.

12 11 10 09 08 07 06 05 04   10 9 8 7 6 5 4 3 2

To order or request information, please call
1-800-759-4447 (individuals); 1-800-245-7894 (trade).
Website: www.heraldpress.com

For those
"who have turned the world upside down . . .
acting against the decrees of Caesar,
saying that there is
another king,
Jesus."
—Acts 17:6-7

And for
Helen Brubaker Kraybill
whose generosity—in the midst
of adversity—was boundless.

Contents

Preface

The seed for this book sprouted one summer when I was teaching an adult Bible study. With two days notice, I found myself pinch-hitting for a teacher caught in an emergency. I had been reading John Howard Yoder's, *The Politics of Jesus* and decided to take the class on a five-session tour of Luke's gospel, which Yoder had used extensively. Midway through Luke's story, a class member exclaimed with enthusiasm and exasperation, "Everything here is so upside down!" It was an unshakable image of God's kingdom. That striking picture, which gave birth to the first edition of this book, has intrigued and stayed with me over the years.

I find myself drawn to Jesus and his upside-down kingdom again and again. His creative stories and powerful images keep pulling me back to the reign of God. Rereading the gospel stories in preparation for this twenty-fifth anniversary edition stirred my spirit once again, in ways only Jesus can. I write as a confessing Christian. A close encounter with the life of Jesus takes me to the heart of Christian faith and the very nature of God. For me, Jesus provides the clearest and the fullest disclosure of God's will.

Although the earlier editions form its core and stretches of text remain unchanged, this third edition has been completely revised, line-by-line and word-by-word. Amid the changes and updates, the original argument remains intact: the kingdom of God announced by Jesus was a new order of things that looked upside-down in the midst of Palestinian culture in the first century. Moreover, the kingdom of God continues to have upside-down features as it breaks into diverse cultures around the world today. An abundance of scholarly studies of the social world of Jesus' time have appeared since the first edition. This revision taps many of those rich resources.

Many things have changed since I wrote the first edition, but much remains the same. The organization of the material remains intact. I have revised the text word by word to enhance its clarity and flow. Recent scholarship on Jesus and the synoptic gospels provided new insights for updating some of the chapters. And while I have leaned heavily on the work of many scholars in preparing this edition, it remains a book for lay readers, not for scholars. Whenever possible I have dispensed with academic jargon, trying to tell the story accurately in a lively and creative style.

It is quite a challenge to shrink a big story into a short book. Many paragraphs could easily be expanded into full-length scholarly tomes. But that was not my aim. Quite the opposite, I tried to capture key ideas of the Jesus story and summarize them for students and lay readers. A trail of sources in the endnotes will aid those who want to pursue more in-depth study of particular topics.

There are many books on Jesus with many different spins on his story. The pages that follow show how I have spun the story. I say story because I have crafted the narrative in ways that reflect my interests as an Anabaptist Christian and as a sociologist. As you read this story, two key questions loom large. First, is this a fair reading of the story? If it is, then what do we do with Jesus and his upside-down kingdom? If in fact he points us toward God, how does the vision and message of the kingdom transform our lives for God's honor and glory?

Sometimes it's hard to see Jesus because he comes to us through the filters of twenty centuries of church history. Our images of him may come from storybooks, bumper stickers, or theological words we hardly understand. In many ways, Christians have domesticated Jesus, taming him to fit our culture and time. In retelling the story, I have tried to peel off some of the filters so we can see him more clearly in his own cultural setting. It's of course impossible to reconstruct all the details, but when we remove some of the filters, we often discover a very different Jesus than the one who came to us in Sunday school. He may be a Jesus we never knew before.

The Jesus we find may startle us. He's somewhat irreverent, certainly not a sweet shepherd walking beside the still waters. In fact, he's not carrying any sheep and he stirs the political waters so much that he gets the Roman electric chair. But this is the Jesus who, according to the Gospels, discloses God's will and nature for all time.

I write from an American perspective as a citizen of a super-power nation. In the global context, I am wealthy simply because I live in the United States and hold a professional job. The Jesus story may sound very different to someone who searches for food and shelter everyday. It will carry a different meaning for those serving an endless sentence for murder, drinking dirty water, dying with AIDS, or tortured because of their faith. I have tried to make the story accessible to all regardless of our social location or the burdens we carry, whether they be wealth or poverty, health or illness. Thanks be to God, the story is big enough and filled with grace enough for all of us regardless of our culture or condition.

I have resisted the temptation to make specific applications for several reasons. First, issues and events quickly become dated. Second, readers in local settings, under the guidance of God's spirit, need to discern what the upside-down kingdom means for them in their own context. My task is to tell the story as carefully and creatively as possible, as Jesus did with the parables, letting the listeners apply the meaning to their own setting. Third, the kingdom of God will look quite different in different cultural settings. The issues for readers in a democratic nation will hardly match those of readers who suffer persecution under a brutal tyrant. For all of these reasons I have resisted the lure to spell out specific applications.

Throughout the text I have spoken of the Old Testament rather than of the Hebrew Bible, even though the latter tends to be the more common practice among many scholars. The books of Moses, the prophets, and other writings before Jesus are considered scripture by both Jewish and Christian communities. The two communities, however, interpret and use these same sacred writings quite differently. In one case they are interpreted in light of the Talmud and the ongoing Jewish tradition. Among Christians, these early writings set the stage for Jesus and the formation of the early church. I write as a Christian within this two-testament tradition and thus use the Old Testament label but do it with genuine respect for its central role in Jewish faith and practice.

My debts are heavy to the many friends and colleagues who have helped with this project over the years. I am especially grateful to those who have helped prepare this twenty-fifth anniversary edition. I deeply appreciate the willingness of Herald Press to undertake the project. I have enjoyed the supportive enthusiasm of Levi Miller, Sarah Kehrberg, and other members of the Herald Press team. As he did for the second edition, Michael A. King's editorial skills have given some of my clumsy phrases greater clarity and more poetic beauty. For the efforts and skills of these fine people I am greatly indebted.

Several colleagues—Christina Bucher at Elizabethtown College and Michael R. Cosby, J. E. McDermond, and John Stanley at Messiah College—provided wise counsel and helped me navigate the growing maze of New Testament studies. Anna Piacentini's comments on an earlier draft helped to improve the text in many ways for which I am grateful. I have been blessed with good clerical assistants—Terri Hopkins at Messiah College and Sandy Metzler at Elizabethtown College—who key-stroked the changes and helped at every turn.

Kudos as well to the library staff at both colleges for their assistance in gathering sources. Linda Eberly kindly prepared the creative illustrations. I am especially pleased to have the art of my friend, Paul Grout, grace the front cover. He has captured the meaning of Jesus and the upside-down kingdom in a series of striking images of art. I am truly blessed to have the support and assistance of these kind and generous colleges.

Previous editions of this book have touched thousands of readers in different languages in many countries. Letters of affirmation have come from prisoners, pastors, professors, students, and others in many cultures. I am grateful that the earlier editions have helped to interpret the Jesus story and energize Christians around the world. I hope this edition continues to do likewise. Thanks be to God.

Donald B. Kraybill
Elizabethtown, Pennsylvania
April 2003

The Upside-Down
Kingdom

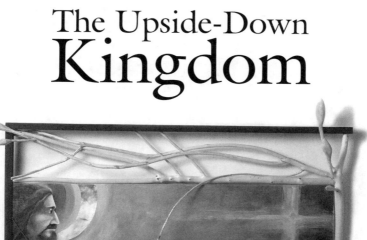

1

Down Is Up

Flat Mountains

The voice of one crying out in the wilderness:
Prepare the way of the Lord,
    make his paths straight.
Every valley shall be filled,
        and every mountain and hill shall be made low,
        and the crooked shall be made straight,
        and the rough ways made smooth;
        and all flesh shall see the salvation of God.
                        —Luke 3:4-6

John the Baptist shouted these words of Isaiah to announce the advent of Jesus. The dramatic pictures portray a revolutionary new kingdom. Paving the way for Jesus, the Baptist describes four surprises of the coming kingdom: full valleys, flat mountains, straight curves, and level bumps. He expects radical shake-ups in the new kingdom. Old ways will shatter beyond recognition. John warns us that the new order, the upside-down kingdom, will transform social patterns but amid the ferment, all flesh will see the salvation of God.

In Mary's song of exaltation, the Magnificat, Mary sings her hopes for the new kingdom. Along with the Baptist, she expects the Messiah to inaugurate an upside-down kingdom filled with surprises.

For the Mighty One has done great things for me, and holy
    is his name.
His mercy is for those who fear him from generation to
    generation.
He has shown strength with his arm;
He has scattered *the proud* in the thoughts of their hearts.

He has put down *the powerful* from their thrones,
and lifted up *the lowly*;
he has filled *the hungry* with good things,
and sent *the rich* away empty.
—Luke 1:49-53, emphasis added

Five types of people are startled and surprised in Mary's vision. Those at the top of the social pyramid—the proud, the rich, and the mighty—topple. Stripped of their thrones, they are scattered and sent away empty. Meanwhile the poor and hungry, at the bottom of the pyramid, take a surprising ride to the top. Mary sings words of hope and judgment. Hope for the lowly, as she describes herself, and judgment for those who trample the helpless.

A poor Galilean peasant girl, Mary expects the messianic kingdom to flip her social world upside down. The rich, mighty, and proud in Jerusalem will be banished. Poor farmers and shepherds in rural Galilee will be exalted and honored. For several centuries the Jewish people had been ruled by outsiders—pagan outsiders. Mary's longing reflects the age-old Jewish yearning for a messiah who will usher in a new kingdom. She spoke for the masses who prayed for the day when the Messiah would expel the pagan invaders and establish the long-awaited kingdom.

An Inverted Kingdom

The central theme in the ministry and teaching of Jesus is the kingdom of God, or as Matthew calls it, the kingdom of heaven. This key idea ties his entire message together. The "kingdom of God" permeates Jesus' ministry, giving it coherence and clarity. It is the undisputed core, the very essence, of his life and teaching.[1]

What did Jesus mean when he announced the advent of the kingdom of God? His fellow Jews expected a political kingdom that would protect and preserve the Jewish faith. Over the centuries, scholars, theologians, and churches have developed different views. Debates on what Jesus meant have swirled down through the ages.

In the pages that follow, we'll explore how the kingdom of God points to an inverted, upside-down way of life that challenges the prevailing social order. It certainly challenged the patterns in ancient Palestinian society and does the same in our world today. We can capture the idea of inversion by thinking of two ladders side by side—one representing the kingdom of God, the other the kingdoms of this world.[2] An inverted relationship between the ladders means that something highly valued on one ladder ranks near the bottom of the other. We find an inversion in the refrain of a Sunday school song when the rain and flood move in opposite directions:

> The rains came down, and the flood came up,
> The rains came down, and the flood came up.

Jesus does not portray the kingdom on the margins of society. He doesn't plead for social avoidance or withdrawal. Nor does he assume that the kingdom and the world split neatly into separate realms. Kingdom action takes place in the world in the middle of the societal ballpark. But it's a different game. Kingdom players follow special rules and heed another coach. Kingdom values challenge the taken-for-granted social ruts and sometimes run against the dominant cultural grain. But don't misunderstand. Kingdom people are not sectarians protesting the larger society just for the sake of being different. Kingdom values, rooted in the deep Love and abiding Grace of God, seed news ways of thinking and living. Sometimes the new ways compliment prevailing practices; other times, they don't. In short, kingdom patterns arise from God's love, not a sectarian impulse to oppose or withdraw from the rest of society.

In addition to being upside down, the kingdom speaks with authority today. In other words, it's more than relevant; it's also normative.[3] More than dusty ideas in the trash bins of history; the message of the kingdom addresses our issues today. Kingdom ethics, translated into our contemporary context, suggest how we "ought" to order our lives. We won't, of course, find specific answers in the Scriptures for all of our ethical questions. The Gospels don't provide cookbook solutions for every ethical dilemma. But they do raise the right questions. They focus important issues and suggest how we can transform our lives today.

A Relational Kingdom

What exactly is the kingdom of God? The term defies definition because it's pregnant with many different meanings. This, in fact, is its genius—this power to stimulate our imagination again and again.

In broad strokes, most biblical scholars agree that the "kingdom of God" means the dynamic rule or reign of God. The reign involves God's intentions, authority, and ruling power. It doesn't refer to a territory or a particular place. Nor is it static. It's dynamic—always becoming, spreading, and growing.[4] The kingdom points us not to the place of God but to God's ruling activities. It is not a kingdom *in* heaven, but *from heaven*—one that thrives *here* and *now*. The kingdom appears whenever women and men submit their lives to God's will.

It means more than God's rule in the hearts of people—more than a mystical feeling. The very word kingdom implies a collective order beyond the experience of any one person. A kingdom in a literal sense means that a king rules over a *group* of people. Social policies shape the collective life of a kingdom. Agreements spell out the obligations citizens have to each other as well as to their king. The king's ruling activity transforms the lives and relationships of his subjects. In the words of one scholar, "The kingdom is something people enter, not something that enters them. It is a state of affairs, not a state of mind."[5]

Kingdom living is fundamentally social. It involves membership, citizenship, loyalties, and identity. Citizenship in a kingdom entails relationships, policies, obligations, boundaries, and expectations. These dimensions of kingdom life supersede the whims of individual experience. Kingdom membership clarifies a citizen's relationship to the king, to other citizens, and to other kingdoms. Living in a kingdom means sharing in its history and helping to shape its future.

Although a kingdom is a social order beyond any person, individuals *do* make choices about kingdoms. We embrace or reject them. We serve or mock them. We enter kingdoms and leave them. We pledge our allegiance to them and turn our backs on them.

The distinction between an *aggregate* and a *collectivity* helps to clarify the kingdom idea. An aggregate is a collection of people who happen to be together in time and space. Consider for example, a cluster of persons waiting for the "Walk" light at an intersection.

Though standing side by side, they usually don't interact with each other. They don't influence one another.

In contrast, the executive committee of a local school board is a collectivity—an interdependent cluster of people. They influence each other, formulate common goals, and together decide how to reach them. A kingdom's subjects have a collective *interdependence* based on the policies of their king.

The kingdom of God is a collectivity—a network of persons who have yielded their *hearts and relationships* to the reign of God. The kingdom is actualized when God rules in hearts *and* social relationships. Kingdom life is more than a series of individualized email connections linking the King to each subject. The reign of God infuses the web of relationships, binding King and citizens together.

What does God's reign look like? What is the shape of the royal policies? How can we translate the lofty idea of God's reign into daily living? The answers lie in the incarnation. Jesus of Nazareth unveiled the secrets of God—the very nature of God's kingdom. We begin to grasp the meaning of the kingdom as we study Jesus' life and teachings because he was God's final and definitive Word. Through Jesus' person and ministry, God spoke in a universal language that everyone—regardless of culture, nation, or race—could understand. God's intentions were not hidden in vague religious doctrines. With undeniable eloquence and clarity God spoke through the concrete acts of a person—Jesus of Nazareth.

The kingdom of God threads throughout the fabric of Jesus' teaching and ministry. At the very beginning, Jesus announced the arrival of the kingdom. He frequently introduced parables as examples of the kingdom. His sermons on the Mount and Plain describe kingdom life. The Lord's Prayer welcomes the advent of the kingdom. The vocabulary of the kingdom frequents Jesus' lips. Indeed the centrality of the kingdom in Jesus' teaching is one of the things on which scholars agree.

In addition to his words, Jesus' acts teach us about the kingdom. The Galilean Jew provides the most concrete example—the most visible expression of God's rule. His words and behavior offer the best clues to solving the riddle of the kingdom. Over the centuries,

Christians have used the words of Jesus to shape doctrine, often to the neglect of his ministry. Who he spoke with, what he did, where he walked, and how he handled critics offer clues to the nature of the kingdom. But in the final analysis it isn't *his* kingdom, nor is it *ours*. Always and foremost Jesus points us to *God's* kingdom.

Why Upside Down?

If Jesus inaugurated the kingdom of God, perhaps we should dub it the right-side-up kingdom. Indeed, if the kingdom portrays God's blueprint for our lives, then surely it merits a right-side-up tag. Nevertheless, I prefer the upside-down image for several reasons.

(1) *Social life has vertical dimensions.* Society is not flat; it has a rugged topography. In social geography there are mountains, valleys, ruts, and plains. Some people stand on high social peaks while others mourn in the valleys. The social clout of individuals and groups varies greatly. The chairperson of a committee musters more power than the average committee member. Lawyers swing more prestige and influence than retail clerks. A central and persistent fact of social life is hierarchy—ranking people on vertical social ladders. We don't play the "game" of social interaction on a level playing field. The upside-down image reminds us of this vertical dimension of social life.

(2) *We forget to ask why things are the way they are.* The upside-down label encourages us to question the way things are. Children quickly learn common cultural values and take them for granted. They learn that cereal is the "right" breakfast food in North America. Socialization—learning the ways of our culture—shapes the assumptions by which we live. We take our way of life for granted. We assume the way things are is the way they ought to be. Eating cereal for breakfast, day after day, makes it seem unquestionably right. We internalize the values and norms paraded on screen and billboard as simply "the way life is." If our economic system sets a minimum wage, we accept it as fair and just without a second thought. If someone trespasses on our property, we happily prosecute. After all, "that's what the law provides for." We charge an eight percent commission on a sales transaction because "that's just the way it is."

The values and norms of our society become so deeply ingrained in our minds that we find it difficult to imagine alternatives. Throughout the Gospels, Jesus presents the kingdom as a new order breaking in upon, and overturning, old ways, old values, old assumptions. If it does anything, the kingdom of God shatters the assumptions which govern our lives. As kingdom citizens we can't assume that things are right just because "that's the way they are." The upside-down perspective focuses the points of difference between God's kingdom and the kingdoms of the world.

(3) *The kingdom is full of surprises.* Again and again in parable, sermon, and act Jesus startles us. Things in the Gospels are often upside down. Good Guys turn out to be Bad Guys. Those we expect to receive rewards get spankings. Those who think they are headed for heaven land in hell. Things are reversed. Paradox, irony, and surprise permeate the teachings of Jesus. They flip our expectations upside down. The least are the greatest. The immoral receive forgiveness and blessing. Adults become like children. The religious miss the heavenly banquet. The pious receive curses—shattering our assumptions. Things aren't the way we expect them to be. We're baffled and perplexed. Amazed, we step back. Should we laugh or should we cry? Again and again, turning our expectations upside down, the kingdom surprises us.

Detours Around Jesus

Is it possible to step back in time and capture the meaning of the kingdom? Are we able to stretch a footbridge across the gulf that separates our world from the biblical one? Centuries of water swirl between the cliffs jutting from each shoreline. Two questions in particular make it difficult to build a bridge between our world and the one in ancient Palestine.

First, can we really grasp Jesus' mission and message from our far-away perch? This question focuses on historical evidence and cultural difference. Do we have enough reliable information to paint an accurate picture of what Jesus said and did? Church leaders through the centuries have created many of our impressions of Jesus. Indeed, the church has focused on the theological meanings of the Christ of doctrine rather than on the ethical teachings of

Jesus the prophet. Is it possible for us to reach back into history and retrieve the message of Jesus?

But even if we can straddle the cultural worlds and gather enough evidence to understand what Jesus was about, does it make any difference? That in essence is the second question. Does Jesus have anything to say to us today—anything of relevance for how we ought to live in our world? Or do the vast differences between our two worlds render Jesus irrelevant? Simple at first blush, these thorny questions underscore the gulf between our world and the Palestinian world of Jesus.

Throughout this book, amid awareness of underlying complexities ever to be debated by scholars, I argue "yes" to both questions. Yes, we know enough about who Jesus was and what he said to unravel the mysteries of the kingdom. Moreover, as we unravel the cultural context of his life, the meaning of the upside-down kingdom comes into focus. Yes, Jesus has much to say to us today, not just about private spiritual things but about how we should live collectively. Jesus, in other words, is relevant. His message and his life speak to our setting in powerful ways today.

However, we may not want to hear what Jesus has to say. We may find his words uncomfortable. His parables may sound interesting at first, but they may also upset us as they sink into our minds. Unhappy with what we hear, we may search for detours around Jesus, detours that enable us to bypass the core of his message. At least five tempting detours make it possible to slip by Jesus. Over the centuries many people have used these cautions to bypass the kingdom message, dismissing its relevance for their lives.

Detour One: Jesus Is Lost in History

We can't hear Jesus if we can't find him. One challenge of New Testament studies involves sorting through many layers of text—layers of stories about Jesus and his message. Layers of archaeological evidence about boats, pots, and other artifacts sharpen our understanding of the cultural context. Sorting through the parallel layers of earth and text helps us discover Jesus.[6]

There are several reasons for all the layers. The gospel writers wrote their stories more than forty years after Jesus' death. They used oral stories handed down, as well as written fragments about Jesus that were floating around. In addition, Matthew, Mark, Luke, and John wrote different Gospels addressed to different audiences. Each writer put his own spin on the story to emphasize a particular point. Sometimes their stories match; other times they don't. Moreover, its not always clear if some of the sayings come from Jesus, the editorial writers, or the confessional memories of the early church who by then claimed Jesus as their resurrected Savior.

These issues have stimulated many searches through ancient documents for the "real" Jesus of Galilee. In the end, we have in the words of one scholar, a Jesus with many faces.[7] Matthew's Jesus looks a bit different from Luke's, and so on. Despite his many faces, we have firm evidence that Jesus was a Jewish prophet who lived in Palestine and was crucified. Moreover, most scholars agree that he preached the good news of the kingdom of God. He welcomed the despised, ate with sinners, preached love for enemies, criticized prevailing religious practices, and was such a threat to both Jewish leaders and Roman rulers that he was tortured on a cross until he bled to death.

Even though we cannot verify every story attributed to him or know the exact wording of each phrase he uttered, we have abundant, reliable evidence of the key themes of his message. Despite his different expressions, we can identify the broad contours of his face. There are of course many things about Jesus we don't know and probably never will, but that is hardly reason enough to say we can't find him. To say he is lost in history becomes an easy excuse to turn our backs on his message.

Detour Two: Jesus Is Wrapped in Culture

Even if we agree that we can find Jesus among the dusty layers of evidence, can we understand him? Isn't he wrapped in an ancient culture that doesn't make any sense today? We hear that Mary wrapped him in swaddling clothes, but what does that mean to us who rarely swaddle? This detour contends that the cultural differences between our world and his are so big that whatever he said will make little sense to us today.

Jesus lived in a small rural village centuries away from computers, the Internet, robots, satellites, nuclear weapons, and global corporations. According to this detour sign, kingdom ethics might work in small villages where Simon knows Martha—in simple folk societies where it's possible to love enemies and forgive neighbors—but not today. Kingdom living might fit gentle shepherds and simple peasants, but not us. Jesus' teaching, according to this detour, is trapped in a quaint rural culture, centuries away from the high-tech world of laser weapons and wireless communication. We surely can't bring any insights, let alone ethical guidance, from his dusty old paths to our digital world today.

According to this caution, we can study the Scripture to learn about biblical ethics in New Testament times, but we shouldn't drag them across the centuries and apply them to our lives. The gap is too big. This detour tells us to make our own Christian ethics from scratch. It tells us to ground them in common sense because the old biblical teachings don't make sense in our complicated world—they're simply irrelevant.

It is foolish, of course, to take words wrapped in an ancient culture and blindly apply them to our times. But thanks to the efforts of many scholars we have a stockpile of information about Jesus' culture setting. With these resources, we can unpack a biblical text in its own cultural context and then transport its meaning across the bridge to our world. Knowing the cultural values, practices, and intergroup relations in the biblical setting helps us to unwrap the full meaning of a particular text. The biblical stories suddenly come alive in new ways when we interpret and understand them in their own cultural context.

Galilean peasant society was strikingly different from our world. Nevertheless, similar human habits persist on both sides of the historical chasm: nationalism, racism, injustice, greed, violence, abuse of power, and arrogant pride. In short, evil lurks within the social structures of both yesterday and today. As we unravel the meaning of the gospel in its own cultural setting it speaks to us in new and powerful ways.

The ancient setting of Jesus isn't a handicap if we stop to understand its cultural context. When we do, the gospel stories swell with meaning and power. Indeed, Jesus' relevance would evaporate if his life had mysteriously floated above culture. He speaks powerfully to us *precisely* because he is wrapped in a particular culture. His cultural wrappings clarify, not hide, his Kingdom message.

Detour Three: Jesus Goofed on the Timing

The issue of the kingdom's timing is a sticky problem in synoptic studies. It has provoked heated scholarly debates.[8] When will the kingdom arrive? Has it already come, or do we still wait? Is the pie in the sky or is it already baked?

The third detour warns us that Jesus goofed by thinking the world would soon end. Thus everything he said must be taken with a grain of caution, if indeed he assumed the world was about to collapse. That didn't happen and, so according to this detour sign, we can't apply his end-of-the-world teachings to our situation.

This view tempers the radical character of Jesus' life. Expecting the world to end in a few years, he offered temporary guidelines for living. They were applicable *only* to the brief interim between his life and the imminent arrival of the kingdom. If you expect the world to end and the kingdom to burst in at any moment, you can love your enemies and give away your cloak. According to this interpretation, Jesus' "interim" teachings are irrelevant for enduring social relationships.

Some scholars think Jesus expected the final consummation of the kingdom during his own lifetime.[9] In Matthew 10:23, for instance, Jesus tells those he is sending out that "truly, I tell you, you will not have gone through all the towns of Israel, before the Son of man comes." In Luke 9:27, after discussing the disciple's cross, Jesus says, "But truly I tell you, there are some standing here who will not taste death before they see the kingdom of God." These and other passages suggest that Jesus expected the kingdom to come soon.

In contrast, other theologians argue that Jesus thought the kingdom was *already* present in his own ministry. Jesus said, "The kingdom of God has come near to you" (Luke 10:9) and "The kingdom of God has come to you," (Luke 11:20). Thus Jesus must have understood that the kingdom of God was already present in his ministry. This line of interpretation stresses the presence of the kingdom in the incarnation and in the later growth of the church, but it may downplay a future consummation.[10]

A third position, the dispensational view, relegates the kingdom to a future and literal reign of Christ on earth. In this perspective, Israel rejected the offer of the kingdom at the first appearance of Christ. This snub forced God to delay the kingdom's arrival until the return of Christ. The futuristic bent of this view dilutes any serious interest in applying the teachings of Jesus to our lives today. Interestingly, both the "interim" and the "dispensational" views reach the same conclusion: kingdom ethics taught by Jesus are meaningless today.

Many scholars stake out a fourth position. They argue that the kingdom of God in Jesus' teachings integrates both present and future. A growing consensus sees Jesus, "speaking of the kingdom as both present and future."[11] There are at least four meanings of the kingdom in the Gospels. (1) An abstract meaning of the reign or rule of God. (2) A future kingdom into which the righteous will enter. (3) A reality that is already present on earth. (4) A realm which persons are entering or turning their backs on now. All four of these views provide us windows for understanding the kingdom.

The kingdom of God is a symbol filled with many meanings. The difference between a *general* symbol and a *specific* one helps to clarify the mystery.[12] Symbols point us to something beyond themselves. The written word "dog" is a symbol. As we read the word it reminds us of a certain kind of animal. A *specific* symbol refers us to one specific thing. A black, female cocker spaniel puppy, for example, points us to a very specific kind of dog. In contrast, a *general* symbol has multiple meanings. The word *animal*, for example, suggests many kinds of creatures.

The kingdom of God is a general symbol, not a specific one. If we view the kingdom as a specific symbol, it limits us to one meaning. If the kingdom is merely a single event, we're forced to ask whether or not the event has occurred—yes or no. A general symbol is elastic. It stretches forward and backward, wide and far, with many meanings. Thus instead of asking questions about time, we ask what the kingdom evokes or represents. For what does it stand?

Toward what does it point us? Furthermore, a general symbol isn't tied to one event. The kingdom is more than an ancient or a future event. Envisioning the kingdom as a general symbol enables us to appreciate both its complexity and power.

Consider the phrase, "It's going to rain." Depending on the context, it means many things.[13] On the lips of someone who just felt a few drops, it means it's already raining. Someone scanning an evening sky may predict tomorrow's weather with the phrase. A meteorologist might use the words in a long-range forecast. The same phrase will sound very different amid two weeks of torrential rains, a six-month drought, or in a desert for that matter. And so it is with the timing of the kingdom.

One scholar notes that the meaning of the kingdom on Jesus' lips did not concern place or time, but *power*. Who rules and how one should rule.[14] Our study embraces the kingdom's *diverse* meanings: The Hebrew hope for it. Its inauguration in the ministry of Jesus. Its power at Pentecost. Its durability in the lives of believers throughout the centuries. And its final future consummation.

Kingdom signs burst forth whenever persons submit their wills and relationships to the way of God. To quote the title of a book, the kingdom is *The Presence of the Future* among us already.[15] The kingdom of God is present today as God's Spirit rules in the lives of believers. Members of the kingdom, even now, are those who obey the Lord of the kingdom. Those who follow in the way of Jesus are already part of the kingdom movement. Jesus didn't goof on the timing; he was simply talking about something bigger than our human understandings of time.

Detour Four: Jesus Only Spoke of Spiritual Things

A fourth detour often softens Jesus' teachings by spiritualizing them. Human communities sort words into boxes. We contrast good and evil, sacred and secular and so forth. In religious circles the term *spiritual* tops the sacred ladder, but the word *social* slips to the bottom.

Spiritual realities, the logic goes, come from God. They are holy. Social realities, on the other hand, come from people. Being far from God's heart, social realities are suspect. In short, spiritual is better than social, in fact, the two realities belong in separate worlds. For example, we may worry that a church activity will become "just a social event"—implying it would have no spiritual meaning. This unfortunate split between spiritual and social often detours us around kingdom ethics.

Spiritual realities do involve great mysterious truths. They include our beliefs about God, salvation, and the mysterious working of God's Spirit. Social realities, on the other hand, point us to mundane concerns—houses, friends, salary, recreation, and our need for love, creativity, and happy relationships.

A false split between spiritual and social leads to a warped reading of the Scripture. It tempts us to turn Jesus' message into sweet, spiritualized syrup. Such a twist can dilute the truth, making it harmless. We marvel at the atoning death of Jesus but forget that it came about because he demonstrated a new way of living.

In fact any gospel without feet isn't gospel. God's love for the world produced social action. God didn't just sit in a great theological rocking chair and muse about loving the world. God acted. God entered social affairs—in human form. Through Jesus, God lived in a real social environment. Jesus in essence disclosed God's social habits. In the incarnation, the spiritual became social.

To put it another way, the incarnation communicated God's spiritual mysteries to us in a practical social form—in a person. Word and deed blended into a single reality in Emanuel (God with us). God spoke to us not through Greek or English but through a Son—a social event (Heb. 1:2). The genius of the incarnation is that spiritual and social worlds intersect in Jesus Christ. To separate them is to deny the incarnation. Social and spiritual are inextricably woven together in the Jesus story.

One scholar argues that repentance "is a purely religious ethical act . . . an act involving only oneself and God and is neutral regarding other human beings and the world."[16] This view mistakenly assumes that repentance is only a personal spiritual experience without social implications. Such a cleavage misrepresents the gospel.

We don't have two gospels. We don't have a spiritual *and* a social gospel, a salvation *and* a social justice gospel. Instead, we have a single, integrated gospel of the kingdom. *This* gospel fuses social and spiritual realities into one. Jesus binds the spiritual and social into an inseparable whole.

On the one hand he says that true faith is anchored in the heart—not in tithing, sacrifice, cleansing, and other external rituals. In this sense he spiritualizes religious faith. On the other hand, Jesus argues that faith in God is always expressed in tangible acts of love for the neighbor. He was, in short, smashing our categories of social and spiritual. In Jesus' view they're a seamless fabric that can't be torn in two.

A pastor once spiritualized the story of Zacchaeus. After telling the tale, he reminded the congregation that if we are spiritually "treed" we can by Jesus be freed. The sermon overlooked the profound economic dimensions of the story. It trivialized a social earthquake with trite spiritual applications. In the text we discover a greedy tax collector who meets Jesus, repents, and corrects his economic wrongs. Spiritual repentance and social retribution form *one* story, a story Jesus calls a "visit by salvation."

To ferret out the social implications of the gospel isn't to depreciate or neglect spiritual insights. It simply means that spiritual insights always have social implications. The integration of social and spiritual into a whole affirms an incarnation that moved beyond the Holy of Holies in the Jerusalem temple to the social realities of Palestinian society. When we spiritualize biblical texts, we evaporate their power and practical meaning.

Detour Five: Jesus Only Addressed Personal Morality

The next barricade suggests that the kingdom only speaks to our personal character. In other words, the teachings of Jesus provide good counsel for our private lives but not for social ethics. One scholar contends that Jesus primarily desires righteous character. Conduct, he notes, should be a manifestation of such righteous character. But he mistakenly concludes "that there is little explicit teaching on social ethics in the Gospels."[17]

Such views strike a cleavage between our personal conduct and our life in community. The distinction between personal and social ethics is tidy, but problematic. It implies that personal actions do not have social consequences. And it assumes that individuals operate in a social vacuum, detached from social forces. Moreover, it makes it easy to focus on our personal behavior while being blind to the social implications of our conduct. Most importantly, it declares Jesus irrelevant for social policy and restricts his authority to personal morality.

Jesus, according to this view, was concerned with the private matters of the inner life. He cared primarily about character, attitudes, motives, emotions, and personality traits. Hence the ethics of Jesus apply only to our inner feelings and private behavior. Jesus transforms our emotional outlook—our sense of hope and inner peace, but not our social relations.

The problem with such a personal/social split is that most behavior is social. Are any actions purely "personal"? Perhaps scratching one's leg would pass the test. But even this creates problems, because the proper way to scratch a leg is learned in a social context. Cultural norms determine the time and method of scratching. Woe to national leaders who scratch their legs with heavy strokes during a press conference!

Our ideas, values, and character traits have social origins. They don't just fall from the sky. We acquire them through a variety of social influences—discussions with friends, reading books, listening to music, watching television, observing parents. This doesn't mean that we lack originality. Nor does it mean we are culturally programmed robots. Our minds are the crucible where a variety of influences are processed together. And each person, of course, blends these social influences in his or her own beautiful way.

Not only do inner feelings and motives have social roots, they have social ramifications. Feelings of despair affect how we treat others. Jesus pinpointed how even private attitudes impact other persons. Hating someone in your heart, he said, is equivalent to murder; sexual lust is tantamount to adultery.

Inner feelings and emotions aren't sealed off from other people. They emerge out of social experience and shape our actions toward others. It's difficult to think of any so-called character traits outside of a social context. Someone stranded on a desert island might ponder the meaning of integrity, honesty, and meekness but would find them hollow words apart from other people. If Jesus had cared only about internal character, he could have spent all his time in a wilderness retreat lecturing on the virtues of inner harmony.

The fact that ideas have social origins and consequences doesn't negate the role of the Holy Spirit. God created us as social beings and God's Spirit stirs us to care for others. Just because our thoughts are social products with social implications, doesn't mean our inner life is unimportant—just the opposite. Thoughts do influence behavior. Jesus stressed the need for genuine internal righteousness in contrast to hypocritical ritual. He knew that the inner life yields social fruit—of one kind or another.

Kingdom ethics, taught and lived by Jesus, can be transported over the bridge linking the first century with our own. This book resists the notion that Jesus should return to his own time because, in the words of one scholar, "He does not provide a valid ethic for today."[18] By contrast, the following pages echo the growing interest of many scholars who tie social ethics to Jesus' teaching about the kingdom of God.[19]

The Gospels don't offer a full-blown system of formal ethics for every conceivable situation. And I certainly don't espouse a sentimentalist mentality of simply "walking in his footsteps." But I do contend that the Gospels provide us with episodes, pictures, and stories, rife with ethical insights that address our situation, however far we stand removed from the shepherds of ancient Palestine. The many pictures of the *good* and the *right* in the kingdom stories aren't impossible possibilities or romanticized ideals. They may be old, but they still intersect in lively ways with the knotty problems of human existence today.

The kingdom vision outlined in the Gospels doesn't spell out a specific program for social ethics or political action. The vision of Jesus does, however, clearly introduce us to basic principles of the right and the good for the collective life of the kingdom. Making specific applications, of course, is the task of believers guided by the Holy Spirit.

These five detours lure us around the teachings of Jesus. They offer excuses for shrugging off the claims of the gospel on our lives.

But such bypasses are not fair to us or to Jesus. We first need to hear his story before we decide how to respond.

The remarkable thing about our attempts to understand the kingdom is the way we dice it into categories. Our questions easily fragment it into bits and pieces. Is the kingdom present or future, we ask. Personal or social? Abstract or concrete? Earthly or heavenly? Spiritual or political? A gift from God or enacted by us?

Our human propensity to pull the kingdom apart into logical categories shreds its integrity. Indeed the kingdom of God in its fullness shatters our puny human categories. It's not an either/or, a yes/no. It's all the above—both/and. It is indeed God's kingdom, not ours!

We want to understand it, examine it, and analyze it. But God enjoins us to enter it. God calls us to turn our backs on the kingdoms of this world and embrace an upside-down world. Underlying all Jesus' teaching about the kingdom is a call to respond. He invites us not to study but to join; not to dissect but to enter. What will we do with it? How will we respond?

2

Mountain Politics

Triple Snares

The synoptic writers report that three right-side-up options lured Jesus before he launched the upside-down kingdom. His three-prong temptation was a forty-day ordeal. The number *forty* represents trial and oppression in Hebrew history. The flood lasted forty days and nights and the Hebrews wandered in the wilderness forty years. Moses was up on the mountain forty days and nights and Goliath taunted the Israelites for the same block of time. Regardless of the actual numbers of days, the number forty signaled agonizing choices for Jesus.

Five key symbols in the temptation story help to unpack its meaning—*bread*, *devil*, *desert*, *mountain*, and *temple*.[1] Each symbol recalls key episodes in Hebrew history. The devil, threat to holiness, brings things to utter ruin. The Israelites faced many temptations in the harsh desert where they ate bread (manna) from heaven. God revealed the Ten Commandments to them on a high mountain. And eventually, God dwelled in the holy temple.

Mark gives no information about Jesus' test, but Matthew and Luke (both in chapter 4) agree that he struggled with three snares symbolized by the mountain, the temple, and the bread. These options formed the legs of a stool. Upon it Jesus could have sat as a powerful political Messiah. The temptation points to a right-side-up kingdom encompassing the three big social institutions of his day: political (mountain), religious (temple), and economic (bread).[2]

Social institutions are the established social patterns that organize a particular aspect of society. Economic institutions, for instance, include a web of rules that govern financial activity by specifying rates of interest and the rights of creditors and debtors.

Participants in an economic system take these "rules" of the game for granted. They make financial behavior predictable and orderly. As in the financial sector, a cluster of social norms organizes educational, recreational, religious, and other social spheres. These social patterns become deeply ingrained in the life of a society.

The temptations faced by Jesus offered *real* social detours. The threefold test promised to fulfill Jewish hopes for a messiah who would defy political oppressors, feed the poor, and bask in miraculous approval from above. Following the test, Luke says the devil departed from Jesus "until an opportune time." This suggests that these enticing shortcuts didn't evaporate after forty days in the wilderness. They continually plagued Jesus throughout his ministry.

For example, when Peter rebukes Jesus for talking about suffering, Jesus emphatically declares, "Get behind me, Satan!" (Mark 8:33). The use of violent force apparently continued to lure Jesus. Amid a squabble over power, Jesus reminds the disciples they have continued with him in his *trials* (Luke 22:28). Throughout his ministry Jesus faced political alternatives which threatened to derail his upside-down commitment to suffering love.

To grasp the nature of the upside-down kingdom, we must explore the three right-side-up alternatives: mountain, temple, and bread. Only as we see what Jesus rejected, can we know what he affirmed. The temptations provide an overview of the social setting of Jesus' ministry. In this chapter and the next two we'll grapple with the temptations in the *political*, *religious*, and *economic* context of his time. Each chapter addresses one of the tempter's offers. We'll begin with the political temptation and then turn to the religious and economic snares in chapters three and four.

Jesus the Great

According to Matthew (4:8), the setting for the political temptation was, "a very high mountain," where "all the kingdoms of the world and their splendor" were offered Jesus. This was Jesus' chance to be a new Alexander the Great, his opportunity to wield political power throughout the vast Mediterranean world. Once again Israel would be supreme, a light and a power to all nations. God's vengeance would roll across the empires of the Middle East. The pivot of world authority and influence would shift from Rome to Jerusalem. Caesar could no longer tax and insult Jews, for Caesar himself would serve Israel.

From that mountaintop Jesus could see himself flexing massive political power. Not only would he rule, his throne would sit upon the highest peak of power, and the crowds would chant their acclaim. This right-side-up option contrasted starkly with the humble servant role. Why was this enticing? Why should Jesus care about the Roman occupation?

A short historical tour will help us understand Jewish political hopes in Jesus' time.[3] Scholars typically divide history with the birth of Jesus. The Common Era, C.E., refers to the common Jewish and

---

Time Line and Key Events

B.C.E.	538	End of Babylonian captivity
	332	Alexander the Great
(Before the	323	Egyptian Control
Common	198	Syrian Control
Era)	175	Antiochus IV "The Madman"
	164	Maccabees gain control
	63	Pompey, Roman General
	37-04	Herod the Great
	05	Birth of Jesus
	04	Death of Herod the Great
	04	General uprising and revolt
	04	Division of Herod's Kingdom
		Herod Antipas
		Philip
		Archelaus

C.E.	0	
	06	Archelaus deported
(The	06	Direct Roman Control (Procurator)
Common	06	Roman taxes
Era)	25-28	Jesus' ministry
	26-30	Pontius Pilate
	66-70	General uprising and revolt
	70	Rome destroys the temple and Jerusalem
	132	Bar Kochba uprising
	135	Roman destruction of Jerusalem

Christian era *after* the birth of Jesus. Before the Common Era, B.C.E. marks the time period *before* the birth of Jesus.

The Old Testament ends with the Hebrews under Persian control. The Persians had allowed the Hebrews to return home in 538 B.C.E., after fifty years in Babylonian captivity. A peaceful coexistence with the Persians permitted the temple to be rebuilt under Zerubbabel. The situation changed rapidly, however, as a young Greek, Alexander the Great, jumped to fame. He conquered the Persians in 334 B.C.E. and within two years all Palestine fell under his control as he rampaged into Egypt. He hoped to usher in a worldwide civilization unified by the Greek way of life (known as Hellenization).

For the first time Greek traders and the Greek language made themselves at home in Palestine. After a fever killed Alexander at the age of 32, his empire fell into the hands of his squabbling generals. Palestine turned into a buffer zone that was shuttled back and forth between his quarreling generals some five times in ten years. One of the generals, Ptolemy, governor of Egypt, along with his successors, finally gained control of Palestine for over 100 years. But they were not happy ones. Ptolemy supposedly entered Jerusalem on a Sabbath day under the guise of offering a sacrifice, only to capture many Jews and export them to Egypt.[4]

The Madman

In 198 B.C.E. Syria captured the Jewish kingdom from the Egyptians. By 175 B.C.E. the Syrian king, Antiochus IV, came to power and created more havoc for the Jews. Nicknamed "the madman," he called himself, "the illustrious." He called himself "Epiphanes," meaning God Incarnate!

The Syrian king promptly set up policies to indoctrinate Jews into Greek life. Foreign Greek culture sprouted in Jerusalem, including the construction of a gymnasium for athletic training. Young Jewish males were shamed by their circumcision, which was openly revealed in nude contests held in the gym. Some underwent operations to hide their circumcision. They also wore Greek clothing, particularly a fashionable broad-rimmed hat associated with the god Hermes.

The Jewish writer of 2 Maccabees (4:14) laments that even Jewish priests had deserted their sacred responsibilities to watch sporting events—wrestling, discus throwing, and horse racing. The Greek language became popular in Jerusalem. All of these activities threatened Jewish identity and heritage. The Hebrews resisted Hellenization, but they couldn't stop the aggressive tactics of the madman, Antiochus IV, to wipe out Hebrew culture.

Twice the Syrian madman plundered the Jewish treasury to support his war activity. He carried off precious furnishings from the temple—the altar of incense, the seven-branched lampstand, and the table shewbread—to Antioch in Syria. One scholar describes his policies:

> The walls of Jerusalem were torn down and a fortress was built on the hill of the ancient city of David. The Jews were forbidden, on pain of death, to keep the Sabbath and to circumcise their children. The king's inspectors traveled throughout the country to supervise the fulfillment of these decrees. In Jerusalem a pagan altar was erected on the site of the altar of burnt offering, and sacrifices were offered there to the supreme god, the Olympian Zeus in 167 B.C.E.[5]

During the madman's reign, two successive Jewish high priests bribed him for their positions with large sums of money. New civil laws decreed that anyone caught with a copy of the Holy Scripture would die. The erection of an altar to Zeus ended sacrifices to Yahweh. Ten days after the altar's completion a pig was sacrificed on it. Killing a pig on a pagan altar was a blasphemous horror to Jewish ritual purity. The temple sanctuary was smeared with blood and soldiers committed the grossest indecencies in the sacred temple courts. Hebrew hearts cried out for God's mercy and deliverance.

In addition, there was economic oppression. The madman's greed for taxes included the following:

> Taxes on the salt mined at the Dead Sea; taxes amounting to a third of the grain harvested, to a half of the all too scanty fruits; poll taxes, crown taxes, temple taxes, to say nothing of the sovereign right to seize cattle and stores in the name of military conscription—all this fomented unrest.[6]

Although the high priests and some of the people welcomed Greek culture, a small group of traditional Jews resented the foreign influence. This conservative element, the Hasideans (meaning pious) protested the Jewish embrace of Greek culture. But they didn't revolt against the policies of the madman. Some other Jews, however, thought they had to fight if their culture, worship, and identity were to survive here in their homeland. They were known as the Maccabeans.

The Hammerers

Rebellion came in the countryside. An old priest named Mattathias and his five sons lived in a small village about twenty miles northwest of Jerusalem. When one of the king's inspectors entered the village to force Jews to offer pagan sacrifices, Mattathias refused. He killed the inspector. Calling all who were zealous for the law to follow, father and sons fled to caves in the hillside. There, pious Hasideans, willing finally to fight to rid the land of Syrians, joined them. From their wilderness base the Jewish rebels directed hit and run campaigns into villages to destroy pagan altars and harass apostate Jews.

On one occasion some rebels, out of respect for the Sabbath, refused to retaliate against Syrian troops. The rebels were attacked and massacred. Fullscale resistance and offensive attacks began. Mattathias soon died and his son Judas the Maccabean ("the Hammerer" in Hebrew) organized a successful military campaign and literally hammered the Syrians. Eventually the Maccabeans regained control of the temple in Jerusalem. In 164 B.C.E., three years after the temple had been defiled by swine's blood, it was rededicated. Still today Jews celebrate Hanukkah, a Feast of Dedication, to commemorate this great event.

Although Jews claimed the temple, the Syrians retained control of the nearby military fortress. With the temple restored, the pious Hasideans stopped supporting the revolt because they had little interest in political freedom. This group eventually formed the cradle of the Pharisee movement.

However, another emerging group, the Sadducees, insisted on political independence. They finally achieved their goal under

Simon (one of Mattathias' five sons) in 142 B.C.E. He declared himself priest and military leader. Moreover, this began an eighty-year period of political independence monitored by the so-called Hasmonean family. During this era the same person often ruled as king and high priest. Coins were minted, and the Jewish state conquered Moab, Samaria, and Edom.

Conflict between the Pharisees and Sadducees soon forced them to side with quarreling factions in the Hasmonean family. A military stalemate between the rival groups opened the door for the Romans in 63 B.C.E., some sixty years before Jesus' birth. Pompey, the Roman general, besieged Jerusalem for three months. Finally, on a Sabbath day, the Romans took the last stronghold, the temple. Over 12,000 Jews were massacred. In an outrageous act of desecration, Pompey entered the sacred Holy of Holies, opened only to the high priest once a year, and to his amazement found it empty. The Roman general's profane act insulted faithful Jews, who viewed it as God's holy judgment.

After nearly 100 years of political freedom, the Jewish state was once again under the thumb of a foreign power. For centuries it would be a tributary of the large Roman Empire. Thus in the 500 years of history before the birth of Jesus, the Jewish people were batted back and forth in a game of political Ping-Pong. They were tossed among the great powers of the Middle East: Babylon, Persia, Greece, Egypt, Syria, and finally Rome.

Although years of turmoil followed Pompey's victory, Rome dominated Palestinian politics after 63 B.C.E. During the period of imperial domination, Roman armies periodically tried to smother peasant revolts through "search and destroy" campaigns of terror. The armies ravaged villages, slaughtered the elderly, and took thousands back to Rome to sell as slaves. As a grim reminder of their brutality, Roman soldiers crucified hundreds of people on crosses along public roads—warnings for other would-be revolters. At times they crucified, butchered, or enslaved entire populations.[7]

About the time Jesus was born, not far from where he likely grew up, the Romans burned houses and enslaved thousands to squelch the popular revolt of 4 B.C.E. But the fire of freedom, ignited by Judas the Hammerer, couldn't be extinguished. It flared again and again in the era of Jesus and eventually erupted into two full-scale Roman-Jewish wars in 66 C.E. and again in 132 C.E. Rome finally smothered the Jewish revolters for good in 135 C.E. when it destroyed Jerusalem.

Great Herod

In 37 B.C.E. Herod the Great, a Jew, came to power in Palestine, as a Roman puppet king. A symbol of oppressive tyranny, he ruled until his death in 4 B.C.E., shortly after the birth of Jesus. He held a tight rein over the people by hiring foreign soldiers, building fortresses, and orchestrating a network of secret informers. This Herod approached the wise men, then killed the male children in Bethlehem because he was frightened by the prospect of a new king.

Under Herod, the territory of Palestine almost doubled. He struck a delicate balance between Roman power and Jewish nationalism. He could keep his crown only as long as he pleased the emperor back in Rome. Herod didn't have to pay taxes to Rome but was required to send troops in time of war. He could maintain his own army as long as it didn't pose a threat to the empire. Above all he was to maintain peace and govern with efficiency.

The outstanding mark of Herod's thirty-three-year reign was a lavish building program. Although he didn't force Greek culture on the Jews, Herod's architecture followed Roman patterns. He constructed temples, gymnasiums, cloisters, aqueducts, and amphitheaters on an enormous scale. He built several new cities, including Caesarea, with its artificial harbor on the Mediterranean coast. Fortresses and palaces sprang up throughout the countryside. Huge construction projects, including pagan temples, were also carried out in the Gentile lands of Sidon, Tyre, Nicopolis, Sparta, and Athens, to name just a few.

Because Herod likely had some Gentile ancestry, Jewish leaders never completely trusted him. To gain their confidence he began a renovation of the temple in Jerusalem in 20 B.C.E.—the eighteenth year of his reign. The Jews feared he would tear down the temple built by Zerubbabel and never replace it. To prove his sincerity he provided a thousand wagons and hired ten thousand workmen. Moreover, he trained 1,000 priests as masons and carpenters, so unconsecrated feet wouldn't desecrate the holy shrine during the reconstruction. He even doubled the size of the old temple area. The magnificent new structure was Herod's pride and glory. It operated during Jesus' life, even while the retrofit continued. It was later destroyed by the Romans in 70 C.E.—seven years after its completion.

Herod's insatiable ambition made him both ruthless and sympathetic to Jewish concerns. He had to maintain Jewish stability to receive Rome's continuing smile. Thus he dared not allow political rivals or Jewish nationalism to gain ground. Although he distributed free corn during a famine and reduced taxes during hard times, his building projects strapped the people with heavy taxes. Some of these revenues went to the new temple, which of course received Jewish approval. Other taxes—used to subsidize lavish pagan temples in faraway places—irritated Jewish leaders. Under Herod the Great the taxes "were ruthlessly exacted, and he was always thinking out fresh ways of subsidizing his vast expenditures."[8] There was popular resentment because Herod squandered much of the common wealth, sucking the lifeblood of the people with his oppressive taxes.

Herod usually tolerated Jewish worship and ritual. But occasionally there were direct confrontations. Out of courtesy to Rome, Herod placed a golden eagle, the empire's royal symbol, over the great east gate of the city. This so enraged some forty pious Jews that in defiance they tore the eagle down. Herod retaliated by burning them all alive. In his later years, the Pharisees refused to sign an oath of loyalty to him and the Roman emperor. They were harshly punished for their civil disobedience.

Although his kingdom grew, Herod wasn't popular. Resentment seethed throughout the land. Suspicion centered on his vicious treatment of his family. His several wives—ten in all—lived in his palace. Over the years he killed two of them, plus at least three sons, a brother-in-law, and other relatives. Even the Roman emperor once reportedly said, "It is better to be Herod's pig than his son."[9]

Soon after Jesus' birth, Herod lay dying. To keep his seething people from celebrating his death, he ordered leading Jews held in the Jericho arena so they could be executed when he died. He wanted to ensure that Jewish tears would flow at his death, even if not for him.[10] Fortunately the prisoners were freed at the time of Herod's death. The demise of the brutal tyrant, however, triggered a widespread popular revolt that swirled across the land during Jesus' childhood.

The Roman Connection

Upon his death, Herod's kingdom was divided into three parts. His son, Herod Antipas, ruled the district of Galilee west of the lake, including Jesus' hometown of Nazareth. The two Herods are frequently confused. Herod the Great, described above, ruled at the time of Jesus' birth but died shortly afterwards. Herod Antipas, his son, was a contemporary of Jesus. It was Herod Antipas who executed John the Baptist and whom Jesus called a fox (Luke 13:32). During his trial, Pilate sent Jesus to Herod Antipas, who happened to be in Jerusalem at the time.

Philip, a second son of Herod the Great, received the territory northeast of the lake of Galilee. He reigned peaceably over his political turf for thirty-seven years but receives little notice in the Gospels.

Herod's third son Archelaus governed the third and southern portion of Herod's kingdom with Jerusalem in its center. Joseph, returning from Egypt with the baby Jesus, was afraid to go to Judea when he heard that Archelaus had succeeded his father. So Joseph settled in Nazareth, ruled by Herod Antipas (Matt. 2:22).

The three brothers—Herod Antipas, Philip, and Archelaus—had to meet the Roman emperor to confirm their father's will and legitimate their power. Archelaus, however, was in trouble with the Jews even before he left Jerusalem to receive the emperor's blessing. He removed the Jewish high priest and appointed a new one. This triggered riots in the streets during the Passover feast in Jerusalem. The crowds demanded lower taxes, called for the release of political prisoners, and protested the removal of the high priest. Archelaus sent a cohort of troops to quell the protest. The mob rushed the soldiers and stoned most of them to death. Archelaus promptly killed three thousand rioters, sent the rest of the pilgrims home, and left for Rome!

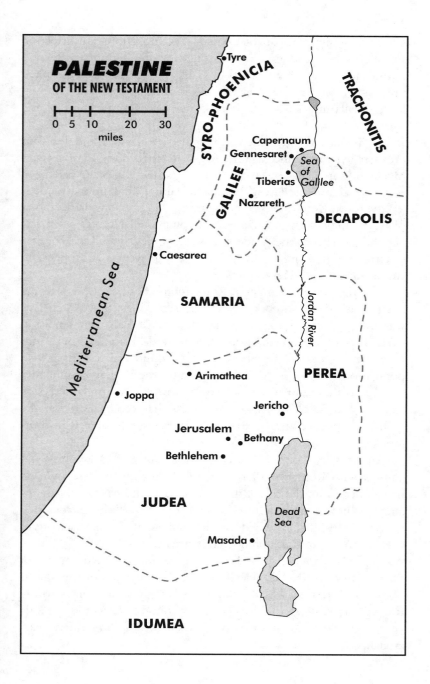

Fervent Jewish patriots could take no more. Insurrection spread. Rebel leaders arose throughout the country. Beyond Jerusalem, the outlying districts of Galilee, Judea, and Perea erupted in bloody disorder.[11] One of Herod's former slaves, named Simon, led guerrilla attacks on the Herodian palaces and estates of the wealthy.

In Judea a former shepherd named Athronges and his four brothers led a resistance against Archelaus for a number of years.[12] Meanwhile in Galilee a Judas, whose father Hezekiah had been killed by Herod the Great, became a flaming revolutionary. Judas led the revolt from the town of Sepphoris, an hour's walk northeast of Jesus' hometown of Nazareth. He plundered Herod's arsenal at Sepphoris. These rebel leaders in various sections of the country ruled as self-proclaimed "kings" for several weeks. Athronges, in Judea, ruled for several months.

But the power of imperial Rome would not be mocked. Rome soon smashed the stubborn Jewish peasant kings. Since Archelaus was still in Rome during the uprising, the Roman commander in Syria intervened from the north. He moved his armies south into Palestine. He burned Sepphoris to the ground and sold its Jewish population into slavery. Continuing south, the Roman commander killed two thousand rebels, leaving the people in the countryside stunned and sullen. Jesus was likely less than ten years old as the violence happened nearby so the memories surely shaped his outlook.

In Jerusalem, diehard Jewish patriots engaged in hand-to-hand combat with Roman soldiers. The rebels hurled missiles down on the soldiers from the top of the temple walls and tried to set fire to a fortress protecting the Romans. Some of the royal soldiers deserted to the rebels, but in the end, the Romans won. Soldiers set fire to parts of the temple and plundered its treasury.

Archelaus soon returned from Rome and regained control of the countryside. Nevertheless, the fuse on the political-religious bomb in Palestine was smoldering. This revolutionary turmoil framed the context of Jesus' early childhood. It would explode again in 66-70 C.E. in a massive Jewish revolt—some thirty years after his death.

Little is known about the short reign of Archelaus (4 B.C.E. to 6 C.E.). We do know that he antagonized Jewish sensitivities, especially by marrying a woman divorced from her second husband. Jewish indignation and hatred was so strong in fact that both the Jews and the Samaritans sent a delegation to Rome to plead for his removal. Surprisingly, the Emperor Augustus agreed and sent Archelaus into exile in 6 C.E., during the childhood of Jesus.

Unfortunately, this changed the political organization of Judea for the worst. Instead of being ruled by a quasi-Jewish king, it now for the first time became a Roman province. This meant that Palestine was now under *direct* Roman control. A Roman ruler, (sometimes called a procurator, prefect, legate, or governor) supervised Judea directly. A procurator such as Pilate was responsible to the Roman emperor. The Empire had two types of provinces:

(1) The more important and wealthy areas received a ruler of senatorial rank called a *legate*. The Syrian legate, Quirinius, controlled Syria to the north of Palestine with a standing army of several legions, each having up to 6,000 foot soldiers.

(2) Minor provinces like Judea required fewer troops to keep order. They received a Roman ruler called a *procurator*, from a lower social class than a legate.

A procurator, such as Pilate, was directly responsible to Caesar and had full military, judicial, and financial authority. Judea had auxiliary troops recruited from the Gentile population. The Jews, however, were exempt from military service because they wouldn't fight on the Sabbath. The procurator had five cohorts of 600 men each under his command and maintained garrisons throughout the country. A cohort of 300-500 soldiers was permanently stationed in Jerusalem in Fort Antonia, overlooking the temple area, to prevent riots. The procurator, Pilate, lived in Caesarea on the Mediterranean coast. But during Jewish festivals he brought extra troops to Jerusalem to prevent bedlam among the thousands of pilgrims.

The first Roman procurator came to Judea in 6 C.E. to replace Archelaus some nine years after the widespread revolt. Along with direct Roman control, came Roman taxes, of course. Thus the Roman commander Quirinius went to Jerusalem to take a census of the population for taxation purposes at the time of Jesus' birth

(Luke 12:2). Passionate Jewish nationalists who wanted a free homeland strongly resisted Roman taxes. The switch from the puppet King Archelaus to direct Roman rule inflamed an already tense situation. Zealous Jewish patriots protested the census. They argued that because the land belonged to God, all taxes also belonged to God. Land taxes and head taxes were, in their eyes, new forms of bondage and idolatry.

The Roman tax census of 6 C.E. enraged zealous Jews, who longed for freedom from oppression and the establishment of an independent Jewish state. Only God was king, they said, declaring it blasphemous to call the emperor "king" and "lord." In their mind, this violated the first commandment prohibiting the worship of other gods. Some thought paying taxes to the emperor was sheer idolatry. Super zealots wouldn't even touch a coin minted with the emperor's image. As one scholar notes, "Of all the peoples within the Roman Empire, none so persistently and steadfastly resisted, both politically and spiritually, the Roman occupation rule as did the Jews."[13]

Protesters, Prophets, and Bandits

In the decades before and after Jesus' birth a variety of Jewish protest movements emerged. The voices of unrest became increasingly violent after his death in the years before the Jewish-Roman war of 66-70 C.E. As shown in table 2.1, four different types of protests arose—public protests, prophets, the messiahs, and bandit groups.[14] In the fifty years before and after Jesus' birth, more than thirty different protest movements appeared.

TABLE 2.1
TYPES OF PEASANT UNREST IN PALESTINE

Type	Number	Dates
Major Public Protest	7	4 B.C.E. to 65 C.E.
Prophets	10	30 B.C.E. to 73 C.E.
Messiahs	5	4 B.C.E. to 70 C.E.
Bandit Groups	11	47 B.C.E. to 69 C.E.

Various factors fueled the public anger, including rural poverty, high taxes, Roman control, inflammatory acts of Jewish puppet kings, and the crushing violence of Roman armies. Political, economic, and religious factors combined together to stir revolt and rebellion. The slogan of many of the zealous resisters was "No Lord but God."

On some occasions large crowds gathered for several days to protest the actions of rulers. Protests and riots frequently broke out during the Jewish Passover and other holy days when unruly crowds and mobs would gather in Jerusalem. Several times Jewish rebels led nonviolent protests to condemn the profane treatment of their sacred objects and places.

Including John the Baptist, at least ten prophets popped up in these years challenging the ruling powers and proclaiming a message of deliverance. Most of them had a sizeable following. Moreover in the four decades after the death of Herod the Great, at least five self-appointed messiahs, not including Jesus, appeared. Coming from poor peasant backgrounds, they too reflected the widespread turbulence. The prophets and the messiahs hoped that God in miraculous ways would eradicate the Romans and establish divine rule as in bygone days.

Social bandits and terrorists also kept rulers on edge. Unlike regular robbers who stole for personal gain, the social bandits championed religious or economic causes and thus often enjoyed support among local peasants. At least eleven bandit groups of various sorts flourished in the decades before the Jewish-Roman war of 70 C.E. Some of the terrorists operated in Jerusalem, killing opponents with daggers, including a High Priest, in surprise attacks and then melting into the crowds. Other freedom fighters fought from the countryside, often to the cheers of local peasants who supported their call for liberation. Many of the social bandits were considered religious zealots because they wanted Jewish independence and declared, "No Lord but God."

Barabbas, released at Jesus' trial, was a political rebel who was considered less dangerous than Jesus. Jesus died between two robbers, likely social bandits who had threatened the "peace," imposed by Rome. The resistance movement pulsated largely among the common folk. Meanwhile, the upper crust of Jewish leaders, living in Jerusalem, collaborated privately and silently with the Romans.

The momentum of resistance turned more violent in the years after Jesus' death. In the 50s and 60s C.E., dagger men (Sicarii) appeared. Their cutthroat tactics involved selective assassinations and kidnapping. Their targets: high priests and other top Jewish leaders in cahoots with the Romans. An organized Zealot faction also emerged after 60 C.E. and eventually plunged into armed combat in Jerusalem. Several other revolutionary factions, ready to slit Roman and Jewish throats, rose to the fore in the 60s. Together these rebel groups led the massive Jewish revolt of 66-70 C.E. that erupted into the first Jewish-Roman War.[15]

Much of the resistance in the sixty years preceding the revolt targeted the Romans. But growing internal squabbles among rival Jewish factions also fueled the unrest. In any event, widespread discontent and disturbance marked the whole period of direct Roman rule (6-66 C.E.) in Palestine.[16]

Thus as Jesus began his ministry about 25 C.E., Palestine was a churning caldron of revolution. Philip, Herod the Great's son, ruled the northeast region as a quasi-Jewish king. Herod Antipas, another son, ruled the Galilee area in similar fashion. A Roman ruler (procurator), from the seacoast port of Caesarea, directed the Judean affairs, including Jerusalem, in the southern region.

Pontius Pilate

Pontius Pilate was appointed the fifth Roman procurator of Judea in 26 C.E. Compared with Jewish leaders, Pilate appears neutral toward Jesus in some accounts of Jesus' trial. But there is another side to Pilate—a brutal one. His ruthless administration often offended Jewish sensibilities.

Shortly after he took office, Pilate ordered troops to go from Caesarea to Jerusalem. They entered the city under cover of night and posted banners bearing the picture of the Emperor Tiberius. This violated Jewish law, which forbade an image in the holy city. The next morning, the idolatrous banners were discovered. Incensed Jews flocked to Caesarea demanding that the images be removed. On the sixth day of the demonstration Pilate herded the mob into a racetrack, surrounded them with soldiers, and threatened to kill them. When he realized the mob would rather die than violate their religious law, he ordered the offending banners withdrawn.

On another occasion in Jerusalem, Pilate dedicated some shields containing the inscription of the Emperor Tiberius. Jewish leaders who wanted Jerusalem consecrated exclusively to the worship of Yahweh were of course insulted. The Jews protested to the Roman emperor, who instructed Pilate to move the shields to the temple of Augustus in Caesarea. In these ways Pilate aggravated the Jewish temper.

Even his one positive contribution brought trouble. Pilate began constructing an aqueduct to bring water to Jerusalem from twenty-five miles away. The water system benefited the temple, which needed huge quantities of water to purify the sacrifice of large animals. Pilate thought the temple treasury should help to pay the bill. Temple authorities protested this secular use of money dedicated to God. But Pilate insisted. Crowds of angry Jews gathered to protest the sacrilege. Pilate's troops dispelled them and killed many.

Pilate's career ended in 36 C.E., after his troops attacked a group of Samaritans assembled on their holy mountain (Mt. Gerizim). The faithful had gathered to follow a self-acclaimed Samaritan Messiah. After the Samaritan incident Pilate was recalled to Rome and lost his procuratorship. Philo of Alexandria described the conduct of Pilate's office as marked by "corruption, violence, degradations, ill treatment, offenses, numerous illegal executions, and incessant, unbearable cruelty."[17]

Suicide at Masada

Following the death of Jesus, Roman and Jewish relations continued to deteriorate. The crisis came to a head in 66 C.E. when the Roman procurator, Florus, stole seventeen talents from the temple treasury. Indignant Jews walked around Jerusalem begging for money for "poor Florus." Enraged, Florus sent his soldiers to plunder the city. The temple priest refused to make the daily animal sacrifice on behalf of the Roman emperor's welfare. Insurgent Jews occupied the temple area, challenging Florus to retreat to Caesarea. Meanwhile Zealots under the leadership of Menahem, son of Judas of Galilee, captured the Roman fort at Masada. The fort sat on the top of a well-protected peak near the Dead Sea.

Bitter clashes between Jewish freedom fighters and Roman soldiers broke out in Jerusalem. By the end of the summer, Jewish revolutionaries had driven all the Roman soldiers out of the country. In fact, it took Rome a year to reconquer Galilee and three more years to retake Jerusalem, but reconquer they did.

Zealots from Masada and Galilee converged on Jerusalem for a final stand against the brutal Roman forces. After recapturing Galilee, the Roman forces moved south to Jerusalem. Systematically destroying villages, they either slaughtered or enslaved the people in their path. During the Passover season of 70 C.E. the Roman general Titus, with an army of 24,000 men, launched an all-out attack on Jerusalem. Roman power crushed the freedom fighters.

Before fire destroyed the temple, Titus grabbed some sacred Jewish symbols—the seven-branched candlestick and the table of shewbread—as trophies for his triumphant return to Rome. The holy temple lay in smoldering ruins. A few rebels entrenched themselves in the Masada fortress until 73 C.E. When Roman soldiers finally gained access to the top of the summit, only several women and children were alive. The zealous patriots preferred suicide to defeat!

The Masada defeat, however, didn't extinguish the flame of Jewish nationalism. In 132 C.E., in response to a Roman edict forbidding circumcision, it burst forth again under the leadership of Bar Kochba. With a force of 200,000 men he set up an independent Jewish state which lasted three years. The Romans lost 5,000-6,000 soldiers before finally cutting Bar Kochba down in the second Jewish-Roman War. In the end, the victorious Romans smashed some 1,000 villages, executed more than 500,000 people, destroyed Jerusalem, and sent thousands away as slaves. The destruction of Jerusalem in 135 C.E. altered, of course, both Jewish and Christian history.

The Low Mountain

Although the Jews could perform their prescribed sacrifices during the Roman occupation, there were underlying irritants. Since

Herod the Great's era, the political rulers hired and fired the high priests. Thus even the high priest was ultimately a Roman puppet. Furthermore, the eight-piece uniform the high priest wore to symbolize the essence of Jewish faith was guarded by Roman soldiers in Fortress Antonia to prevent possible uprisings. The soldiers gave it to the high priest only on festival days. A final insult was the requirement of a daily sacrifice, offered in the temple to Yahweh, on behalf of the Roman emperor.

This turbulent political context framed Jesus' face-off with the devil on the high mountain. Revolutionary turmoil filled the valleys below. The Palestine of Jesus' childhood was not serene. It was a caldron of revolutionary fervor. Only against this backdrop can we grasp the meaning of his political temptation. The possibility of a political kingship was not an idle offer. It was the fervent goal of many messianic prophets with whom Jesus surely was familiar.

The temptation Jesus refused was not merely an invitation to join the ranks of Jewish patriots. It was not only a temptation to unshackle Roman control. It was also a snare to endorse violence—the accepted mode of governing.

On the high mountain Jesus rejected brute force as the proper mode for governing others. The rules of political power sanctioned force, violence, and bloodshed. Jesus spurned this right-side-up institution of coercive political power. He chose to demonstrate a new power, a new way of ruling. He refused to play the game by the old rules. But in the end, his upside-down way so threatened the old kingdoms that he was crucified as "King of the Jews."

The mountain in the temptation symbolizes divine power.[18] It was on the mountain that God met his people through Moses (Exod. 24). Preaching on a mountain, Jesus later described the people of his new kingdom as merciful, meek, pure in heart, and peaceful (Matt. 5). And on a mountain, he called his disciples (Luke 6:12-13).

After feeding the five thousand, Jesus returned to the mountain for prayer and rejuvenation (Mark 6:46). The divine confirmation "this is my Son, The Beloved," came from a cloud atop a high mountain (Mark 9:2, 7). And from the Mount of Olives Jesus began his kingly descent into Jerusalem on a donkey (Matt. 21:1).

He was arrested a few days later on the same Mount of Olives when he didn't resist capture (Luke 22:39). After the resurrection the disciples met him on a mountain in Galilee (Matt. 28:16). Finally, on the Mount called Olivet, the risen Jesus told his followers: "You will receive power when the Holy Spirit has come upon you" (Acts 1:8, 12).

The mountain symbolizes the strength of divine power and the nearness of God. Jesus redefined the meaning of power when he refused to use violent force. Nevertheless, it was hard for him to toss the lure of force aside. Matthew and Mark report three occasions when Jesus spoke of suffering as the new form of messianic power. Each time the disciples were arguing over how much power and authority they would have in the kingdom. In all three cases, Jesus responded by teaching them about suffering discipleship.

He made one thing abundantly clear: the heroes of the upside-down kingdom are not warrior kings riding in chariots or peasant kings carrying pitchforks. The heroes of this kingdom are children and servants. These lowly ones carry the new flag of the servant regime. They operate not by the power of might and force but by the sustaining power of the Holy Spirit flowing from the mountain of God.

Did Jesus Use a Dagger?

Was Jesus a terrorist? Some argue he was.[19] He supposedly espoused the bloody tactics of the dagger men. Proponents of this position argue that the Gospels, written more than forty years after Jesus' death, deliberately camouflaged his violent streak so early Christians wouldn't appear threatening to Roman authorities.[20] In other words, gospel writers may have masked Jesus' violence with images of a peace-loving shepherd.

Several reasons are given for placing Jesus with the zealous rebels.[21] He instructed the disciples to sell their clothing and buy swords at the Last Supper (Luke 22:36). With a whip he drove the money changers and their animals out of the temple (John 2:15). The Romans, considering him a political seditionist and agitator, crucified him as "king of the Jews" (Luke 23:38). Barabbas, a known rebel, had led a political insurrection. But considered less dangerous than Jesus, he was released, whereas Jesus was killed (Luke 23:25).

Jesus himself said he came to bring not peace but a sword (Matt. 10:34). Like other zealous prophets, Jesus did proclaim a kingdom. He criticized kings who ruled over people (Mark 10:42). He even called Herod a fox (Luke 13:32). At least one of his followers, Simon, was called "the Zealot" (Luke 6:15). Some interpreters use these things to align Jesus with violent revolutionaries.

In the gospel accounts we find that Jesus was indeed a revolutionary—of sorts. He did defy the ruling religious, political, and economic powers. His statement that the law of love supersedes the dictates of human institutions made him a revolutionary. But he hardly was a violent one.

Without refuting the charge that Jesus was a zealous rebel point by point, considerable evidence, suggests Jesus wasn't among the violent rebels of his day.[22] Zealous terrorists thought humans should help God usher in the kingdom. In contrast, Jesus told his followers, "Fear not, little flock, for it is your Father's good pleasure to give you the kingdom" (Luke 12:32). Although Jesus strongly criticized the rich, he never resorted to violence. His teaching on wealth would have also threatened Roman interests and would likely have been erased by Gospel writers had they merely been trying to appease Roman officials. Pilate may have viewed Jesus as a political threat, but that doesn't mean Jesus acted in violent ways.

Purging the temple of money changers wasn't a mandate for violence despite the fact that Jesus was dramatic and forceful. Had a major riot erupted, the 600 Roman soldiers in Fort Antonia, overlooking the temple, would have quickly intervened. The temple drama was a prophetic condemnation of profiteering by money changers and a sign that the temple should be opened for Gentile worship. The prophetic Word—not action—stood at the center of the temple purge.

Jesus severely rebuked the ear-cutting resistance of his disciple when he was "captured" in Gethsemane. If the disciples had been heavily armed, a major clash would have likely developed. Had the disciples been deemed a violent threat, they would certainly have been captured and crucified, not allowed to flee into the darkness.

Perhaps the most convincing evidence that Jesus wasn't in the revolutionary camp was his warm embrace of tax collectors and publicans. Zealous rebels hated tax collectors—traitors who exploited fellow Jews under the power of Roman rule. The rebels were willing to kill Jewish tax collectors, but Jesus embraced them. He even invited them to join his disciple band. Jesus taught that the radical call of the kingdom undercuts loyalties to other human institutions. This unique message stood apart from the coercive and sometimes violent tactics of the zealous.

Persuasive evidence that Jesus rejected violence permeates his message and his life. As we've already seen, he turned down the political temptation to rule with force. He instructs us instead to love enemies, bless cursers, and forgive up to 490 times. In short, he calls us to serve, not rule. He shows the way of love in stories where enemies help enemies. The paramount lesson, of course, is his own example on the cross. Though violated and tortured, he refused retaliation. With nails searing his flesh he refused to curse. He begs, instead, for forgiveness for those who "know not what they do"—forgiving at once both ignorance and stupidity.

The final evidence for a nonviolent Jesus comes from the teachings of the early church. For two and a half centuries after his death, the early church forbid members to enter military service. This practice would hardly have developed if in fact Jesus had espoused the use of violent resistance during his life.[23]

Jesus was a revolutionary in violating Sabbath laws, criticizing the greedy, eating with sinners, and provoking the Pharisees. His message of the kingdom threatened the power of vested interest groups. The Romans considered him a threat to their false political tranquillity. The right-wing Sadducees hated his condemnation of their lucrative temple operation. Progressive Pharisees decried his disrespect for their laws of ritual purity. And the freedom fighters couldn't stand his talk about suffering. The temptation to use violence was difficult to shove aside. But to endorse violence would have negated his entire platform of suffering love.

Jesus was revolutionary when he attacked the root of the problem—the evil which often laces human intentions and institutions. He called for repentance. He pled for love. He announced that only

God should be worshiped. He admitted before Pilate that indeed he was Lord of this new kingdom. But his upside-down revolution replaced force with suffering and violence with love.

Jesus did threaten the status quo. He rocked the cozy boats of Sadducees, Pharisees, Romans and rebels alike. In some ways he looked like other insurrectionists of his day. But his revolution was upside-down. It touted acts of compassion, not daggers. Love was the new Torah, the standard of his upside-down kingdom.

3

Temple Piety

A Heavenly Parachute

Ruling the world by force wasn't the only enticement Jesus faced. There was religion itself to contend with. The devil's next trick invited Jesus to embrace institutionalized religion. There were many devout Jews in the first century; however, as can happen in any faith, some aspects of formal religion had gone stale. A complex code—interlaced with do's and don'ts, pilgrimages, and sacrifices—encompassed much of Jewish life, from civil law to national festivals. Some rituals had become empty and self-serving.

Religious fervor nevertheless ran deep and strong. Jesus' upside-down way would clash with the religious heavyweights who guarded the sacred rites of Hebrew ritual in God's holy name. The authorities would rage as Jesus demolished their cherished assumptions and practices. Their teeth would grind at the blasphemous suggestion that God's ambassador was in their midst, upsetting tables in the holy temple—in the very apex of their entire system.

A miraculous appearance, a sudden bolt from heaven, would certainly convince even the most skeptical Sadducee of Jesus' divine authority. And so the devil offered Jesus an attractive option: why not miraculously certify your mission? This would eliminate any harassment by religious leaders. A miraculous, divine blessing near the sacred temple would erase any doubts about Jesus' messianic authority. The masses would quickly follow if the scribes and wise men embraced the newcomer. Parachuting into the temple court would make Jesus an instant the Messiah.

And so the devil taunted, "Come on, Jesus, go for it. Bypass the anger of the Pharisees. Forget the poverty and disease. Don't stir up the anger of the rich. Why worry about a cross? Go for it Jesus. Just parachute in and everyone will know you're Messiah."

Thirty-Five Acres of Piety

What lay beneath the temple temptation? The temple was the pinnacle of religious life, the very heart of Jewish worship, ritual, and emotion. The temple at Jerusalem stirred passions. It was shrouded in mystery and awe. It was the seat of wisdom, law, and Scripture. It housed the *one* Jewish altar on which the high priest performed the sacrificial rites of atonement *once* a year for the entire Jewish world. Here and *only* here was forgiveness possible with the proper sacrifice. In the one and *only* Holy of Holies, the high priest entered the presence of God. The Holy of Holies was the literal home of God. Jerusalem was the "city of the temple." The arteries of Jewish religion pulsated with the heartthrob of the temple. It was the obvious place for the cunning devil to test Jesus.

We may visualize the temple as a contemporary church building, but a modest shopping mall offers a better comparison. The temple itself—about 100 feet long, 35 feet wide, and 60 feet high—stood inside a thirty-five acre plaza area. Herod the Great doubled the size of the temple plaza. Magnificent marble colonnades and towering walls ranging from 100 to 300 feet high enclosed the entire complex. Some of the stones in the walls weighed 70 tons and foundational ones topped 500 tons. Guards stationed at various entranceways monitored the flow of traffic.

The open temple plaza was divided into two areas: Gentile and Jewish. The court of the Gentiles, open to all, covered about two-thirds of the plaza area. A low stone wall barred Gentiles from entering the three-part Jewish area: the Court of Women, the Court of Israelites, and the Court of Priests. Jewish men brought their animal offerings to the Court of Israelites and gave them to the priests who killed and sacrificed the animals on the altar in the Court of Priests. The Holy of Holies was inside the sanctuary directly behind the altar. A completely dark and empty room, about 30 feet square, it was Almighty God's sacred abode.

The temple complex included two additional structures. The large Royal Stoa, inside the 900-foot southern wall, housed the commercial operations of the temple. Here, money changers traded the pristine Tyrian half shekel required for offerings and sold animals for sacrifice. Outside the northern wall stood the Antonia

Fortress, where Roman soldiers overlooked the entire area ready to squelch any disturbance.[1]

The temple building, which housed the Holy of Holies, wasn't used for public worship because it was considered the literal "house of God." Worship, sacrifice, and other rituals took place in the large open courts outside the temple. Gold and silver covered much of the temple building including the furnishings and the roof. From the distant countryside it appeared as a glittering peak on the holy mountain. There was so much gold in the temple that after its destruction and plunder in 70 C.E., the province of Syria was glutted with gold, halving its value.

A Hebrew proverb exclaimed, "He who has not seen the holy place in its detailed construction has never seen a splendid building in his life." Even the disciples of Jesus were impressed. They remarked with awe, "Look, Teacher, what large stones and what large buildings!" (Mark 13:1). The size of the temple is underscored by the fact that nearly 20,000 workmen lost their jobs when its reconstruction was finally completed in 62 C.E.

Roughly 18,000 *priests* and *Levites*, divided into twenty-four groups called "courses," were involved in the temple operation. These lay priests and Levites lived in the countryside of Galilee and Judea and came to the temple for weeklong tours of duty twice a year. They also helped during three annual festivals attended by Jewish pilgrims from many countries. When the temple veil was purified, 300 priests were needed to dip it in a tank of water. Two hundred Levites were required each evening just to close the temple doors. Dozens of money changers sold pilgrims "pure" money for tithes and hucksters peddled animals for sacrifice. The temple had three functions: ritual, economic, and administrative.

An elite group of chief priests managed the whole operation. The temple treasury also functioned as a huge national bank. It held the tithes and offerings required of Jews throughout the world. The elaborate temple operation generated the major source of revenue for the city of Jerusalem, and its tentacles stretched into the countryside where it owned large estates farmed by poor peasants.

Devout Jews living beyond Palestine came to the temple three times a year to celebrate religious festivities. In springtime the Feast

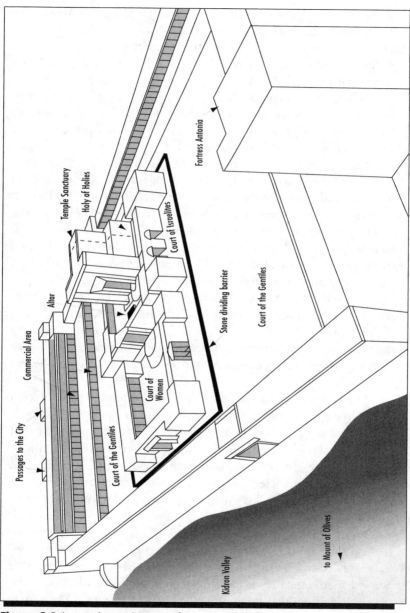

Figure 3.1 Approximate Layout of 35 acre Temple Plaza

of the Passover chronicled the deliverance from Egypt. About fifty days later the Feast of Pentecost offered thanks for the first fruits of the harvest. In the fall the Feast of Tabernacles included a solemn march around the altar in gratitude to God for the completed harvest. Most importantly, the great Day of Atonement was celebrated in autumn. On that day, the high priest sacrificed a goat for his own sins and sent another one into the desert for the sins of the people. During these pilgrim festivals, Jerusalem's normal population of about 25,000 swelled upwards of 180,000 people.

The temple stood as a monumental reminder that God's elect people had direct access to him through their sacrificial ritual. Each morning and each afternoon, day after day, the "continual" burnt offering of an unblemished lamb was sacrificed on behalf of the community. These perpetual offerings likely required some 1,200 animals per year.[2] An offering of incense mixed with spices burned daily. Devout Jews also offered private sacrifices. The smell of smoke, burning meat, and animal fat filled the air of the temple. The priests held various duties in the sacrificial system. They removed ashes from the altar, prepared firewood, killed the lamb, sprinkled blood on the altar, cleaned the lampstand, and prepared the meal and drink offering.[3] At least twenty priests, chosen by lot each day, performed the regular sacrifices while others attended to special offerings.

The temple was the centerpiece of Jewish faith. It symbolized God's living presence on earth. Folks came to the temple to pray, believing that from this site their prayers went directly to the ear of God. Here both Nazarite and Gentile convert offered sacrifices. Here was brought the wife suspected of adultery. Here the first fruits were offered. Here mothers presented purification offerings at the birth of each child. This holy place was the fountain of forgiveness.

From all over the Mediterranean world flowed Jewish taxes to support the temple. Three times a year the people themselves flooded here for festivities.[4] This was home to the seventy-member Sanhedrin, the final Jewish authority in religious, political, and civil matters. Here resided the high priest. In all these ways the temple throbbed with the worldwide heartbeat of Jewish faith. It is quite impossible to overstate the importance of the temple and of sacrifice. Place and ritual formed the sacred core of Hebrew religion.

Sanitized Ritual

Contemporary images of the temple as stately sanctuary in a quiet suburb are historical distortions. Think again! Imagine a huge slaughterhouse on the edge of a thirty-five acre plaza surrounded by high walls. Animals squealed as their throats were slit. Gallons of blood flowed underground into the special ducts built for that purpose at the bottom of the outdoor altar. The slaughter struck tens of thousands of animals a year.

The sacrificial ritual was a huge system of purification. Like a large kidney, it filtered the impurities of sin out of personal and collective lives making them acceptable to a holy God who demanded purity. Some six different offerings required a sacrifice at the temple: burnt, cereal, peace, purification, reparation, and the thank offering.[5] Three major occupational groups—*priests, Levites,* and *scribes* served the large temple operation.

The high priest, priest of all priests, was the symbolic head of both faith and nation. He wore a splendid eight-part outfit with each piece invoking power to atone for specific sins. *Only* the high priest, in perfect purity, could part the curtains and enter the Holy of Holies in the very presence of God once a year on the Day of Atonement. He officiated at sacrifices on the Sabbath and during pilgrim festivals. Even his death had atoning power. Slayers who fled to a city of refuge after accidentally killing someone could only return home upon the high priest's death.

The high priest was subject to strict laws of ceremonial purity. He couldn't touch a corpse nor enter a house of mourning. "Arab spittle" once contaminated a high priest on the evening before the Day of Atonement. Thereafter, high priests were required to undergo a secluded, seven-day purification before officiating at the Day of Atonement. No one was to see the high priest naked or when shaving or taking a bath. His pedigree had to be immaculate. It required direct ties to the family of Aaron. Strict rules required him to marry only a twelve-year-old virgin of pure descent. Many priests married the daughters of priests.

The high priest's role wasn't only pompous and ceremonial. He wielded considerable power as president of the Sanhedrin. This supreme council had complete judicial and administrative authority in religious and civil matters. Its judgment on religious issues was respected far beyond the borders of Judea. It was a self-perpetuating body composed of chief priests, scribes (usually, though not always, from the Pharisee party), and nobility. Although lower courts met in various districts of Judea, the Sanhedrin was the supreme court of Jewish authority.

The power of the high priest grew considerably under the Roman procurators. He became the key Jewish spokesperson, not only for ceremonial matters, but also for political negotiations with the Romans. Sixteen of the eighteen high priests between 6 C.E. and 67 C.E. came from five prominent and wealthy Jerusalem families.

An extensive pecking order of religious officials stretched below the high priest and the Sanhedrin. The captain of the temple managed the temple staff. He ranked next to the high priest because he often helped the priest perform solemn duties. On the next rung were twenty-four priests who directed twenty-four groups of some 7,000 ordinary priests. They lived throughout the countryside and participated in temple ritual at least five times a year. Next were 156 priests who served as daily managers of other priests working in the temple that particular day.

The temple's administrative affairs were the responsibility of seven permanent overseers. Next in line came three treasurers who managed the temple treasury by collecting taxes, purchasing sacrificial materials, and supervising the sale of animals to pilgrims. They also maintained the ninety-three gold and silver vessels used for daily rituals and managed the property owned by the temple. Next in rank were the ordinary priests who lived in the countryside and trekked to the temple five times a year to perform their sacred duties. Zechariah, John the Baptist's father (Luke 1:5), was one of these.

At the bottom of the ritual ladder stood almost 10,000 Levites. Living in surrounding villages, they helped in the temple when their weeklong shift was on duty. Levites were considered inferior to priests, although some Levites served as singers and musicians. The rest did the temple's dirty work—serving as gatekeepers, security guards, trash collectors, and sanitation workers throughout the temple area.[6] Scribes served as clerks, recorders, legal experts, and accountants. There were likely a variety of clerical or, as we might say today, "secretarial" roles the scribes played—copying documents, writing letters and agreements, recording taxes, and drawing up legal papers. Although not an organized social group, the scribes served clerical functions from village life to royal court. Many scribes were also students of the Torah: the Law.

Laying Down the Law

Jewish piety and passion were rooted in temple and Torah. At the heart of temple activities and at the core of Jewish religion was the Torah.[7] Usually known as the "Law," it's better translated "doctrine" or "religious teaching." Technically it refers to the five books of Moses. In addition, students of the Torah composed oral interpretations or commentaries on the Scripture. These oral "fences around the Torah" translated the Torah into practical guidelines for daily living. So the Torah included not only the five books of Moses but also the oral commentary which grew up around it.

The Torah, Jews believed, contained God's absolute and unquestionable will. To obey it was to obey God. A cult of worship developed around the Torah, personifying it as the "well beloved daughter of God." It was said that Yahweh devoted leisure hours to the study of the Torah, even reading it aloud on the Sabbath. Jews saw it as the absolute standard for all aspects of religious life. It was *the* source of God's truth.

Continual reading and discussion of the Torah was a prime sacred activity. In the oral commentary that encrusted the Torah, pious Jews could discover whether it was lawful to eat an egg laid on the Sabbath. They could learn if water, poured from a clean bucket into an unclean one, contaminated the clean one from which it was poured. The Torah guided sacrifice in the Jerusalem temple and worship in village synagogues.

As we've seen, *priests* and *Levites* provided the expertise and labor to operate the temple. In addition to their clerical roles, the *scribes* explained the Torah's secrets.[8] The better educated and upper level scribes unraveled the complex traditions surrounding the Torah. Carefully trained, the scribes were sometimes known as "doctors of the Law." They were reverently called "rabbi," "teacher," "master," and "father." The scribes wore a special robe, a long mantle reaching to their feet, etched with a fringe. People rose respectfully when these men of wisdom and learning passed by on the streets. The highest seats of honor in the synagogue were reserved for them.

In their early teens, some young men would embark on a scribal career by taking a regular course of study. The young student would apprentice with an older rabbi for several years until he had mastered the fine points of the Torah and its commentary. At about forty years of age, the student was ordained as a full-fledged scribe with all the rights of a wise scholar. After ordination he could make decisions on religious legislation and ceremonial purity, as well as on criminal and civil proceedings. Only ordained scholars could create and transmit the traditions of the Torah.

Except for high priests and those from noble families, scribes were the only persons who could sit on the powerful Sanhedrin. Young Jews from around the world streamed to Jerusalem at the time of Jesus to study with esteemed scribes because Jerusalem was the theological center of Judaism. Influential scribes, in short, "were venerated, like the prophets of old, with unbounded respect and reverential awe.[9] As teachers of sacred knowledge; their words held sovereign authority."

Party Politics

In our exploration of Jewish religion we've scanned the formal roles of priest, Levite, and scribe. We've looked briefly at the temple, Sanhedrin, and synagogue. In addition to these roles and organizations, there were two religious political parties—the *Sadducees* and the *Pharisees*. These parties developed in the second century B.C.E. because of religious and social differences.

The watershed dividing them was their understanding of the Torah. The Sadducees considered the written Torah, the five books of Moses, their final authority. They rejected the oral commentary on the Torah, which the Pharisees accepted.[10] The Sadducees also denied the resurrection, personal immortality, and the future life. Moreover, they were skeptical of demons and angels. In short, the Sadducees represented the conservative element of Judaism. They were the defenders of the *true* faith of Israel handed down by Moses.

The Sadducees lived primarily in Jerusalem. They were drawn from the governing class and the wealthy aristocracy. Some of the chief priests were members of the Sadducean party. They were closely involved with temple operations and dominated the Sanhedrin. In short, the Sadducees steered the religious and social affairs of the wealthy Jerusalem upper class. The Sadducees supported both the political and religious status quo in Jerusalem. They accepted Roman control and collaborated with it, as long as they could keep the blood flowing on the altar and retain their privileged status.

In contrast, the Pharisaic party represented the progressive wing of Judaism.[11] As progressives in the pursuit of holiness, the Pharisees applied the Torah to practical, everyday issues. Known as "separated ones," the Pharisees had developed the oral tradition to apply the Torah to each and every situation a Jew might face. The

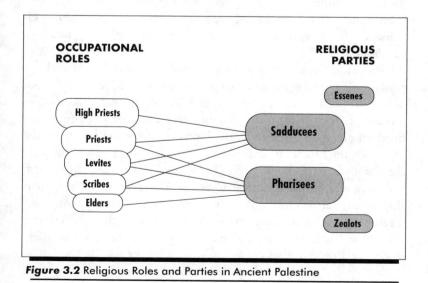

Figure 3.2 Religious Roles and Parties in Ancient Palestine

Torah spelled out rules of purity for officiating priests. The Pharisees sought to extend these rules, these habits of holiness, to the everyday life of the common people. By encouraging average people to be pure, pious, and holy, they hoped to eventually mold all Israelites into a holy priesthood—a kingdom of priests, a holy nation.

The Pharisees are often confused with the scribes. Some scribes joined the Pharisee party while other ones affiliated with the Sadducees. Some members of the Pharisees came from pious common folk. The Pharisees operated primarily in the rural countryside, promoting their doctrine in local synagogues. As champions of holiness for the common people, they stood in opposition to the rich Sadducean elite. Jesus' appeal to commoners threatened the rural political base of the Pharisees and stirred their barbed criticism of him.

Although they enjoyed widespread support, the Pharisees numbered only about 6,000. This was due, most likely, to their strictness. Prospective members had a probationary year to prove their compliance with the meticulous laws of purity. The Pharisees challenged the ruling establishment in Jerusalem, but they also disdained common people who were careless about ceremonial purity and tithing. Strict legalists they were, but they also welcomed new interpretations—ever seeking to apply the Torah to new issues.

Two additional political movements were the *Essenes* and the *freedom fighters*. As we have seen, the freedom fighters were not organized until several decades after Jesus' death when the Zealots formed. Before that, social bandits and protesters championing freedom emerged independently. However, near the shores of the Dead Sea, the Essenes took a different tactic than the freedom fighters: they withdrew from society. These separatists created a self-sufficient communal society at Qumran. Unhappy with the leadership of the Jerusalem temple, they opted out of the system. They created their own purification rituals and expected the world to end in a great battle between the sons of light and the sons of darkness—the Romans.[12]

Messianic Hopes

Regardless of their political views, the Sadducees, Pharisees, Essenes, and freedom fighters were all expecting a messiah who would rout out the Romans and set things straight in Palestine. They differed, of course, in how much they thought God needed their help. Thus, at the birth of Jesus, messianic hopes were alive in the Jewish community. There were many stripes of hope. But the deepest yearning was for a new ruler anointed by God—one who would reestablish the Davidic throne in all its former glory and usher in a peaceable kingdom of God.

Such hope had intensified in the century before Jesus. The Psalms of Solomon, written during that time, picture the Messiah as overthrowing rude Gentiles who intrude in God's holy place and expelling corrupt Jewish priests who pervert the worship of Yahweh. The Anointed One will gather the scattered tribes in the Promised Land. He will bring blessed days in every way. Under him, Jerusalem, the holy city of God's presence, will reign supreme—"a place to be seen in all the earth."[13] In Luke (1:32-33) the angel Gabriel offers Mary a fresh vision of the messianic reign.

> He will be great, and will be called the Son of the Most High,
>   and the Lord God will give to him the *throne* of his ancestor
>   David.
> He will *reign* over the house of Jacob forever,
>   and of his *kingdom* there will be no end
> (emphasis added).

A similar refrain comes from the mouth of Zechariah, the father of John the Baptist, recorded in Luke (1:68-72.)

> Blessed be the Lord God of Israel,
>   for he has looked favorably on his people and redeemed them.
> He has raised up a mighty savior for us
>   in the house of his servant David,
>   as he spoke through the mouth of his holy prophets from of old,
>   that we would be saved from our enemies
>   and from the hand of all who hate us.
> Thus he has shown the mercy promised to our ancestors.

It was uncertain how the Messiah would appear. Some thought he would come from the skies, riding a cloud. Others expected him to be human-born but suddenly revealed in a decisive disclosure. Jerusalem, home of the sacred temple, was the very site where such messianic texts were carefully studied. It was the obvious place for the devil's snare.

The temptation account doesn't specify exactly where the devil wanted Jesus to jump. Was it over the edge of the temple wall, falling hundreds of feet into the Kidron Valley below? Or was he to plummet inside the plaza courtyard at the temple's entrance? Regardless of the mode, a miraculous parachute would certify, beyond all reasonable doubt, the Messiah's arrival. He would stun everyone at the center of religious life where things were done properly, in exact compliance with the law. The scribes, the Sanhedrin, the high priests—all the religious heavyweights—would witness the miraculous arrival. Seeing the miracle with their own eyes, they would quickly claim Jesus as the real Messiah.

Such divine certification would mute any confrontation with the religious establishment. Opponents would fall silent. The Jerusalem aristocracy would welcome the new miracle worker. Jesus could avoid wandering among poor peasants in Galilee. There would be no doubt—Jesus the Messiah had arrived!

Upside-Down Messiah

The thought of basking in the religious establishments' doting approval must have tantalized Jesus. But he turned away. He rejected right-side-up religion. The temptation apparently nagged him, nevertheless, right up to the crucifixion. As the guards arrested him in Gethsemane, he reminded the ear-cutting disciple that he could call a cloud of angels to defend him. But he didn't. Instead of succumbing to institutionalized religion, Jesus uprooted its very foundations. His parables wreaked harsh judgment on Jewish leaders. He willfully violated sacred Sabbath laws. "Blasphemer!" cried the religious leaders when he chased merchants from the temple and called the holy shrine a den of robbers.

Yet he didn't completely spurn established religion. He taught in synagogues and in the temple. He endorsed the Torah. He asked cured lepers to show themselves to the priest, according to tradition. He directed Peter to catch a fish to pay the temple tax. Truth be told, he was a Jew, a Jewish prophet in the eyes of most people. He supported the virtues of the Law and the piety of genuine Hebrew faith. He took on the hard task of critiquing Judaism from within.

But when religious practices grew stale he turned them upside-down and inside out and called them back to their original purpose. He refused to bless religious structures, which ranked people by their pious deeds. He replaced the machinery of formalized religion with compassion and love. Jesus, the upside-down Messiah, would become the new high priest. God's Spirit would vacate the Holy of Holies in the temple and abide in the heart of each believer. No longer would people worship God in the holy temple or on a sacred mountain. Now they could approach God anywhere in spirit and in truth (John 4:23). Now the Spirit would dwell in the temple of each believer. Worship would be freed from elaborate buildings and complicated ritual. In the words of the Gospels, "Something greater than the temple is here" (Matt. 12:6). Greater than the temple! Such an idea—almost impossible to grasp—was outrageous to Jewish ears.

As the story unfolded, Jesus would become the final and definitive sacrifice. He would be the unblemished Lamb of God slain for the sins of the world. Jesus would reveal the secrets of the new Torah of love. This Torah would end ceremonial cleansing and sacrifice. He would offer forgiveness to sinners directly from God without trekking to the temple or slitting sacrificial throats.

Jesus affirmed the new, upside-down religion when he told a scribe that he was close to the kingdom of God if he placed love for God, self, and neighbor above *all* the burnt offerings (Mark 12:34). In Jesus we see upside-down religion—no building, no program, no elite clergy. In Jesus we have a final sacrifice, a definitive offering, a new temple in each believer's heart, and a new Torah—the law of love.

Jesus rejected the temptation for spectacular display. He preferred the messianic secret—the role of the servant Savior. Throughout his ministry, he was slow to disclose his identity. He spoke in riddles and parables. People he miraculously healed he forbade to speak. This was no arrogant, horn-blowing Messiah. This was no magician performing special signs so the crowds could clap. His life itself was the sign. Care for the lost, compassion for the poor, and love even for enemies. These were the messianic signs.

The new heroes were the castaways of institutional religion. They were repentant sinners, publicans, confessing tax collectors, and harlots. And what of the old heroes—scribes, priests, Pharisees, and Sadducees—the guardians of sacred ritual? They now were dethroned, brought low, and told to become like children. No wonder his message annoyed them. No wonder they killed him.

4
Wilderness Bread

Welfare King

Jesus rejected pompous power and spectacular religion, but the devil had one more snare. Would Jesus be a welfare king? Why not miraculously feed the poor?

Was Jesus tempted to turn stones into bread merely because he was hungry? This interpretation may hold one grain of truth. But the fuller significance of the temptation lies in the economic plight of Palestine's masses. Bread symbolizes the heart of material life. The core of many diets, it appears on tables meal after meal, week after week. In the Lord's Prayer—"give us this day our daily bread"—bread represents basic necessities. Through his literal hunger, Jesus identified with the thousands of poor peasants whose daily existence revolved around the search for bread. His gnawing appetite stirred him to act on behalf of others who shared his pain.

Jesus' temptation, however, isn't to gobble down boulders of bread to relieve a forty-day fast.[1] Thinking of bread reminds him of God's manna freely distributed during the Israelites' forty-year roam in the desert. Perhaps memories of hometown Nazareth also come to mind. He sees ruthless creditors pushing poor peasant farmers off their land and a system of double taxation oppressing the masses. He hears the lepers, the blind, and the poor—trampled by the pious and greedy—crying for help. Why not miraculously feed the masses and throw a divine banquet for his followers? Free food would surely bring a groundswell of public support in Galilee. "Feed 'em, Jesus, feed 'em," the tempter whispers, "You have the power. Go ahead. Bake the bread!"

Even the religious authorities were afraid of the masses. The nighttime arrest of Jesus was prompted by their fear of the crowds. Jesus himself realized that a well-fed mob could seize him and make him king by force (John 6:15). Bread was the quickest way to the heart of the crowd. Mark peppers his Gospel with references to multitudes (numbering in the thousands) following Jesus. Luke (12:1) notes that the surging multitudes once squeezed so tightly they trampled each other. Neither Pilate nor the high priest could defuse the contagious frenzy of mob action. Feeding the crowds offered Jesus a shortcut to galvanizing their political support.

The bread temptation involved more than an abuse of power. It would reduce God incarnate to a welfare king. The enticing thoughts flow on: "Lessen their poverty without suffering. Let the religious authorities continue their idolatry. Don't preach God's judgment on the greedy—just distribute bread to the hungry. Don't criticize economic injustice, the temple, and Roman control—just toss bread to poor Galilean peasants and let the world go by." Such devilish suggestions would have reduced humans to soulless organisms—to mere bread-eating animals.

Very Rich and Very Poor

Most members of developed societies belong to a large middle class. In sharp contrast, first-century Palestine had basically two economic classes: *upper* and *lower*.[2] In peasant societies rooted in agriculture, ninety percent or more of the people are usually poor peasants. Wealth is based on land ownership, but much of it is held by wealthy absentee landlords.

So it was in Palestine. A small *upper class* accounted for ten percent or less of the population. These were the landowners, hereditary aristocrats; appointed bureaucrats, chief priests, merchants, government officials, and various official servants who served the needs of the governing class. The rest of the people— likely ninety percent or more—were in the *lower class*. Mostly poor peasants living precariously, hand-to-mouth, they were at the mercy of weather, famine, pestilence, bandits, and war.

There were some layers within the lower class. Near the top were craftsmen, carpenters, masons, fishermen, and traders.[3] Most, however, were farmers. Some were tenant farmers or sharecroppers on large estates owned by absentee landowners. Others farmed their own plots. Still others were day laborers picking up work wherever they could. On the fringe of the lower class were "unclean" occupations such as leather tanning. At the bottom of the bottom were the outcasts—peasants forced off their land, wandering vagabonds, beggars, and lepers. These down-and-outers may have numbered some ten percent of the peasant class.

In Galilee, where much of Jesus' ministry took place, the middle class was also absent. One historian describing Galilee says, "It can be safely concluded that there existed both the extremely rich and the miserably poor, the latter being the lot of the majority of the people."[4] The parables and sayings of Jesus assume a two-class system of rich and poor. Despite many small distinctions, one stark reality dominated the economic landscape: the *few* lived in luxury while the *many* lived in poverty. The large middle class of modern capitalist societies was simply absent.

Plush Aristocrats

Jerusalem was more than a high religious peak—it towered above the country in social and economic prestige as well. An elite aristocracy, including chief priests, wealthy landowners, merchants, tax collectors, and Sadducees, called Jerusalem home.[5] The upper class—landowners living off the rent of their estates, skilled artists, clever traders, and poets—all flowed toward the city that held the great temple.

Extravagance oozed from the affluent elite. Gold bindings bundled the palm branches they carried to festivities. They brought offerings of firstfruits in golden vessels on Pentecost day. A city ordinance prohibited covering their phylacteries with gold. Two men reportedly wagered the equivalent of more than a year's salary on being able to anger one of the leading rabbis. Archaeological evidence readily documents the rich lifestyles of the small aristocratic class living in the upper city of Jerusalem adjacent to the temple.[6]

Many of the rich in Jerusalem derived their wealth from vast country estates farmed by slaves, hired men or tenants. One of Herod's chancellors owned an entire village. It was said that another person had inherited 1,000 villages, 1,000 ships, and so many slaves that they didn't know their master. According to the sages, a wealthy man was one who had a hundred vineyards, a hundred fields, and a hundred slaves. Some of the special artists working in the temple received the equivalent of 300 dollars a day. Unskilled workers in Jerusalem received their food and about twenty-five cents a day.

On the Day of Atonement, everyone was required to go barefoot. To protect her feet, the wife of a high priest carpeted the path from her house to the temple. A snobbish attitude permeated Jerusalem's elite. They wouldn't sign a document as a witness unless the other witnesses were also well to do. They accepted dinner invitations only if the other guests matched their own high status. The arrogance kept the elite from mingling with common people, except to employ them as servants.

The rich gave large dowries when their daughters married. Indeed, one dowry exceeded a million gold denarii, the financial equivalent of a million days of work. In the unlikely case a poor

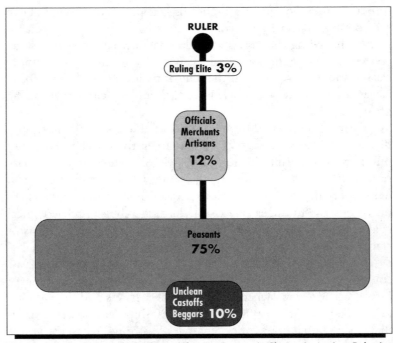

Figure 4.1 Approximate Distribution of Socio-economic Classes in Ancient Palestine

peasant married an urbanite, the poor had to pay enormous sums. A village man who took a Jerusalem bride was required to give his weight in gold as a betrothal gift. A country bride also brought her weight in gold to her city groom. Joseph of Arimathea (Matt. 27:57), friend of Jesus and a rich man, no doubt belonged to this rich upper crust. Jerusalem also had a sizable middle class of retail traders and craftsmen as well as many poor.

The Poor Masses

Out in the countryside, the bulk of the people were poor. The poor masses were called "people of the land." At one time this simply meant *common people*, who lived outside the city. Later, it became a label hurled at those who didn't observe religious laws.[7] The Pharisees, avoiding contact with the "people of the land," even refused to eat with them. The religiously careless were so scorned they couldn't testify in court nor be the guardian of an orphan. Pharisees wouldn't marry them and considered their women unclean vermin.

Galilee, sixty miles to the north of Jerusalem, was a heartland of common folk. Rich in resources, Galilee was the most densely populated area of Palestine. Before the reign of Herod the Great, many Gentiles bought land there. But in the years before Jesus' birth, Jewish immigrants were resettling it. By the time of Jesus' birth, Galilee was predominantly Jewish. Herod Antipas, ruler of the area, built the capital city of Tiberias along the Sea of Galilee. The region, however, still carried its former stigma: "Galilee of the Gentiles."

The Galilean population included a large number of slaves and many Jews who had absorbed some Greek culture. Most Galileans were poorly educated and ignorant of the finer points of religious law. Overwhelmed with making a living, peasants had little time to worry about the minute details of ritual purity. The sarcastic words of a Pharisee show his disdain for the people of the land.

A Jew must not marry the daughter of the people of the land for they are unclean animals and their women forbidden reptiles. And with respect to their daughters the Scriptures write,

"Cursed be he that lieth with any manner of beast" (Deut. 27:21). . . . Said R. Eleazar: one may butcher a people of the land on a Day of Atonement that happens to fall on a Sabbath (when any kind of work such as butchering constitutes a violation of a double prohibition). His disciples said to him, master, say "slaughter" (instead of the vile word butcher). But he replied "slaughtering requires a benediction, butchering does not."[8]

Although exaggerated, this attitude reveals the spite which religious leaders held for the poor. The feeling was mutual, for it was said that the "people of the land" hated the Jewish scholars more than the heathen hated Israel. Another rabbi, once a person of the land himself, said,

When I was a people of the land, I used to say, "I wish I had one of those scholars, and I would bite him like an ass." His disciples said, "You mean like a dog." He replied, "An ass' bite breaks the bone; a dog's does not."[9]

It was from these backward people that the fierce streak of Jewish nationalism burst forth some years after Jesus' death. This revolutionary fervor, directed at the occupying Romans, also targeted the rich Jerusalem aristocrats who courted the Romans. Nazareth, in the heart of people-of-the-land country, was Jesus' home. It was situated in a fertile farming area of Galilee, which also exported fish. The masses of Nazareth lived in poverty. Most had to get along with one set of clothing. There was even a saying that "the daughters of Israel are comely but poverty makes them repulsive."

The social ferment in first-century Galilee was stirred not only by Roman rule and patriotic nationalism but also by the harsh economy. Taxes had been high during the era of Herod the Great, although many dollars were funneled into the magnificent temple at Jerusalem and consecrated to God. At Herod's death, a delegation of Jews complained to the Roman emperor that Herod derived too much of his wealth by confiscating land and the goods from common people. Herod may, in fact, have owned one-half to two-thirds of his kingdom.[10]

Much of Galilee was divided into large estates owned by wealthy merchants and Sadducees living in Jerusalem, as well as

Gentile landowners in other countries. The parables of Jesus refer to absentee landowners who placed a steward over their property and servants. Some peasant farmers owned small plots of land, but rising debt often pushed them off their land. They were forced to mortgage their property to pay taxes amounting sometimes to half of their harvest. Tax collectors and estate owners then snatched the land from indebted peasants, who couldn't pay their bills. In agrarian societies, such as Palestine, the ruler and the wealthiest five percent often control as much as sixty-five percent of the national wealth.[11]

Peasant families were often trapped on the plot, working as day laborers for wealthy and absent landholders. One writer describes their plight.

> Within a few decades, small and middle-sized plots of land had disappeared, whereas the properties owned by the temple and the imperial crown grew beyond proportion. . . . Driven to misery, many peasants abandoned their land and joined bands of robbers that survived by pillage and lived in caves in the mountains.[12]

The Roman IRS

The poverty was intensified by a double system of taxes: *civil* and *religious*. It's impossible to calculate the exact proportion of taxes. Most scholars agree, however, that thirty to sixty percent of the peasant's annual income eventually fell in the hands of various tax collectors and creditors.[13] The total tax bite was much worse than the tax burden in developed nations today. In addition to taxes, the cost of seeds and rent left many peasants with as little as one-tenth of their produce for food and subsistence.

The efficient Roman bureaucracy collected taxes on people, houses, animals, sales, imports, and exports.[14] First a land tax took about one-fourth of the crop. Then a poll, or per capita tax, was levied on each male over age fourteen and each female over age twelve. The taxes were gathered by *Jewish* tax collectors appointed by the Roman government from within the ranks of well-to-do families. The police who accompanied the tax collectors to insure and protect the payments were sometimes also guilty of abuses making it easy for fraud to flourish.

There were also many other tariffs and tolls, including import duties, road tolls, and market fees. The collectors of these tolls were known as publicans. They exploited the public's ignorance of toll fees and were seen as utter deceivers. The publicans worked for a "tax farmer" who supervised the tax collecting of a large district. The tax farmer had paid the Romans the highest bid for the toll income from his district. Most tax farmers were Jews who worked for the Romans. The tax farmers collected the designated Roman taxes, then added their own additional fees. The produce market in Jerusalem, for example, was given to a "farmer" who taxed the produce merchants. Zacchaeus was likely a tax farmer.

The bite of Roman taxes irked many in Jesus' time because they were no longer used to rebuild the temple, as they had been under Herod the Great. Now Jewish taxes were financing a foreign army and the luxuries of a faraway empire.

Since the Jews never regarded Roman rule as legitimate, many viewed Roman taxes as outright robbery. They saw Gentile rulers in Palestine as robbers without rights over the land or its people.[15] Indeed, the rabbis made no distinction between tax collectors and thieves. Even the Gospels portray tax collectors as sinners. The taxation was so oppressive that Syria and Judea begged Rome for a reduction. After Jewish Zealots gained control of Jerusalem in 66 C.E., they burned all the debt records in the Jerusalem archives hoping to prevent future retaliation by the rich.

God's IRS

On top of the Roman taxes, Jewish law prescribed some two dozen or so religious tithes and offerings. Jewish males over age twenty paid a temple tax each year. The equivalent of two denarii, or two days' wages, this half shekel tax was due at the beginning of Passover each spring. A few weeks before Passover, tax collectors traveled to outlying districts to gather the tax from those who wouldn't go to Jerusalem for the festival. In Matthew (17:24), these collectors ask Peter for the half shekel tax. Used for operating and maintaining the temple, this tax could only be paid in high quality Tyrian silver. The

Roman denarius, however, was the common currency. Adding to the tax burden, money changers at the temple made a profit by exchanging Tyrian silver for the denarius.

Jewish farmers offered the first fruits of their crops in gratitude for the coming harvest. They also gave a tithe of the harvest itself and a tithe of the herd to support the Levites. In the time of Jesus, the priests in Jerusalem sometimes took the tithe by force, short-changing the Levites. Another tithe supported the poor. And an additional offering was possibly collected for the poor every third year, as well.

Farmers were required to leave gleanings on their fields for the poor. On top of this came the sabbatical year practice of letting land lie fallow every seventh year. This "involved the loss of at least a year-and-a-half of agricultural produce in every seven year cycle—a crushing burden, indeed, upon a people which was unable in any year to save a substantial part of the crop."[16] In addition, there were required personal contributions—peace and sin offerings—as well as offerings for the dedication of a child. The Pharisees at the time of Jesus were tithing herbs from their gardens—a practice Jesus mocked in light of their neglect of justice and mercy (Matt. 23:23).

The religious tithes and taxes were not viewed as free will offerings, but as ordinances commanded by God. There was, however, no legal way to enforce them. The exorbitant taxes tempted many rural people to let their tithing slide. Such carelessness infuriated religious leaders, especially the Pharisees, who saw tithing as the path to holiness. One scholar contends that the press of Roman taxes forced this "crisis of holiness." It solidified the Pharisees' insistence on careful observance and spurred their disgust toward nonobservant peasants.[17] In any event, without a middle class, the tax money—both Roman and Jewish—flowed upward to benefit the small upper crust at the expense of the poor.

The Carpenter's Son

We find Jesus growing up in this peasant setting. Several shreds of evidence place him with the poor of Galilee. Mary describes herself as a person of "low estate" in her song of exaltation (Luke 1:48). The prescribed offering for the dedication of a child in Jerusalem was a lamb and a dove. But Mary and Joseph brought only two doves, an acceptable practice for poor families unable to afford a lamb.

Although this evidence suggests Jesus came from a poor family, he probably didn't spring from the poorest of the poor. His father was a craftsman—a skilled worker, likely a mason, carpenter, or cartwright.[18] Joseph probably belonged to the higher ranks of Galilee's poor class—as did Jesus, who was also a craftsman. Among Jesus' followers were independent fishermen and tax collectors. Thus Jesus and at least some of his followers came from the upper levels of Galilean peasantry.[19]

Even though he was a skilled craftsman, Jesus identified with the poorest of the poor.[20] He told enthusiastic followers that he had no place to lay his head. The foxes and birds were better off than he was (Luke 9:58). His disciples were caught on a Sabbath shelling wheat in the field. Such grain was left for the poor according to the Deuteronomic code.

When grilled about paying Roman taxes, Jesus asked for a coin, showing an empty pocket. He held no job after beginning his ministry. As with other rabbis, he wasn't paid for his teaching. He had no formal support beyond the pittance given by several women along the way (Luke 8:3). Jesus and his followers were a band of wandering itinerate preachers who lived from hand-to-mouth. Their ethical radicalism led to their homelessness, meager possessions, and distance from family.[21]

Although he grew up in poverty-ridden Galilee, Jesus didn't join the zealous rebels who endorsed violence for political purposes. The rebels captured the imagination of youngsters who came of age amid poverty. They dreamed of someday burning the records of debt in the Jerusalem archives. Jesus surely heard the revolutionary rhetoric—but left it behind. His message didn't promote a violent reaction to economic oppression. Although he despised economic injustice, his primary passion was the inauguration of a new kingdom that would grapple with poverty in a new way.

Living Bread

Jesus' bread temptation involved more than easing personal hunger. He was enticed to go back to Galilee and miraculously feed the masses. We can't second-guess all the dimensions of the test. Perhaps he thought of picking up the mantle of Judas the Galilean and joining other freedom fighters to resist Roman taxes. Perhaps, like other bandits of the day, he dreamed of raiding the stockpiles of rich estates. If he had the miraculous touch, why not use it to feed the masses in one grand smorgasbord? Why not achieve economic justice in one bold stroke?

But Jesus finally rejected the live-by-bread-alone option. A miraculous feeding was a short-term fix. Hunger would return with the miracle baker's death. Jesus offered a new alternative. His life, his way, his teaching would form a new foundation for living. This would be a permanent bread of life. As people digest this new bread, it would fill them with new spirit and vision. And those so blessed would begin to share their material bread in new ways.

Near the midpoint of his ministry Jesus fed the five thousand and the four thousand with loaves and fishes. The feeding sprang from his compassion for the crowd's hunger (Mark 6:34; 8:2). But the big picnic was also a messianic sign: Jesus *himself* was the living bread, the long awaited Messiah (Mark 6-8). The breaking of the bread came just before the scene at Caesarea Philippi where Peter confesses that Jesus is the Christ. The crowd feeding wasn't a ploy to establish Jesus' identity as a miracle worker. Indeed, a few days later Jesus told the crowd the only reason they followed was because they were fed (John 6:26). He understood that miraculous feedings didn't cultivate serious disciples.

However, by breaking the bread, Jesus disclosed his messianic identity, not as miracle worker, but the architect of an upside-down kingdom. In John 6, Jesus declares, "I am the bread of life . . . the living bread which came down from heaven. . . . Whoever eats of this bread, will live forever."

As he prepared for a violent crucifixion, Jesus ate the Passover meal with his disciples. While breaking bread he announced, "This is my body" (Luke 22:19). After the resurrection, the Emmaus road walkers suddenly recognized Jesus in the breaking of bread (Luke 24:30-31). His messianic identity as Savior of the world was revealed not by turning boulders into loaves but by allowing his life to be broken for others.

When the values of Jesus' upside-down kingdom become our bread of life, the economic institutions of society lose their grip. Rich folks who accept the eternal bread freely share their daily bread. This is an upside-down way of feeding the hungry. It is neither revolution by angry peasants nor miraculous loaves from heaven. Rather, those with abundance, those moved by God's mercy, stop hoarding and give generously.

If the upside-down way of Jesus pulled the rug from under conventional politics and religion, it yanked even harder at the carpet beneath the wealthy. Again and again, story after story, Jesus preaches against economic injustice. "Woe to you who are rich. . . . Blessed are you who are poor" (Luke 6:20, 24). His teaching condemns economic practices that trample the poor to benefit the rich. As we shall see in later chapters, the heroes of Jesus' upside-down kingdom aren't the wealthy landowners relaxing in Jacuzzi's in Jerusalem but the poor, the maimed, and the weak.

Jesus challenged the three major social institutions: politics, religion, and economics. And as often happens, the three were woven together. The rich aristocrats—the chief priests and Sadducees in Jerusalem—owned large estates in Galilee, which trapped small tenant farmers. This ruling elite also controlled the mighty Jewish supreme court—the Sanhedrin. This body, in turn, supervised the temple ritual and religious regulations. Indeed, this same upper crust of Jerusalem was in cahoots with the Romans. The wealthy welcomed the Roman occupation because it protected them from bandits and supported the system that fed their wealth.

This ruling Jewish elite cheered when the Romans crushed zealous freedom fighters. The religious leaders were likely part of the crowd that shouted, "Crucify him, crucify him." They too considered Jesus more dangerous than the rebel leader Barabbas. A lone bandit could be caught again and killed. But a new teaching, a new way of living, which overturned political, religious, and economic tables, was simply too dangerous for Jerusalem's ruling powers.

So the mountain, the temple, and the bread symbolize the three social institutions Jesus struggled with in the wilderness. The temptations invited him to affirm corrupt politics, empty religion, and unjust economics. He was wrestling with the big issues of his day.

If indeed Jesus' vision offered new modes of living for God's people, it makes little sense to view the temptations as merely personal enticements. This reading of the temptations lets us appreciate the anguish of Jesus as he grappled with the powerful forces of politics, religion, and wealth. It also reminds us that in Jesus, God was introducing a new upside-down kingdom—one based on a new source power, a new temple, and a new type of bread. We turn now to exploring the new kingdom in the following chapters.

5

Free Slaves

Hometown Boy Lynched

Jesus gave an emphatic "no" to the three right-side-up kingdoms.
But what was his upside-down kingdom all about? Mark (1:15) and
Matthew (4:17) report that after his temptation, Jesus announced
the arrival of the kingdom of God. Luke (4:16-30) begins his
account by describing Jesus' appearance in his hometown of
Nazareth.[1] Although Matthew (13:53-58) and Mark (6:1-6) agree
the audience was stunned by Jesus' appearance, they place the event
later in their sequence of his ministry. Luke, however, sees greater
significance in this hometown ruckus. For Luke, Jesus' inaugural
sermon in front of familiar faces unravels the mysteries of the new
kingdom.

The decisive moment arrives. Jesus strides to the front of his
hometown synagogue. The leader hands him the scroll. Jesus turns
to Isaiah.[2] But he doesn't read. He quotes forcefully from memory.
The hometown folks can't believe their ears. The carpenter's son,
Joseph's boy, declares that *he* is the anointed one. He is God in flesh.
He is the long-awaited Messiah, standing before them.

In a terse quote from the prophet, Jesus summarizes his identity
and mission.

> The Spirit of the Lord is upon *me*,
> because he has anointed me
> to bring *good news* to the *poor*.
> He has sent me to proclaim *release* to the *captives*
> and *recovery* of *sight* to the blind,
> to let the *oppressed* go *free*,
> to proclaim the year of the Lord's favor.
> —Luke 4:18-19, emphasis added

Proclaiming liberty. Setting free. Announcing the favorable year of the Lord. These words ring Jewish bells. The people know what Jesus means. They've heard these phrases again and again. Releasing, liberating, letting go, forgiving, restoring. Yes, yes! These are images of messianic hope. This is what the Messiah, "the Anointed One," is all about.

Three elements stand out in Jesus' use of Isaiah's passage (Isa. 61:1-2). First, Jesus reveals *he* is the Messiah. Second, his role is to bring liberating news to the poor, the blind, the slaves, and the oppressed. Third, this is the proclamation of God's favorable year. Then Jesus concludes with dynamite: "*Today* this Scripture has been fulfilled in *your* hearing." The messianic announcement is alive today in your presence. You are living witnesses to it. You are seeing it fulfilled before your very eyes! I am much more than Joseph's little boy, *I* am the *Messiah*!

The reaction of Jesus' friends and neighbors is fascinating. As the full impact of his words sank in, they were astonished. So astonished they tried to kill him by chasing him out of town and shoving him off a cliff. Why this murderous reaction to the hometown boy? What did he say that goaded them to violence?

In his simple announcement of the outbreak of God's reign, Jesus omitted a phrase from the Isaiah passage concerning a Day of Vengeance when God would punish the wicked. Indeed, he told several stories at the end of his sermon that confirmed just the opposite. God, in fact, would extend mercy and liberation even to the wicked. This upside-down announcement infuriated the crowd (more on their reaction later).

The usual reading of Jesus' inaugural sermon spiritualizes its meaning. We often assume Jesus proclaimed release to the captives of sin, gave sight to the spiritually blind, and offered liberty to those oppressed by spiritual bondage. Although this is true, the Old Testament background of the text expands its meaning by rooting it in practical social realities. The "year of the Lord's favor" refers to the Hebrew Jubilee. Jesus thus links his messianic role back to the Jubilee.[3] The sermon is, in essence, a Jubilee proclamation.

Is Jesus calling for a concrete program of social and economic reform? New Testament scholars disagree on this point. There is more agreement that Jesus expected his followers to embrace Jubilee practices *among themselves*.[4] What is clear, however, is that the social vision heralded by Jesus suddenly takes on new meaning in the Jubilee perspective. The Jubilee vision offers an interpretive framework, a metaphor that enables us to understand the teaching and ministry of Jesus in new ways.[5] But what was this Jubilee that Jesus proclaimed?

A Hebrew Turnover

Three books—Exodus, Deuteronomy, and Leviticus—describe the Jubilee vision. We're familiar with a weekly cycle of six workdays followed by a *Sabbath*. This pattern emerged from the creation story when God relaxed on the seventh day. The Hebrew calendar however, didn't stop with the weekly cycle. It counted six work years and then celebrated the seventh as a year of rest. This seventh, or "Sunday" year was called a *sabbatical* year. Scholars aren't sure if the *Jubilee* actually fell on the forty-ninth or fiftieth year; either way the year of Jubilee celebrated the end of the seventh seven-year period. To summarize:

The Sabbath ended a week of six days.

The sabbatical year ended a "week" of six years.

The Jubilee ended a "week" of sabbatical cycles.

The term Jubilee means "a ram's horn." A special horn, taken from a mountain goat, was blown on the Day of Atonement. This signaled the start of Jubilee festivities. The priests blew the special horn only on the Jubilee year. Other years they used an ordinary ram's horn. The sabbatical and Jubilee years established a chronological rhythm for Hebrew society. The vibrations of this rhythm could turn social life upside down. In brief, three shake-ups were expected in the seventh, or sabbatical, year.

(1) *Land* was given a vacation in the seventh year. Crops weren't to be planted or harvested. Unplanted "volunteer" plants were to be left for the poor. The Lord promised a plentiful yield in the sixth year, large enough for both sixth and seventh years. Like a Sabbath rest after six days of work, this practice granted the land a vacation after six years of productivity (Exod. 23:10-11; Lev. 25:2-7).

(2) *Slaves* were released on the seventh year. Some folks became slaves because of rising debts. After working for six years as a hired servant, the Jubilee freed them in the seventh year. It's not clear if slaves were always released on the sabbatical year, but the expectation of freeing them after six years of labor appears in several passages (Exod. 21:1-6, Deut. 15:12-18).

(3) *Debts* were erased in the sabbatical year. Since Israel had an agricultural economy, debts were mostly charitable loans to needy persons not commercial ones. Charging interest on loans to other Hebrews was prohibited. The principal of any debt was also canceled in the sabbatical year (Deut. 15:1-6).

(4) The fiftieth, or Jubilee year, brought a big shake-up. The ownership of *land* returned to the owners who held it at the beginning of the fifty-year period.

> And you shall hallow the fiftieth year, and you shall proclaim liberty throughout the land to all its inhabitants; it shall be a Jubilee for you: you shall return every one of you your property and every one of you to your family. (Lev. 25:10)

This fifty-year turnover helped to preserve the original pattern of land ownership. The Jubilee prevented greedy barons from buying up more and more land at the expense of the poor. Although land was bought and sold throughout the forty-nine years, the Jubilee restored land ownership at least once in each generation. The Hebrews really didn't *buy* the land in the intervening years; they bought its *use*. As the Jubilee approached, the cost of using the land dipped because fees were calculated according to the number of harvests remaining before the Jubilee (Lev. 25:13-16).

It's difficult to know how carefully the sabbatical and Jubilee practices were followed. Historical references outside the Scriptures suggest that the practice of letting land idle on the sabbatical year continued until the destruction of the temple in 70 C.E. and perhaps even later. It's uncertain, however, how often slaves, debts, and land were restored. Some evidence suggests at least partial observance of these practices. During the reign of Zedekiah, before Jerusalem fell to Babylon in 586 B.C.E., the rich released their slaves but soon recaptured them. Jeremiah fumed at their disobedience:

> You turned around and profaned my name when each of you took back your male and female slaves, whom you had set free according to their desire, and you brought them again into subjection to be your slaves. Therefore, thus says the Lord: "You have not obeyed me by granting a release . . . behold, I am going to grant a release to you says the Lord, a release to the sword, to pestilence, and to famine. I will make you a horror to all the kingdoms of the earth." (Jer. 34:16-17)

Jeremiah viewed the sabbatical violation as one of the reasons for the impending destruction of Jerusalem (Jer. 34:18-22).

About 423 B.C.E., Nehemiah (5:1-13) rebuked the people for not observing the Jubilee after returning from captivity. He told the nobles and officials to free their slaves and return their land to its original owners. In the last chapters of Ezekiel, the prophet calls for reestablishing the Jubilee (Ezek. 45:7-9; 46:16-18).

Although many scholars think the Jubilean land reform was never practiced, others believe it was periodically observed. There is firmer evidence that debts were released. A leading Pharisee, Hillel, living about the time of Jesus' birth, started a legal practice called *prosbul*.[6] This legal procedure ended the devastating effect of canceling debt every six years. Creditors were slow to lend money when they knew the approaching sabbatical year would wipe out their loans. In short, people refused to lend money because they would never see it again. The prosbul allowed lenders to deposit a certificate with the courts when the loans were made. This paper prevented debts from being erased on the sabbatical year. Borrowers then knew that their debts would be binding, despite the sabbatical teaching.

The need for the prosbul to bypass the sabbatical suggests that debts were indeed being canceled. Despite erratic practice, the sabbatical and Jubilee were important symbolic markers of Hebrew time. Above all, they embodied key theological values.

Level Pyramids

More important than the details of the Jubilee are the theological principles undergirding it. There can be no question that the Jubilee vision called for social upheaval, for upsetting the social order. As the social blueprint for the people of God, the Jubilee touched three factors which can generate inequality. (1) Control of the land represents access to natural resources. (2) Ownership of slaves symbolizes the human labor necessary for production. (3) Borrowing and lending money involves the management of capital and credit.

The use and distribution of these resources—natural, human, and financial—tilts the balance of justice in any society. In the modern world, technology has become a fourth variable in the equation. By controlling these resources, some people become wealthy as others slide into poverty. Six Jubilee principles highlight the divine vision for the age-old problem of social injustice.

(1) *Divine Ownership.* A bold message reverberates through the Jubilee Scriptures: God *owns* the natural and human resources.

Why shouldn't the land be sold perpetually? Because "the land is mine" (Lev. 25:23).

Why should slaves be released periodically? "For they are my servants, whom I brought out of the land of Egypt; they shall not be sold as slaves are sold" (Lev. 25:42, 55).

The land and the people are the Lord's! We are not to abuse them. We who manage land and people are not *owners*. We are *stewards* accountable to God, the true owner. We dare not use land and people selfishly to build economic pyramids, create social dynasties, or feed greedy egos. Giving the land a vacation in the sabbatical or seventh year fits this understanding. Since the land is the Lord's, it shouldn't be abused. On the seventh year it's given back—restored to God—its original Owner. A theology of stewardship underlies the entire Jubilee vision. Natural, human, and financial resources are, very simply put, *God's*. These resources are ours only on loan. As short-term stewards of them, we are accountable to God for their proper use and care.

(2) *God's Liberation.* Why were God's people called to participate in this unusual vision? Why were the people to forgive debts, liberate slaves, and restore land? Was this some human concoction to prevent rebellion and revolution?

Not at all. God's liberation is the driving motivation. God's decisive act in the exodus from Egypt provides the theological base for the Jubilee. Let no one forget: "Remember that you were a slave in the land of Egypt, and the Lord your God redeemed you; for this reason, I lay this command upon you today" (Deut. 15:15). "I am the Lord your God, who brought you out of the land of Egypt to give you the land of Canaan, to be your God" (Lev. 25:38).

In other words, God is saying "For 450 years you worked as slaves carrying bricks for the Egyptian taskmasters. Not long ago you were whipped and beaten slaves. You too cried out for freedom. But I, the Lord your God, intervened on your behalf. I liberated and redeemed you from Pharaoh's enslavement. I freed you from bondage and brought you back to the Promised Land."

Time and again the memory of God's liberating acts flash across the pages of Holy Scripture.

(3) *Jubilee Response.* The Jubilee was a response to God's gracious liberation and deliverance. As the people recalled how God freed them from slavery, their joyous response was to pass that freedom on by forgiving debts, releasing slaves, and redeeming the land. To our minds, releasing a slave sounds like a noble act. But the Jubilee prescription didn't stop with a self-righteous pat on the back. Simply freeing a slave wasn't enough. "And when you send a male slave out from you a free person, you shall not send him out empty-handed. Provide *liberally* out of your flock, out of your threshing floor, and your wine press" (Deut. 15:13-14a, emphasis added).

Why such generous mercy? Isn't it enough to free the slave? Why this extra dose of goodness?

The biblical refrain is clear. "Thus giving to him [the slave] some of the bounty with which the Lord your God has blessed you" (Deut. 15:14b).

As God liberally redeemed you out of Egypt, so you ought to graciously liberate your brothers and sisters.

Jubilee acts of social justice aren't motivated by divine badges of merit. They're the natural and joyful response to the good news of God's liberation.

(4) *Jubilee Compassion.* The Jubilee response has one eye on history, on God's gracious acts of deliverance. The other eye is on the less fortunate. Jubilee behavior responds to God's acts in history

and to the cries of those crushed by social injustice. The sight of trampled outcasts, according to the biblical writer, should remind the Hebrews of their own slavery in the past.

The poor are the reason the land lies fallow. God commands that "the seventh year you shall let it rest and lie fallow so that the poor of your people may eat" (Exod. 23:11).

God promises that "There will, however, be no one in need among you . . . *if* only you will *obey* the Lord your God, by diligently observing this entire commandment that I command you today" (emphasis added). Then God continues, "Do not be hardhearted or tight-fisted toward your needy neighbor. You should rather open your hand, willingly lending enough to meet the need, whatever it may be. . . . I therefore command you, open your hand to the poor and needy neighbor in your land" (Deut. 15:4-5, 7-8, 11, emphasis added).

God warns the people not to refuse loans to the poor just because the sabbatical year is near. What they loan may not come back because of the sabbatical cancellation; *nevertheless*, "Give *liberally* and be ungrudging when you do so, for on this account, the Lord your God will bless you in all your work and in all that you undertake" (Deut. 15:10, emphasis added).

There is a double motive in Jubilee forgiveness: a gracious response to God's liberation *and* compassionate eyes that see human hurt.

(5) *Upside-Down Revolution*. The Jubilee envisions a social revolution. But it's certainly a unique one. Revolutions usually erupt at the bottom of the social ladder. Exploited peasants, angered by their oppression, grab pitchforks or machine guns and lash out at rich oppressors. If successful, they gain power. More often they're crushed. Motivated by anger, the successful revolutionaries of today often become the oppressors of tomorrow as they continue to use the same weapons of violence.

Jubilee is upside-down revolution. Here the flame of revolution burns at the top. God's grace moves those in seats of power, the rich and influential. They now see with compassionate eyes and join the Jubilee by redistributing natural and human resources. Such generosity flattens the socioeconomic pyramids as those at the top begin freely giving to others as God has freely given to them.

(6) *Institutionalized Grace.* The Jubilee concept is rooted in a keen awareness of human sin and greed. Without social controls, economic pyramids rise. Without constraints and periodic leveling, the weak at the bottom are stamped into the dirt. Societies must have special provisions to defend and protect the helpless. Without these, power and wealth accumulate in the hands of the elite.

The Jubilee is a splendid example of a social—yes, an institutional—plan to harness personal desire and ambition. Benevolence can't be left only to the personal whims and wishes of the rich. A few personal gifts won't alter the evil structures which perpetuate opulence at the expense of the poor. Jubilee levels the pyramids of social life by making justice a new rule of economic practice.

The Jubilean vision doesn't squelch individual initiative. It doesn't call for communal living nor prescribe legalistic equality. It allows personal aspirations their place. But it knows such things easily get out of hand. So it wisely mandates structural change at regular intervals to equalize the disparities which would otherwise run rampant. As we've seen, the Bible understands such institutionalized grace as a response to the grace of a God who has already taken the initiative. Divine grace stirs economic change.

In true biblical fashion, the Jubilee integrates spiritual and social dimensions. It weaves religion and economics into one fabric. Pulling the two apart prostitutes the biblical truth, which holds spiritual and economic life together.

Meanwhile Back at Nazareth

Good news for the poor. Release for the captives. Sight for the blind. Liberty for the oppressed. God's favorable year! The old words ring with new meaning as Jesus quotes them in hometown Nazareth. Some New Testament scholars think Jesus may have actually preached these words in a sabbatical year.[7] One scholar even argues it was the actual year of Jubilee, but that's uncertain.[8]

In any event, the Old Testament background embellishes Jesus' use of these words. Now they strike us with new meaning. The Hebrew word for liberty is used only seven times in the Old

Testament—but each time with the year of liberty.[9] The literal meaning of Jubilee was certainly good news in Nazareth. The poor could say good-bye to their debts. Those driven into slavery because of debts could now come home. Peasants forced to sell land would see it returned once again to their family. No question about it—this was *very* good news!

But there's more. Jesus wasn't just making another Jubilee proclamation. "The Lord has anointed me," was a messianic announcement. It's remarkably similar to Jesus' response when John's disciples asked if he was indeed the Messiah. Jesus didn't say yes or no (Luke 7:22-23). Rather, he said that "the blind receive their sight, the lame walk, the lepers are cleansed, the deaf hear, the dead are raised, the poor have good news brought to them." These are exactly the same folks Jesus mentions at Nazareth.

This isn't the first time such a list appears. In fact, we find the same catalog in the messianic prophecies of Isaiah (29:18, 35:5, and 61:1). What do these images mean? They're all age-old descriptions in Eastern culture for the time of *salvation,* when tears, sorrow, and grief will end.[10] Jesus surprises us by adding lepers and the dead to the list of the saved. Both are missing from Isaiah's passages. Alert listeners in the synagogue that day would have heard Jesus using these messianic code words from the Scripture. They would have heard him saying, "The Messiah is *here*! Salvation is dawning. The kingdom of God is *near*. It's no longer far away in the clouds. God's presence has broken in among you *now*. It's happening before your very eyes!"

The theme of restoration links together the Jubilee, Jesus' Nazareth sermon, and his reply to John's disciples. Things will be restored, returned to their original state. Images of paradise—no debts, no poverty, no slavery—shine forth. These images of the garden take us back to Genesis and creation. Enacting the Jubilee vision will restore things to their original garden perfection.

Jubilee talk also clarifies the role of the Messiah, the one who announces God's release. The Messiah lets us go, forgiving our debts, redeeming our sins. Jesus Christ remolds us into the image of God. He cuts the chains of sin. Our eyes open. The handcuffs of evil drop off. This is true liberation. We repent and turn back to the garden, rekindling harmony with God—finding a place once more in God's family.

And so at Nazareth, Jesus announced God's acceptable year of salvation. But his punch line insulted Jewish pride when he claimed that God used Gentiles in Hebrew history. The Jubilee restoration wasn't only for Jews. Now, in the words of Jesus, it restored *everyone*—even Gentiles. Jesus outrageously offered Gentiles words of grace instead of vengeance. The day of favored people was over. The Jubilee kingdom was universal. It knew no ethnic barriers, no ethnic favorites.

This was the startling news that incited rage in the Nazareth crowd. Instead of a day of God's vengeance against Gentiles, Jesus had announced a day of universal mercy and forgiveness.[11] There could be no doubt about it. Jesus, Gentile-lover, was a false prophet. And so they chased him out of town and tried to shove him over a cliff.

The Jubilee Habit

A redemptive rhythm emerges from the Jubilee. It echoes from garden to empty tomb. The drummers of holy history pound out a four-beat message vibrating down through the ages:

Garden—Egypt—Exodus—Jubilee

Perfection—sin—salvation—mercy

Freedom—oppression—restoration—forgiveness.

The first beat reminds us of God's perfect creation. The second beat recalls oppression in Egypt. God's mighty intervention brings restoration and salvation. Finally, we can respond to God's salvation by extending mercy and forgiveness to others.

Once we were oppressed. Once we were captives. But now, the Jubilee reminds us, we're forgiven debtors. We're released slaves. What should be our response? Suddenly the reciprocal rule from Deuteronomy 15:14 strikes home: "Provide liberally out of your flock . . . giving to him some of the bounty with which the Lord your God has blessed you." Jesus echoes the chain reaction. Forgive as I have forgiven. Be merciful as I have been merciful. Love as I have loved. Give freely as I have given to you.

In the Jubilee model God's graciousness moves us to forgive others. God's mercy nudges us to cancel debts. We release our slaves because God released us. In short, we pass the Jubilee on—extending grace to others.

Just as the Hebrew response to God's liberation had real consequences, so must ours. It's not enough to sit and ponder the Jubilee's theological beauty. We must act. The biblical model calls us to start forgiving not only interpersonal insults but financial ones as well. We lower rents and raise salaries. In the words of the Lord's Prayer, "forgive us our debts, as we also have forgiven our debtors" (Matt. 6:12).

Two points stand out here. One is that accepting and granting forgiveness are linked. We're eligible to accept God's forgiveness as we repent and forgive others. Moreover some scholars note that the word *debts* in the Lord's Prayer may refer either to sins or to financial debts.[12] Are we to forgive not only bad feelings but also financial debts? In any event, couched in the heart of the Lord's Prayer we find the Jubilee principle.

The parable of the unforgiving servant (Matt. 18:23-35) also underlines the Jubilee posture. A king forgives a servant's large debt. The forgiven servant grabs a fellow servant by the throat and demands repayment of a small debt. When the friend can't pay, the forgiven servant locks him in prison. When the king learns this, he's irate and throws the forgiven servant in jail until he repays the debt. The story concludes with a blunt Jubilee moral: "So my heavenly Father will also do to every one of you, if you do not forgive your brother or sister from your heart" (Matt. 18:35).

The Jubilee principle of reciprocal forgiveness pervades New Testament teaching. Jesus' words about wealth suddenly make sense in the context of the Jubilee model. In this framework his teachings take on new meaning. They invite us to respond in concrete, economic ways, to God's liberating initiative.

The Dog's Tail

We've seen how Jubilee links spiritual and social spheres. Although tied together, they represent different starting points. In fact, the way they mesh has stirred much philosophical controversy. Social scientists argue that our beliefs often reflect our material environment. Hence the chicken and egg question. Do our ideas influence our economic lifestyles or do our lifestyles influence our ideas?[13]

Philosophers and theologians tend to line up on one side of this argument. They contend our beliefs shape our economic behavior. On the other side, many social scientists argue that our convictions merely mirror our economic status.

In the latter view, our economic niche shapes the beliefs we hold dear. For instance, a person born into a wealthy family will likely believe affluence is a sign of God's blessing. In contrast, those born poor are more likely to believe God will bless them in heaven with divine pie in the sky. Peasants eking out a harsh and meager living will likely dream of God's future heavenly blessing while their oppressors view the here and now as already quite heavenly.

The songs of American slaves, for example, focused on the future hope of crossing Jordan's stormy banks to enter the Promised Land. Meanwhile, their masters quoted Bible verses to support their belief in a slavery system that made them rich, here and now. Likewise, today's affluent upper crust, surrounded by luxury homes and cars, have little need for a heavenly escape from financial woes.

At stake here is the relationship between religion and economics, spiritual and material realities, our faith and our pocketbook. This raises the question of the dog and the tail. Does our faith wag our wallet, or does our bank account wag our convictions? What controls what? This oversimplifies, of course the complex relationship between pocketbook and piety. Nevertheless it's important to ask how our faith impacts our pocketbook.

Economic factors do powerfully shape the way we look at things. Our salary, the income of our friends, the value of our house, and our social status—all these factors impact our thinking. They provide a set of lenses that screen our view of the world. We cling to theological beliefs that support and legitimate our economic status. Our financial status filters our view of the Bible and encourages us to interpret it in ways that endorse our economic lifestyle—whether we are rich or poor.

In short, our wallets too often wag our beliefs. This contradicts the biblical pattern. The scriptural vision calls for a faith which opens pocketbooks. Economic forces do shape our views. We can't jump out of our social environments. But we can hear and obey the biblical message, which urges us to place our economic decisions *under* the reign of King Jesus.

The Jubilee provided a Hebrew solution to this dog-tail problem. Faith in a God who graciously delivered from slavery motivated people to open *wide* their hand of mercy. God's saving acts in holy history moved the community to forgive debts, free slaves, and return land. Sometimes the Hebrews balked at practicing the Jubilee. Their stubbornness attests to the firm grip of economic loyalties over faith. The biblical model, nevertheless, is clear: faith should wag wallets. This biblical principle undergirds the teaching of Jesus, which we will explore in later chapters.

Christian obedience today doesn't mean duplicating the historical details of the Jubilee. Many people no longer live in a theocracy where civil and religious legislation flows together under God's kingship. Moreover, a small band of Christians can't impose their brand of economics on the larger society. Restoring land to its original owners won't help families who have never owned land in the first place. Land exchanges can't correct injustices resulting from unequal access to technology, information, capital, and natural resources. Allowing wheat to stand every seventh year in Nebraska fields won't feed the hungry in New York and Bombay. Although many of the details aren't applicable today, the theological *principles* of the Jubilee do offer a biblical framework for Christian economic practice.

The Jubilee vision weaves together social and spiritual, political and personal, inward and outward. It also blends God's initiative with ours. Prodded by divine liberation, we forgive. As we forgive, so we are forgiven. As we are merciful, so we receive mercy. These truths lie at the heart of the Jubilee. And the Jubilee vision permeates Jesus' teaching, not only at Nazareth but throughout his entire ministry.[14] Mercy, liberation, freedom, compassion, release. These are the code words of Jubilee. And these same words energize Jesus' economic vision. They shape his forgiveness for the poor and lowly.

Jesus' theological vision has social consequences. The Jubilee declares God's kingship. And God's decree brings release from enslavement to old authorities, forgiveness from indebtedness to old kingdoms, and liberty to those in spiritual *and* social bondage. This lavish grace is Jubilee. It is the favorable day of the Lord, the day of liberty, the day of salvation. And it is Jesus of Nazareth who articulates and embodies it in his words and deeds.

6
Luxurious Poverty

Perpetual Jubilee

Jesus pays an astonishing amount of attention to wealth. Particularly in Luke's Gospel, he ties economic conversion to the new kingdom. We'll follow Luke's story with cross-references to the other Gospels.[1]

Jesus doesn't condemn private property. He doesn't call for a new Christian commune. He does, however, condemn greed. And as we have seen, there was much to criticize. Jesus holds up the Jubilee model as the new way for his disciples. People on the way with him respond to God's gracious love by sharing with the needy around them.

Wealth doesn't simply drop from the sky. Clusters of social rules regulate its acquisition and use. In chiding the greedy, Jesus questioned the economic norms of his day, which allowed the affluent to oppress the poor. He didn't say material things are inherently evil. But he did warn of their danger. Money and material goods can quickly become idols, which can control us and unseat the rule of God in our lives. We'll begin by exploring six dangers of wealth, which, according to Jesus, can undercut our allegiance to the kingdom.[2]

Beware: The Strangler

Tucked away in the parable of the sower is a sermonette on the threat of riches to kingdom citizens.[3] The seed is the Word of God.[4] Its growth symbolizes the emergence of the kingdom. The seed that falls among thorn bushes is choked. "As for what fell among the thorns, these are the ones who hear; but as they go on their way, they are choked by the cares and riches and pleasures of life, and their fruit does not mature" (Luke 8:14; Mark 4:18-19; Matt.

13:22). The seeds do sprout. There is growth and new life. But prickly thorns quickly smother vitality. The cares, riches, and pleasures of life suffocate the new plants. The synoptic writers all use the word *choke*. Spiritual life is gagged. Fruit buds appear, but there is no harvest. The pods never mature. Today, the cares, riches, and pleasures of life may include professional advancement, houses, resort homes, luxury vacations, exotic hobbies, financial investments, designer clothing, high performance cars, and many other things. These pleasures of life can abort the kingdom's growth. They divert us from its true ministry and spoil the harvest.

Beware: The Worrier

Yesterday brings guilt. Tomorrow brings worry. Jesus understood that wealth generates anxiety. Will we be secure tomorrow? What if a terrorist strike throws the economy into chaos? What if the stock market crashes? Could the burglar alarm fail? Owning property makes us fret about its defense and protection. In Luke (12:22-34) and in Matthew (6:19-21, 25-33) Jesus urges the disciples four times not to be anxious about food and clothing.

> And do not keep striving for what you are to eat and what you are to drink, and do not keep worrying. For it is the nations of the world that strive for these things, and your Father knows that you need them. Instead, strive for his kingdom, and these things will be given to you as well. Do not be afraid, little flock, for it is your Father's good pleasure to give you the kingdom. Sell your possessions, and give alms. Make purses for yourselves that do not wear out, an unfailing treasure in heaven, where no thief comes near and no moth destroys. For where your treasure is, there your heart will be also. (Luke 12:29-34)

The Greek text means "do not make anxious efforts for." Pagans are anxious about material things. They are strivers. They worry and fret about what they will wear, what they will eat, where they will live, and how much they will earn. The nations of the world seek these things.

Not so Jesus' disciples. They relax about such things. They concentrate fully on the kingdom! God will care for them. In the context of the sabbatical year, when crops weren't planted, this wisdom takes on new meaning. One scholar offers this paraphrase.

> If you work six days (or six years) with all your heart, you can count on God to take care of you and yours. So without fear leave your field untilled. As he does for the birds of heaven, which do not sow or harvest or collect into granaries, God will take care of your needs. The Gentiles who pay no attention to the Sabbath are not richer than you.[5]

In the context of the sabbatical year, these words don't prescribe sloth; they're not a recipe for laziness. They remind us that amassing *things* distracts us from the kingdom. Jesus urges us to place our priorities on kingdom values, not material ones. And when we embrace his vision, God's kingdom, we will be moved by God's grace to share our goods with the needy. The poor are the focal point of Jesus' discourse. Hoarding is the pagan way. Giving alms to the poor reflects the upside-down way. The Jubilee principle rides again. Children of a loving God respond to the gift of the kingdom by using their possessions for the sake of the poor.

This same spirit permeates the Beatitudes when Jesus instructs us to give to those that beg and to lend without expecting a return (Luke 6:34-35, Matt. 5:42). Excessive profits don't tantalize those whose hearts the kingdom captures. When the kingdom is our treasure, we switch from hoarding to giving. When we elevate kingdom priorities we liberally share our wealth. And in the process we not only restore and liberate the poor but also ourselves! We free ourselves from anxiety and the bondage of worry, from the shackles of endless consumption.

We don't inherit worry. Possessions bring worry. Healthy children rarely worry. For example, a four-year-old, listening to a song about emotions, was troubled. The singer asked, "What are you sad about?" and "What are you mad about?" Hearing the question "What are you worried about?" The child came sobbing to her mother saying, "I have nothing to worry about." A few days later, quite relieved, she chimed, "I finally found something to worry about." To enter the kingdom as a child, as Jesus calls us to do, is to allow God to care for our tomorrows.

A pithy saying from Matthew's Gospel sums it up. "So do not worry about tomorrow, for tomorrow will bring worries of its own. Today's trouble is enough for today" (Matt. 6:34). The number of insurance contracts sold each year may reflect the amount of collective anxiety in a society. An obsession with possessions enslaves us to the demon of worry. Jesus invites us to change our priorities, focus on the kingdom, and share with the needy.

Beware: The Blinder

In one of his most stinging parables Jesus shows how the trappings of riches can blind us.

> There was a rich man, who was dressed in purple and fine linen and who feasted sumptuously every day. And at his gate lay a poor man named Lazarus, covered with sores, who longed to satisfy his hunger with what fell from the rich man's table; even the dogs would come and lick his sores. The poor man died and was carried by the angels to be with Abraham. The rich man also died and was buried. In Hades, where he was being tormented, he looked up and saw Abraham far away with Lazarus by his side. (Luke 16:19-23)

Usually known as the story of Lazarus and the Rich Man, a better title might be, "Surprised by Hell." Jesus likely aimed the story at rich Sadducees in Jerusalem who doubted the existence of an afterlife. It may also be Jesus' answer to incessant requests for a miraculous sign.

In any case, the teaching is clear. The rich man lives in a large house and throws parties every day. He wears fine purple robes and the most expensive Egyptian underwear. He's not a robber or cheat. He hasn't gained his riches illegally. He has simply taken advantage of the economic system. His wealth may have come through inheritance, family connections, or hard work. He was an upright and decent man, perhaps a Sadducee, but certainly not a swindler.

At the edge of the rich man's estate lay a poor beggar suffering from a skin disease. Lazarus, the only character named in any of

Jesus' stories, means "God helps."[6] Day after day he reaches out for tidbits of bread. Household guests toss leftovers to him while they are feasting. According to local custom, guests did not use napkins, but wiped their sticky hands on chunks of bread and threw them under the table. The Greek word for *beggar* is related to the word for *spit*. Lazarus was a "spit upon" person despised by the revelers. The beggar embarrassed the rich man and spoiled the spirit of his party.

But the dogs had no favorites. They licked the wounds of poor Lazarus. The puppies symbolized the unsaved, the Gentile outcasts. The upside-down moment dawned. The rich, religious Sadducee spit on the beggar in contempt. But the dogs, of all things, showed compassion. Instead of spitting, they used their saliva for healing. They licked the sores of poor Lazarus. What a stinging sarcastic punch line—dogs have more compassion than rich Sadducees.[7]

Suddenly, as the story unfolds, the world turns upside-down. The rich man roasts in hell and old spit-upon Lazarus sits at Abraham's right hand. He holds the place of honor, the most prestigious seat in the congregation of the righteous. The tables turn. High and low reverse. Earlier, Lazarus had reached up to the rich man, begging for crumbs. Now, sizzling in hell, the rich reveler reaches up to Lazarus and begs for a drop of water. Echoes of Mary's Magnificat ring in our ears. "He has filled the hungry with good things, and sent the rich away empty" (Luke 1:53).

The message is clear. The rich man, blinded by luxury, refused the Jubilee and faced a scorching end. The huge gulf in the story symbolizes his distance from God. Almighty God had not forgotten weak, spit-upon Lazarus. But careful, this isn't a story to comfort beggars. The parable doesn't ask the poor to patiently await their reward in the sky. No, the ending of the story focuses on the five rich brothers who are still living.

In the heat of the moment, the rich man feels compassion. He suddenly begs Abraham to let Lazarus rise from the dead and warn his brothers. Abraham refuses. Again the rich man begs for a miraculous messenger to rise from the grave and warn his brothers. Each time Abraham says, "They have Moses and the prophets; they should listen to them. . . . If they do not listen to Moses and the prophets, neither will they be convinced even if someone rises from the dead" (Luke 16:29, 31).

In other words, the rich man's brothers have known about Jubilee since their childhood. Their ears have heard the Jubilee laws read aloud Sabbath after Sabbath in the synagogue. The harsh conclusion is obvious. No special messenger will warn the rich. Judgment will singe those who refuse Jubilee and scoff at God's reign.

Scrumptious feasting and a lavish lifestyle blinded the rich man. Wrapped in the good life, he couldn't see the sores or hear the nearby cries of despair. He was trapped in a cultural system that was callous to compassion. How much more serious is the blindness of those who have not only Moses and the prophets, but also Jesus, Paul, and church history. Surely, Jesus would tell us, "Let those that have ears to hear, listen."

Beware: The Boss

In another parable Jesus informs us that riches not only blind, they also boss. They dominate and order our lives. A rich man, likely an absentee landowner, has a steward to manage his estate (Luke 16:1-9).[8] The absentee landowner has contracts with merchants who sell his produce. The steward writes the contracts on behalf of his boss and includes a hidden interest charge.

The owner learns that the steward is squandering the estate. So the owner asks for a complete inventory of his goods before firing the cheat. Learning he is about to be fired, the steward realizes that he faces possible doom in other jobs such as digging or begging. He's too weak to dig and if he begs, he'll likely become ill and die a beggar's death. So he concocts a surprising solution. The shrewd steward, sensing his impending demise, quickly calls in his master's debtors and reduces their debts. Learning of the surprise, the landlord commends the steward for his swift action.

This story has perplexed many commentators. The Jubilee perspective and knowledge of the financial practices of the time clarify the riddle. At the heart of the story is the fact that the steward was likely charging a hidden interest, probably twenty-five to fifty percent, on the contracts with the debtors. The steward had probably written the contracts, but it's not clear if the hidden interest was for him or the owner.

Interest, considered usury and against God's law, was forbidden in the Old Testament. The Pharisees, however, had concocted ways to charge a hidden interest condoned even by Jewish civil courts. When loaning grain, wine, and oil, hidden interest *could be charged* if the loan was not of "immediate necessity." Most loans weren't considered of immediate necessity. Thus interest was in fact typically charged, violating the law of God. For example, if a woman had one drop of oil and wanted to borrow more oil, the loan was *not* of immediate necessity. She already had *one* drop of oil! Thus her creditor could charge interest on her loan.

The rule of immediate necessity applied primarily to commodity loans like wheat and wine. Monetary loans were often translated into commodity values so hidden interest could be charged. The interest, however, was never written into the contract, for that would have violated God's law.

Back to the story. The steward is in a crunch. He'll soon be jobless, lacking references. His reputation will be smudged. In a jam, he decides to forgive the borrowers the interest he had *unjustly* added to their loans. He likely had translated the loans into commodity values—oil or grain—to hide the forbidden interest he would collect for himself. By canceling the illegal interest, the steward lost a considerable sum. He didn't have the power to forgive the entire debt since the principal was owed to the master. "Our steward, then, lending at interest to Jews was *morally* a transgressor but *legally* secure, so long as his contracts hid the fact that the loan was usurious."[9]

The steward acted righteously by releasing the forbidden interest on the loan. According to the law of the land, the steward could have forced the debtors into slavery if they defaulted on their interest payments. But the interest wasn't the property of the master, according to Old Testament law. The master, in fact, may not have known the steward was charging interest. Under the oral law of the Pharisees, if the steward forgave interest without the owner's authority, the owner had to accept the steward's decision. Indeed, the owner had nothing to lose and all to gain. The steward's decision made the owner appear like a caring and forgiving creditor. Moreover, the owner wouldn't have gained the interest anyway since it likely was headed for the steward's wallet.

The story begins with animosity—masters who distrust stewards, merchants who hate stewards, and stewards who cheat masters and merchants. It ends, however, in an upside-down fashion with everyone happy—merchants are pleased with lower debts, the master praises a steward for eliminating dishonest contracts, and the happy steward just saved his job.[10]

The steward, in the end, models righteousness by forgiving unjust debts. Moreover, by granting favors to the debtors, he can now expect favors in return from them. They will offer warm hospitality and support if he ever needs it. The owner commends his steward for following biblical law and acting righteously (Luke 16:8). Then comes the upside-down saying: "the sons of this world are more shrewd in dealing with their own generation than the sons of light."

The Pharisees, supposedly the sons of light, had devised these ingenious ways to skirt the law of God because they were "lovers of money."[11] The worldly steward acted righteously by canceling the interest. If the Pharisees couldn't be faithful in a little thing like loaning money, how could God trust them to handle the larger wealth of the kingdom?

According to Luke, the parable of the shrewd steward launched Jesus into a biting sermon: "No slave can serve two masters for a slave will either hate the one and love the other, or be devoted to the one and despise the other. You cannot serve God and wealth" (Luke 16:13). The Pharisees, lovers of money, heard this and scoffed at him.

Yet Jesus said, "You are those who justify yourselves in the sight of others, but God knows your hearts; for what is prized by human beings is an abomination in the sight of God" (Luke 16:15).

The steward was caught between two masters. The law of God forbade interest, but the law of the Pharisees permitted it. The demands of the two masters collided. The fraudulent steward realized the impasse and chose to obey God's law. In upside-down fashion, the scoundrel turns hero.

Mammon, an Aramaic term, means wealth, money, property, or profit. The striking truth here is that Jesus sees mammon claiming divine status. In his view it competes directly with God. Wealth, more than anything else, can act like a god. Jesus doesn't grant deity status to knowledge, skill, appearance, occupation, nobility, or nationality. It is wealth, he says, which clamors to control and boss us like a deity.

Jesus is not, in this case, attacking money or possessions, but enslavement to them—obsession with them. It is the difference between fully surrendering to the reign of God or devoting our passion to material possessions. We must choose. It's impossible, says Jesus, to freely serve God if we are entrapped by wealth.

Fluctuations of the stock market can become our obsession. We easily become engrossed with new gadgets and begin serving them. As new toys captivate children, so material pursuits can captivate grownups. We too easily bow down and worship at the altar of materialism. Luxuries begin to manipulate and dictate our lives. Mammon turns into a god. Jesus contends that we can't serve God and wealth simultaneously. We can use wealth to serve God's ends, but that's quite a different thing than serving wealth itself.

Particularly irksome is the accumulation of wealth beneath a veneer of pious slogans. When Jesus sanitized the temple, he struck at profiteering that oppressed the poor in the name of religion. "My house shall be called a house of prayer for all the nations. But you have made it a den of robbers" (Mark 11:17; Matt. 21:13; Luke 19:46; John 2:16). The merchants operating in the temple weren't acting illegally. They were exchanging "pure" money for offerings and selling animals for sacrifice at a high profit. They had concocted a "legal" system that robbed the poor. Jesus called them "robbers," for they engineered a system that exploited the poor in the name of religion.

The Pharisees, engaged in their own version of fraud by charging secret interest, sneered at Jesus' rebuke. He declared that amassing wealth to impress others is an abomination in the eyes of God (Luke 16:15). Glamorous goods, an easy buck, and large financial assets top many ladders of success. The material goodies, however, fall to the bottom of the upside-down kingdom. According to Jesus, mercy, love, and compassion are the new yardsticks of success in God's inverted kingdom.

Beware: The Damner

Wealth can even have a damning effect on our lives. Jesus underscores this point in a story about a rich fool (Luke 12:13-21).[12] A man in the crowd runs up to Jesus and asks for legal advice. He's pouting because his brother won't share the family inheritance. The man begs Jesus to reprimand his stingy brother. Jesus refuses to mediate. Instead he tells a story about barns, for he detects a spirit of greed with all the worry about getting a fair share of the family farm.

The forty-nine-year Jubilee pattern protected the inheritance rights of the poor. If land returned to former owners each generation, a family couldn't accumulate large tracts. Inheritance practices usually favor the children of the rich, who receive silver platters. Perhaps Jesus was pricking not only this man's greed but also the habits of inheritance, which gave one person a free farm while others had none.

Back to our story.[13] A farmer enjoys good yields. He expands his storage space and locks up the grain. He plans a party. That night God calls him a fool and demands his soul. Jesus summarizes the inversion, "Those who store up treasures for themselves . . . are not rich toward God" (Luke 12:21). The barn this fellow builds isn't a holding shed to keep grain until threshing, but a warehouse for permanent storage. Rather than practicing the Jubilee by sharing his surplus, he hoards it like a fool. This is no righteous, sabbatical storage of the sixth year's yield. This is selfish expansion at the poor's expense. His selfish motive is clear: "Relax, eat, drink, be merry" (Luke 12:19-20).

Amid his party God knocks on the door and calls him a fool. In everyday use "fool" means stupid or a little crazy. The biblical meaning, however, is harsh. The fool is one who says there is no God (Ps. 14:1). A practical atheist trapped by greed, the rich man lives as though there is no God. In Matthew's Gospel (5:22) the person who calls his brother a fool is worthy of hell. When God dubs the farmer a fool, God damns him.

In the short span of four verses (16-19), the rich fool makes eleven references to himself. His only focus is the good life for "me and only me." God doesn't ask about his motives; he snatches away his life. Wallowing in self-obsession, the fool is callused to the needs of others. He was not a monster but merely a typical member of the rich elite. He was simply securing his future and expanding his investments.

But the story is not just about greed; it's a warning about the fragility of life and the true goods that count for eternity. The *fool's* refusal to practice Jubilee—his captivity by wealth damns his soul. Stacking up his own treasures makes him a pauper in God's sight. Again inversion strikes. Those who pile it up down here are poor in God's kingdom. Their tacky goods won't endure. The rich who enter God's reign give generously. In so doing they save their souls from wealth's damnation.

Jesus warns, "Be on your guard against all kinds of greed; for one's life does not consist in the abundance of possessions" (Luke 12:15). Again we find an inversion between kingdom values and societal standards. After the coffin is buried, the gossipers ask, "How big was his estate?" "How much did she leave?" Successful folks leave large financial holdings. The seductive voices of our age proclaim that financial success *does* determine significance. Life *does* consist of possessions. Abundant possessions *do* equal abundant life. In an age of consumerism dictated by fads and fashions and slick commercials, we are tempted to believe the lie of advertising: the goodies of this world will satisfy our soul.

Jesus is very clear. Other values govern the upside-down kingdom. Here, investment portfolios don't measure a person's worth. Financial growth doesn't equal higher status in the kingdom. In God's new order, covetousness and the pursuit of excessive profit and privilege are wrong. The mindset which builds bigger barns for selfish purposes is clearly named: it's greed, no more, no less.

Beware: The Curse

The Beatitudes sharpen the contrast between rich and poor. Here Jesus, in upside-down fashion, awards the poor and spanks the comfortable. In normal social life we often do the opposite. We applaud the superstars, the celebrities, and the media sensations. Valuing monetary success, we give the "winners" enticing rewards. We shower them with private estates, public awards, prestigious positions, glamorous attention, and access to political power.

We assume, as did Jesus' contemporaries, that wealth equals blessing from God. Thus we deplore and stigmatize the "losers," the castaways, on the edge of society. We condemn the poor as shiftless nobodies who lack motivation and drive.

Jesus demolishes our assumptions by flipping them upside-down. "Blessed are you who are poor, for yours is the kingdom of God. . . . But woe to you who are rich, for you have received your consolation" (Luke 6:20, 24). Instead of rebuking the poor for being lazy, Jesus exalts them. The despised, the forlorn, and the weaklings are the recipients of God's happy blessing. To the rich, whom we applaud, Jesus delivers woes.[14]

Does Jesus really mean that raw poverty is a virtue? Is he suggesting that the poor automatically enter the kingdom? Likely not. The term *poor* in the biblical context has at least three meanings. First, it refers to the materially poor—destitutes living in squalor with meager food, housing, and clothing. The term occurs more than sixty times in the Old Testament and usually refers to material poverty.

Second, in a broader sense, the poor in the Bible are the oppressed.[15] They are the captives, the slaves, the sick, the destitute, and the desperate. These nobodies are, in fact, the same ones whom Jesus offers good news in his Jubilee sermon in Nazareth (as explored earlier in this book, in chapter 5). They are the down-and-outers, the outcasts who can't defend themselves. Living on the fringe of society, they depend on the mercy of the powerful. The multitudes following Jesus often included the disreputable, the uneducated, and the stigmatized. By Pharisee standards, their social blemishes blocked any hope of salvation. Jesus' followers, in fact, were often called the "little ones," and "the least ones."

The third connotation of poor comes out of an Old Testament tradition. Here the poor are the humble in spirit—those who are poor toward God. Regardless of their economic status, they stand before God as beggars with outstretched hands. They plead for

mercy with contrite and broken spirits. It was this poorness of spirit—
this humility—which Matthew highlighted in his version of the
Beatitudes, "Blessed are the poor in spirit, for theirs is the kingdom
of heaven" (Matt. 5:3). Matthew underscored inner spiritual poverty
while Luke clearly had the materially poor in mind.[16] Luke's
Beatitudes (6:20-26) consist of a quartet of blessings and woes.

Blessed are	Woe to
You who are poor	You who are rich
You who are hungry now	You who are full now
You who weep now	You who are laughing now
You when people hate you, . . . exclude you, revile you, and defame you . . .	You, when all speak well of you

What does all this mean? Luke is clearly thinking of those who
are indeed financially poor, really hungry, actually crying, actively
persecuted. These are the people who share one thing in common:
suffering.[17] These are the little ones who shed tears of grief because
they carry great burdens. Poor peasants and beggars—they are in
fact hungry, crying, and poor. But they are also lowly in spirit—little
ones—on the edges, at the bottom of society. Their poverty is both
attitude and circumstance.

The words of Jesus bring good news to them. Discarded on the
human trash pile, they have not, however, been trashed by God.
Almighty God hasn't thrown them out. Indeed, God's blessing falls
on them. God cares about them. Meanwhile, the rich and haughty
in Jerusalem, who refuse to practice Jubilee, may be indicted for
snubbing the law of God. But they too will have new life in the
kingdom if they cast off the shackles of possessions.

But is Jesus applauding sheer poverty? Is he saying that the destitute are automatically in God's kingdom just because they are
poor? Probably not. More likely he is making it clear that the poor
have God's unconditional welcome. Unlike the rich who despise the
poor, God welcomes them. Moreover, in many ways the poor are
closer to the kingdom than those who are caught in the snares of

wealth. Indeed, it's easier for the poor to enter the kingdom because they aren't entangled in property and prestige. The grip of mammon often blocks the pathway to the kingdom. The outcasts—sinners, prostitutes, children, homeless—can enter the kingdom more readily than the elite, the righteous, the strong, and the pious.

The poor understand dependence, simplicity, and cooperation. They know the difference between needs and luxuries. Having fewer entanglements, they are freer to abandon all else for the kingdom. They have little to give up. They can simply walk in. And they are grateful. They know what it's like to be forgiven. The haughty, the arrogant, and the rich find it difficult to stoop in humility at the kingdom's door and acknowledge any dependence on God.

Jesus offers good news to the poor. Their poverty isn't a sign of divine disapproval, a common view of the time. Jesus signals salvation by transforming the destitute. The blind see. The lame walk. The deaf hear. The lepers are cleansed. The oppressed are released (Matt. 11:5; Luke 4:18-19; 7:22). God welcomes the poor through Jesus Christ. Social outcasts they certainly are, but no longer bums in God's sight. Their poverty brings no divine spanking, in fact, the opposite. They are just as welcome in the kingdom as anyone else. That is good news indeed!

It was probably this good news to the poor that brought Jesus to add: "And blessed is anyone who takes no offense at me" (Matt. 11:6; Luke 7:23). Healing lepers and curing the sick carried little offense. But Jesus insulted Sadducee and Pharisee ears when he blessed the poor and welcomed nobodies into the kingdom. Jesus also made it clear that the rich too were welcome—if they shucked off the shackles of wealth, obeyed God's economic laws, and practiced Jubilee.

Jubilee Refused

We've surveyed six warnings of Jesus about wealth. Now we turn to three biblical characters: the rich young ruler, Zacchaeus, and the widow with a coin. Jesus uses their stories to expand his teaching about riches.

The story of the rich young ruler (Luke 18:18-30) features a young professional who poses the big question to Jesus; "What must I do to inherit eternal life?" Jesus' dialogue with this bright fellow is sharpened when it's placed alongside the story of Zacchaeus, which follows (Luke 19:1-10). Side by side, Zacchaeus and the ruler make opposite choices about Jubilee. Both are rich and in positions of power. Both meet Jesus, but they walk away in different directions.

The adjective *rich* isn't strong enough for this darling upstart. He was *very* rich. He had everything that counts. He was young, wealthy, powerful. This triad sent him soaring to the top. We can only speculate about how he became rich at such a young age. Was it hard work, inheritance, luck?

Why does he stop Jesus? Had his abundant life turned sour? Did emptiness stalk his days? Whatever the prod, the big question haunts him. What must he do to inherit eternal life?

Here again, as with the Lazarus story, Jesus links eternal life to wealth. The rich ruler is sincere and conscientious, not a cunning robber. He grew up in a devout family. He knows God's commandments. He has studied in the synagogue. His attendance at Sunday school, Bible study, choir, church camp, and mass is perfect. He knows Scripture and denominational doctrine by heart. His theology is orthodox. He not only knows the creeds—he lives them in his daily life.

Jesus answers his big question by pointing to one deficiency. He must sell his possessions. They are ruling his life—not God. To experience the reign of God, to gain eternal treasure, he must sell his possessions. Why should he sell out? Because the poor are hungry and needy. Wealth has captured his heart and claimed his allegiance. Selling out will not only feed the hungry; it will also refocus his attention on the heavenly kingdom. Jesus invites him to "come, follow me."

We should accent the "follow" rather than the "sell." This is an invitation to join the people of the kingdom and selling all was, in this case, a necessary first step. Jesus didn't always counsel persons to sell everything, as we shall see in the story of Zacheus. But in this case he does. The ruler's decision was likely negative, because he turns away sadly. The grip of mammon is simply too strong. He forfeits eternal life.

Jesus summarizes the event harshly: "How hard it is for those who have wealth to enter the kingdom of God! Indeed, it is easier for a camel to go through the eye of a needle than for someone who is rich to enter the kingdom of God" (Luke 18:24-25). Some scribes changed later versions of the manuscript to soften the hardness of this teaching. One later edition said that getting a rich man into heaven was like pulling a cord or rope through a needle. Another version said it was like getting a camel through a small gate. Neither of these are likely authentic interpretations.[18] Jesus probably *meant* a camel and a needle. The camel was the largest animal and the needle had the smallest opening. Such exaggeration fits his other teachings on wealth. Today Jesus might put it like this: it's harder for the wealthy to enter the kingdom than for a casino owner to slip through the slot of a cash machine.

The outburst of the crowd was predictable. "Then who can be saved?" The answer: "What is impossible for mortals is possible for God" (Luke 18:27). This doesn't mean God will miraculously drag the wealthy through the kingdom's gate. It means, rather, that God's grace can free even rich people from wealth's demonic grip. As we shall soon see, even a rich person can turn around and practice Jubilee. Everything is possible when people open their lives to God's reign.

Luke builds a bridge between the sad ruler and Zacchaeus with two short stories. Stitched with irony, the stories surprise us. In the first story, the disciples who "see" are blind to the truth. In the second one, a blind man opens his eyes and sees. When Jesus speaks about his impending doom on the cross, the disciples don't get it; they don't understand. They're perplexed. What kind of a victorious Messiah is this that talks about crosses? The disciples, who should know about these things, don't. Perhaps they symbolize the blindness of the rich ruler. The next story features a blind beggar outside of Jericho. He can't see. But he understands who Jesus is and yells for mercy. Jesus heals him. Suddenly the blind person sees; the people glorify and praise God. Luke is preparing us for Zacchaeus.

Jubilee Embraced

Zacchaeus might have been short, but he ran a sizable business (Luke 19:1-10). Jericho was no small farming village. It was a city with pools, parks, and typical Greco-Roman buildings. The surrounding area, irrigated and extremely fertile, made it wealthy. The rabbis spoke of the "fat lands of Jericho." Wooed by its balmy weather, Herod the Great made it his winter capital. The region claimed the distinction of cultivating large groves of balsam trees. They sold for an enormous price, often bringing their weight in gold.[19] Furthermore, Jericho was the gateway for a trade route that ran between Jerusalem and the whole Gentile area east of the Jordan.

Zacchaeus was rich because he was the chief tax "farmer" of the district. A team of subordinates actually collected the taxes for him. It was a lucrative job in a lucrative area. Zacchaeus had outbid other contenders to win the right to collect the taxes. Tax collectors often used force and fraud to make a financial killing. Tax bosses like Zacchaeus sometimes even embezzled from their employees.

Understandably, then, tax collectors and especially the tax bosses were despised. This was not only because they were Jews collecting taxes for the Romans, but because they often cheated and used force to collect the taxes. Tax bosses were stigmatized. They weren't allowed to be judges nor could they serve as witnesses in court. Like Gentile slaves, they were even denied the civil and political rights granted to blemished bastards.[20] Money from a tax collector couldn't be given for alms because it was tainted. Eating and associating with tax collectors would contaminate the righteous.

It would have been unthinkable for a Pharisee to lunch with Zacchaeus. The people sneered at him. Perhaps they nicknamed him Zacchaeus out of contempt, for his name means "the righteous." He was, in fact, anything but righteous. Yet Jesus took him to lunch. The rabbis and scribes would have joyfully spit in his face. Jesus deliberately contaminates himself by eating with this outcast at his elaborate mansion. One of the finest in Jericho, it was built on the excessive profits Zacchaeus had squeezed from the poor.

We don't know the details of their conversation, but somehow a miracle happens. Jesus' care and compassion move Zacchaeus.

They so move him that he decides to practice Jubilee. He calls a crowd together on the front lawn. Flabbergasted, they hear crabby old Zacchaeus say, "Look, half of my possessions, Lord, I will give to the poor; and if I have defrauded anyone of anything, I will pay back four times as much" (Luke 19:8). The people cheer and applaud. They can't believe the miracle unfolding before their eyes. What has happened to this scoundrel?

We don't know the final balance in Zacchaeus' bank account. Depending on how much he returned because of fraud, it may have been empty. Or he may have had a pile left over. It doesn't matter. What counts is a change of heart that produces economic change.

Jesus affirms his action. "Today *salvation* has come to this house, because he too is a son of Abraham. For the Son of man came to seek out and to *save* the lost" (Luke 19:9-10, emphasis added). This man has been saved! He has joined the people of God. He is in the royal family, a son of Abraham. This is what the day of salvation is all about. Jesus ties personal salvation to social ethics. What is impossible with humans is possible with God. By the grace of God, a rich man has walked through the eye of the needle. Jubilee is under way.

Things are quite upside-down. The rich young ruler has perfect theology but lacks obedience. Zacchaeus has a lousy or nonexistent theology but practices Jubilee. The ruler calls Jesus a "good teacher." Zacchaeus, the cheat, calls him "Lord." The ruler hopes for eternal life but refuses to share and can't squeeze through the needle's eye. Zacchaeus probably gives little thought to life eternal, but his new care for the poor opens the needle's eye. The religious leader runs up to Jesus. In contrast, Jesus invites himself to lunch with a sinner who is moved by his compassion.

In the first story economic concerns stagnate faith. In the second story faith drives the economic agenda. Here we have two contradictory responses to the gospel, opposite reactions to the poor. On the one hand, good theology, no Jubilee, and condemnation. On the other hand, scant theology, Jubilee, and true salvation. In both stories private spiritual experience connects to social justice, no, to economic justice!

Upside-Down Jubilee

We conclude Jesus' teaching on wealth with a case of inverted Jubilee. Near the end of his ministry, shortly after cleansing the temple, Jesus returns to it. He stands in the massive temple treasury where offerings are placed in large golden vessels. Again we find a comparison of rich and poor. Jesus sits opposite the treasury, and watches the multitude dropping their offerings into golden vessels. Many rich people put in large sums. Then a poor widow comes by, and drops in two copper coins, which make a penny.

Jesus stands and calls his disciples. Pointing to the widow, he says, "Truly, I tell you, this poor widow has put in more than all those who are contributing to the treasury. For all of them have contributed out of their abundance; but she out of her poverty has put in everything she had, all she had to live on" (Mark 12:41-44; Luke 21:1-4).

In the verse preceding this account, Jesus condemns those "who devour widows' houses and for the sake of appearance, make long prayers. They will receive the greater condemnation" (Mark 12:40). A widow in Palestinian society was an outcast. She had no inheritance rights from her husband's property. When the husband died, the oldest son acquired the property. If there was no son, a brother of the deceased husband might marry the widow. If the brother refused or there was none, she would return to her father's house or to begging. Widows, like other women, had no role in public or religious life. They often wore black clothing to signal their plight. Moreover, the rich often oppressed them.

Jesus condemns the scribes for devouring widows' houses. The scribes had developed religious rules, which pushed widows out of their own homes. But the religious leaders glossed over their injustice with long and pretentious prayers. After searing the scribes for "devouring widows' houses," Jesus turns and highlights the widow's faithfulness. The rich—probably Sadducees and nobles from aristocratic families—were putting "large sums" into the golden vessels, pure and proper silver coins.

The poor widow plunks in two copper coins worth a penny. The copper lepton was the smallest Greek coin in circulation. It took 128 of these leptons to equal one denarius—a day's wage. So the widow drops in a sixty-fourth of a day's wage!

Jesus is impressed, so impressed in fact that he lectures the disciples. This widow, he says, has put in more than all these rich persons together. How can this be? Unlike them, she put in everything she had. They just skimmed off the top of their abundance. The actual amount of money was insignificant. What counted was the amount left over for consumption. The rich were still quite rich, even after giving a sizable offering. The poor widow gave everything, not a self-righteous tithe. Jesus, the story suggests, looks at what proportion of our wealth we give, not the raw amount.

Jesus affirms the Jubilee attitude of the poor widow. Certainly she could have found convincing excuses for not giving the last coins in her purse. Upside-down Jubilee occurs when the poor give out of their poverty "bigger gifts" than the rich.

The stories in this chapter summarize the core of Jesus' economic message. The amount of material in the Gospels dealing with wealth is enormous. Few other topics, except for the kingdom of God itself, appear more frequently in the Gospels! Economic issues are central to Jesus' vision of the new kingdom. Conversion, which doesn't involve economic change, isn't complete conversion. Jesus not only condemns greed in first-century Palestine; he calls for a perpetual Jubilee.

The upside-down message reverberates again and again.

- Blessed are the poor . . . woe to the rich (Luke 6:20, 24).

- What human beings prize is an abomination in the sight of God (Luke 16:15).

- Lazarus goes to be with Abraham while the rich man faces torment (Luke 16:22, 23).

- Those who store up treasure for themselves are not rich toward God (Luke 12:21).

- The nations of the world strive after things. . . . Instead, strive for God's kingdom (Luke 12:30, 31).

- The rich young ruler refuses to share his wealth, but salvation visits the home of Zacchaeus, the cheat (Luke 18:18—19:10).

• Do not store up for yourselves treasures on earth . . . but store up treasures in heaven (Matt. 6:20).

• You cannot serve God and wealth. You will be devoted to one and despise the other (Matt. 6:24).

Several key ideas emerge from Jesus' message. Attachment to wealth can compete with and unseat the rule of God in our lives. When God becomes truly King of our lives, God transforms our economic values and practices. Although Jesus rebuked "rich people," he was also attacking the practices of Palestinian society that trampled the poor to benefit the rich. Unjust structures carried a double offense when religious leaders endorsed them with pious language. Jesus turns things upside-down by arguing the true religion stimulates compassion and generosity. It never sanctifies injustice.

The teachings of Jesus emerged in the first stage of a new religious movement, which eventually became the church. Because leaders of new movements are often outside the social mainstream, they typically criticize established practices. Many Christian disciples today find themselves inside institutions concerned with continuity and self-preservation. Stable and predictable financial arrangements are necessary for organizations to continue. Protecting financial self-interest is basic to institutional survival.

How, then, do we relate the economic teachings of Jesus, the "outsider," to the issues faced by "insiders" in mainstream organizations, corporations, schools, and churches? How can the wisdom of Jesus inform the economic practices of modern organizations without jeopardizing their survival?

Jesus doesn't prescribe policies or give us specific guidelines. He does, however, offer a new vision—one that heralds grace rather than greed, compassion rather than competition. It is a Jubilee vision based on a new spirit and kingdom values: one that changes both hearts and economic practices. Nevertheless, change of heart and practice comes hard. We often search for detours around Jesus' call for economic transformation. We'll explore some of those detours in chapter seven.

7

Right-Side-Up Detours

Our economic commitments often distort our reading of the Scripture and divert us around the biblical teaching on wealth. We're tempted to lift verses out of their context and twist their meaning to "bless" our personal economic philosophy. In addition to spinning Scripture our way, we often use nonbiblical folk wisdom to rationalize affluence. We'll consider nine detours—nine examples of ways wealth may wag our theological beliefs. The bypasses permit us to slip by the substance of Jesus' message. Often based on an isolated verse or proverbial saying, these evasions enable us to maneuver around Jesus' call for economic conversion.

Detour One: What About the Parable of the Talents?

A frequent excuse clings to a familiar parable (Matt. 25:14-30; Luke 19:11-27).[1] It's ironic that we sometimes use the parable of the talents, immediately following Luke's story of Zacchaeus, to contradict Zacchaeus' behavior. Readers in the Western capitalist world are tempted to think the story affirms a homespun version of capitalism. We also easily confuse the word *talent* in the text, meaning about 6,000 drachmas (monetary units), with the modern English usage of talent as personal gift and ability.

The popular interpretation of the parable often runs along these lines. God has given each of us different abilities or personal talents—singing, managing, counseling, and so forth. The talents also refer to our financial assets and expertise—especially our ability to make money. God will hold us accountable for how we use these personal gifts and material resources. God will reward us for expanding them.

Punishment, on the other hand, will strike those who sit on their resources. Thus if making money is our gift, we should make money like mad. We should multiply capital assets and property as rapidly as possible. Indeed, such a reading can justify profiteering. Matthew's Gospel quotes the master telling the unfaithful steward, "You ought to have invested my money with the bankers, and at my return, I would have received what was my own with interest" (Matt. 25:27). A literal interpretation of these lines misses the point entirely.

Just because Jesus uses money as the key symbol in the story doesn't mean the parable addresses financial stewardship. The actual objects in a parable are usually not literal prescriptions for Christian behavior. Everyday symbols are used to craft a story with a deeper meaning. We don't say that the parable of the sower means Christians should actually sow grain. Nor do we say that the parable of the lost sheep implies we should raise sheep! On the other hand, example stories such as the Good Samaritan *do* show Christian behavior when they conclude, "Go and do likewise" (Luke 10:37).

So what's the point of the talents? A nobleman entrusts his servants with a commodity and holds them accountable for it. His unexpected return causes a crisis. The master judges the servants by how they cared for his property. The commodity in the story is our knowledge of Christian faith. Perhaps Jesus was thinking of the scribes or Jewish people in general. How had they managed the faith and Scriptures, which had been given them? Jesus was now judging their stewardship of the law. How well had they handled their stewardship of the commandments? Had they preserved and interpreted the Law of Moses properly? Or had they buried their knowledge of the law in the sand?

The early church thought the parable meant Jesus, like the nobleman, was going away. Upon his return, he would judge them on how they had multiplied the kingdom. In fact, Luke (19:11) reports that Jesus told the parable precisely *because* some disciples thought the kingdom would appear immediately when they arrived in Jerusalem. Jesus may be saying, in effect, the kingdom is not here yet in its fullness, but we are responsible to invest (spread and apply) our knowledge of the kingdom. Luke likely thought Jesus would judge his followers' stewardship of the kingdom upon his return later, not immediately. Jesus might then ask how well they had practiced the teachings of the kingdom. Had they invested and multiplied their knowledge of his message?

As one writer puts it, we're to "trade" or "barter" with kingdom ideas.[2] So, rather than a story which justifies the acquisition of wealth, we have the opposite. The more we know about the upside-down way of Jesus, the greater our obligation to live it. The parable of the talents echoes the story of the rich man and Lazarus. The rich man knew about Moses and the prophets. He understood the Jubilee. He had been given a talent, knowledge of God's economic way, but had buried it. He didn't feed the beggar Lazarus. So he faced condemnation.

Luke places the parable of the talents immediately after Zacchaeus. Perhaps Luke is suggesting that we are responsible for the stewardship of the ideas of the Zacchaeus story. Will we, like Zacchaeus, allow the lordship of Jesus Christ to open our pocketbooks? A similar interpretation fits the wisdom saying at the end of the parable. "To all those who have more will be given; but from those who have nothing, even what they have will be taken away." The key issue here is more of *what*? This hardly means that those who have money will make more—even though that's often true. The meaning of the parable is clear: those who invest and multiply their kingdom knowledge will be given more. Those who waste it may lose the kingdom completely.

Detour Two: Seek the Kingdom and Get Rich!

After teaching about anxiety, Jesus instructs the disciples to "strive first for the kingdom of God and his righteousness, and all these things will be given to you as well" (Matt. 6:33; Luke 12:31). Does this offer biblical proof that those who pursue the kingdom will become rich? May we view riches as a sign of God's blessing? We have already seen that wealth in Jesus' eye was more of a curse than a blessing.

What does it mean that kingdom seekers will have the material things of life as well? In the context of the sabbatical year, Jesus is simply saying that God will provide an adequate six-year yield to cover needs in both the sixth and seventh years. If folks follow his command, he will care for them. The "things" God will supply are basic food and clothing—not luxurious homes and estates. God will provide the basic necessities. In the context of the sabbatical year, this passage isn't a scheme for getting rich off the kingdom. It simply offers basic survival in the seventh year.

A business venture or a household managed in harmony with Christian principles—honesty and integrity—will likely be successful. But managers and owners who truly allow the rule of God to operate in their lives won't hoard gain. They'll share it in the spirit of Jubilee. Our material stockpiles may be one barometer of our willingness to follow kingdom principles.

Matthew counsels us to strive for the kingdom and God's "righteousness," which could be interpreted as God's "justice." Seeking the kingdom doesn't mean bread will mysteriously fall out of heaven. Nor does it mean we'll automatically get rich. Seeking the kingdom with the intention of getting rich perverts the kingdom's very essence. It mocks the message of Jesus about wealth and it implies that we can achieve God's blessing by our good works.

Detour Three: Give and Gain!

We find another evasive route near the end of the rich young ruler story. Jesus concludes, "Truly, I tell you, there is no one who has left house or wife or brothers or parents or children, for the sake of the kingdom of God, who will not get back very much more in this age, and in the age to come eternal life" (Luke 18:29, 30; Mark 10:29-30; Matt. 19:29). Matthew and Mark include land in their list of things forsaken. Does this mean Jesus will multiply our property if we follow him?

A pastor warming up his congregation for an offering used this verse. He promised that God would literally return 100 dollars for every dollar placed in the offering. Giving with the hope of getting rich distorts the spirit of Jubilee. Such an interpretation would also multiply wives, husbands, and parents in this age!

Jesus doesn't expect our spouses and lands to multiply. He means that when we join the kingdom we join the family of God. Disciples who sell property or leave homes will find a warm welcome in other Christian homes as they travel. They will discover a new network of sisters, brothers, and parents in the kingdom that will welcome them with beds and teapots. Those who argue that God will double our wealth if they forsake everything for the kingdom usually are the ones who have *not* left houses or lands. They are, rather, trying to find an isolated verse to justify expansion. Their motives mock the spirit of Jubilee, which focuses on the needs of others—not personal gain. Jesus says that those who sacrifice for the kingdom's sake will receive both material and spiritual rewards now and in the age to come.

Detour Four: The Poor Are Always with You!

All four Gospels report the story of the woman pouring expensive perfume on Jesus (Matt. 26:6-13; Mark 14:3-9; Luke 7:36-50; John 12:1-8). There is considerable variation in the four accounts. All writers (except Luke) report that the onlookers condemned this waste of a year's wages. They wondered aloud why the perfume wasn't sold and the money given to the poor. Jesus said, "For you always have the poor with you, but you will not always have me" (Matt. 26:11).[3] Is this a clear example of Jesus' fatalism? He apparently acknowledges the perpetual existence of the poor and shows the priority of worship over social justice—or does he?

Interestingly, Jesus quotes directly from Deuteronomy 15, the chapter with Jubilee and sabbatical instructions. Earlier in the passage God tells the Hebrews that if they're obedient there will be no poor in the land. However, if they harden their hearts, there will be poor. As long as greed and selfishness continue, the poor will be among them. Does this fact justify a callous neglect of the poor? Just the opposite! "Since there will never cease to be some in need on the earth, I therefore command you, 'Open your hand to the poor and needy neighbor in your land'" (Deut. 15:11).

In light of his continual plea on behalf of the poor, it's hardly conceivable that Jesus now contradicts himself by telling us to neglect the poor who, after all, will always be around and there's not much we can do about it. Such a sarcastic sense of fatalism flies in the face of everything else he says about caring for the poor. He's likely suggesting that as long as greed and ambition govern the lives of people, there will always be poor. His observation of this fact *does not* justify its perpetuation. Rather than excusing us from social obligation, Jesus is reminding us that the alleviation of poverty is a never-ending struggle.

A detailed study of Jewish law shows that pouring the perfume was an act not, of worship, but of charity.[4] A prostitute couldn't give her offering in the temple because her profession contaminated it. Contaminated earnings and ointment could, however, be used to prepare a corpse. Preparation for burial took precedent over feeding and clothing the poor. In the words of Jesus, "She has done it to prepare me for burial" (Matt. 26:12).

The prostitute takes a tool of her trade—perfume—and uses it in an act of charity to prepare Jesus' body. She joyfully gives the perfume, which once seduced other bodies, to prepare the body which soon will be broken for the sins of the world. Splashing perfume over Jesus' body symbolized the rejection of her old ways and her spontaneous joy of forgiveness, for she had many sins. Upside-down indeed!

Detour Five: It All Depends on Your Attitude!

It's tempting to summarize Jesus' teaching on wealth by saying, "It's only our attitude toward money that matters. As long as we have the right attitude, things will work out okay." Now obviously attitudes are important because they influence our behavior. Jesus taught that wrong attitudes are as bad as wrong behavior. And the poor can be just as materialistic, if not more so, than the rich.

Jesus didn't say, however, that we can substitute good attitudes for good behavior. Good sentiments are a fine place to start, but Jesus clearly wants us to go beyond them. He condemns the rich fool for expanding his barn and the rich man for throwing crumbs to Lazarus. He encourages us to distribute wealth. Several times he tells his disciples to sell their possessions. He describes Zacchaeus as a child of God because his change of attitude alters his economic behavior. The rich young ruler has good attitudes, but they aren't enough to feed the poor.

Warm feelings in our heart, good intentions in our head, and proper attitudes in our mind are an essential first step. But they don't clothe and feed the poor. Behavior is the real test. Jesus calls for attitude changes that produce action.

Detour Six: What About Stewardship?

Stewardship is a core concept in understanding our relationship to wealth. Ironically, sometimes we use stewardship itself to mask greed. Oddly enough, Jesus doesn't use the word *stewardship* to discuss wealth. Instead, he warns of the dangers of mammon and calls for compassion. In Hebrew, steward means "manager over the house." The steward is an official who controls a large household for the master. It's certainly fitting for Christians to use the term stewardship to describe our relationship to property because the concept reminds us that God in fact owns the property. But what do we mean by stewardship?

It's helpful to distinguish between the wishes of the owner and the wishes of the steward. The steward is responsible to manage the property according to the master's wishes, *not* the steward's. We sometimes use the term stewardship to whitewash our own desires. We may, for example, say stewardship means taking whatever resources we have, multiplying them as fast as possible, and using them for our own purposes.

This twists the biblical view of stewardship. The biblical view begins with God's vision for the use of natural and human resources. In the Hebrew Jubilee and in Jesus' teachings, God's resources are to be widely shared. They're not to be used to elevate some people and put others down. They're to be given freely to those in need. Good stewards of God's resources generously share and distribute them. We're not stewards of God's resources when we stockpile and multiply them for personal gain. Good stewards are prudent and careful guardians of the resources that have come their way. They despise waste and callous abuse of resources. Faithful stewards are frugal when calculating their own needs and generous when responding to others.

Detour Seven: Just Give a Tithe!

Even tithing can serve as a self-righteous diversion around Jesus' message. It can become a mechanical rule to justify luxurious living. The New Testament doesn't explicitly instruct us to tithe. Jesus and the apostle Paul both encourage liberal giving. Liberal offerings, however, go beyond tithing, as we've seen in the case of the poor widow. Tithes were an integral part of the Old Testament system of sacrifices and offerings. The New Testament simply assumes the tithe as a minimal standard for giving.

The weakness of the tithe as the primary guideline for giving is obvious. A person earning $10,000 a year gives $1,000 and retains $9,000. Someone else earning $100,000 and giving $10,000 has $90,000 left for personal use. Tithing unfortunately focuses our attention on how much we *give* rather than on how much we *keep*. In upside-down fashion, God cares more about what we *keep* than what we *give*. It's less important that one person gives $1,000 while another gives $10,000. What counts is that some struggle to make ends meet with $9,000, while others can justify spending $90,000 lavishly because, after all, "we have tithed."

Token tithes don't necessarily exemplify good stewardship, compassion, or Jubilee. They easily become self-righteous maneuvers to justify opulence. Rather than using the tithe to excuse upscale living, we might explore ways of shrinking our standard of living so we have more surpluses to give.

A graduated tithe is one way of working at this issue.[5] A family might establish a baseline budget of, say $30,000. They might then give a regular ten percent tithe on this basic figure.

Five percent is added to the tithe for each thousand above the baseline.

A $31,000 income is tithed ten percent on the first thirty thousand and fifteen percent on the next thousand, and so on.

When the income reaches $48,000, all of the last thousand is given since the graduated tithe has jumped to 100 percent.

At $48,000, a family following this scheme would give $13,350 and retain $34,650 for personal use and savings. Under the traditional tithe, they would give $4,000 with $43,200 left for personal use.

These hypothetical numbers illustrate how some form of graduated tithe might work. Such a tithe embodies the Jubilee spirit and nudges us in the direction of generous stewardship. Specific guidelines can help to discipline our giving, but our gifts should flow from a heart of joy, not legalistic rules.

A one-tenth tithing mind-set also promotes the notion that the good life is fine "if we can afford it." The popular adage of "live within your means" suggests that those of meager means must follow an austere budget. Those with larger means can, of course, consume freely. "If you can afford it; you can have it." As our means expand, so does our appetite for so-called "necessities." The things that we couldn't afford in the past become things we simply cannot live without as our incomes rise. Living within our means is obviously necessary—especially for lower-income families. The phrase often, however, becomes a convenient excuse to endorse an upscale lifestyle. "Live within your means" is a cultural rule of thumb that can steer upper income people away from the spirit of Jubilee and giving in abundance.

Detour Eight: Maintain the Witness!

"Maintain the witness" is a pious argument that also evades the Jubilee model. It suggests that a high standard of living is necessary to "witness" effectively to affluent persons. To reach upper-class folks with the gospel requires Christians to communicate with them through upper class symbols. In other words, we can't witness meaningfully to the Jaguar crowd if we drive a Ford. Christians need to splurge to effectively communicate the gospel in an affluent context. The advocates of "luxury evangelism" certainly wouldn't encourage Christians to steal as a witness to burglars. Nor would they encourage sexual promiscuity as a witness to prostitutes. Yet they sometimes use this logic to rationalize an extravagant lifestyle. In the process, the good news becomes diluted.

Such upscale "witnessing" calls people to a simple "yes" to

Jesus in their heart with few expectations for social and economic conversion. This leads to a cheap gospel—one that makes service to mammon appear righteous. The gospel of Jesus Christ frees us from enslavement to other idols. Maintaining a high standard of living to "effectively" witness not only mocks true faith, it also points others to a diluted gospel.

Detour Nine: Children of the King!

A final detour reminds us that we are, after all, children of a King. The Scripture promises manifold blessings to God's faithful children. Since earthly kings live in extravagant palaces, we Christians should also live luxuriously. Children of a king should dress and eat in regal fashion. By living this way, we show our membership in God's royal court because the material blessings show God's smile upon us.

Jesus is, of course, our King. But that hardly gives us license to indulge in lavish living. Just the opposite. In his triumphal ride into Jerusalem on a donkey, for example, Jesus makes clear that he is, in harmony with his teachings, an upside-down king. Thus if Jesus is indeed Lord and King of our life, we'll seek ways to demonstrate comparable humility, generosity, and compassion. Jesus does promise to "bless us," to provide wholeness, peace, and joy. But he never promises financial riches to his children.

Jesus, in fact, was very clear: God's rain falls on the just and the unjust. God's sun shines on everyone. God doesn't have pets. We can't manipulate God like a puppet. To say that rich people are blessed—that their riches are a sign of God's smile—implies that the poor are not. Such an attitude is a harsh and callous condemnation of the poor because it suggests that their poverty is a sign of God's curse.

To struggle to survive in squalor every day is bad enough, but to have rich Christians suggest that material goods are a blessing, and poverty a divine curse, is blasphemy. Material well-being and poverty are fed by many complicated factors but not by God's blessings and curses. For wealthy Christians to say that their riches are a sign of God's blessing not only insults the poor but God's very nature and message.

Meanwhile Back Home

What does all this mean? God's rule in the lives of believers is the key to Jesus' economic message.[6] The nearness of God's reign robs economic demons of their power. We've seen the Jubilee principles woven throughout the Gospels. As we experience God's forgiveness, we can in turn forgive. As we learn of God's goodness, we no longer fret about necessities. Once we were beggars, strangers, slaves, and debtors. Now God has made us new, filling us with compassion for those trapped as we once were.

God's love for us transforms our economic behavior. Mercy, not accumulation, becomes our new yardstick for measuring success. Generous giving replaces conspicuous consumption. God's highest command forms the core of this upside-down way. Loving God with all our heart means loving our neighbors as much as ourselves. And this means caring, sharing, giving—valuing our neighbors' welfare as much as our own. Care for our neighbor strips the old demons of their grip.

Jesus doesn't offer specific answers, but he does prod us toward the right questions. He pushes us beyond rules and regulations by calling for a perpetual Jubilee. He doesn't reject private property nor insist on communal ownership. In fact, much of his teaching assumes our ownership of private property. We can't lend or give to those in need if we have no property. What Jesus asks of us may vary, but he does invite us to treat the poor as our neighbor, indeed as our self.

Although he addressed individuals, Jesus' words rocked the foundation of the Palestinian economy. Even today, his call for Jubilee challenges economic policies which encourage disparities between rich and poor. Does working hard to earn money justify spending it lavishly and selfishly? Are there times when the legal acquisition of wealth is immoral? Jesus warns us that wealth can turn into a powerful god, capturing our imagination, demanding our allegiance, bending our knees, and ruling our lives.

The Jubilee perspective nudges us to question cultural assumptions we take for granted. Is it morally right to pay only a minimum wage even when it's legal? Should we charge exorbitant professional fees, even though they're legal and customary? Charging exorbitant commissions may hinder the Jubilee by perpetuating economic structures which keep poor people poor while rich folks feast.

Is getting the "best price" for a property or product always "good stewardship"? Selling for a lower figure to a needy person might be more in the spirit of Jubilee than demanding the "best price." Is charging the highest fees the "market will bear" consistent with Jesus' way? Does "good stewardship" mean squeezing the last nickel out of every deal? In many subtle ways our economic systems may distort our faith. We dare not assume that just because "that's the way things are" means they are necessarily ethical, moral, or Christian.

Who's Rich?

Jesus talked of the rich and the poor. These terms needed little clarification for his audience. In a two-class society the rich were obvious. It's easy to toss aside Jesus' comments about wealth because we may assume we're not rich. A moment's reflection, however, shows the relative meaning of the term. A person rich in one context may be poor in another. It depends on whom we compare with whom. There are simply no absolute standards to define the slippery term *rich*. Middle class folks tend to brush off Jubilee because Jesus was talking about the *really* rich, not them.

Social scientists note that happiness doesn't automatically rise with wealth. In fact, one psychologist posed the perennial American paradox: Why are so many people sad amid prosperity?[7] We're satisfied when we *feel* we have enough resources to meet our perceived needs. The people around us shape what we think we need. Our needs, and thus our happiness, are based on soft social comparisons with others, not on absolute standards. If we don't think we need much we can be happy with little. If we try to match our upscale peers, a modest salary hike may leave us sulking. What we need, what makes us happy, all depends on our point of comparison.

When I think about rich people, I think of the Bill Gates, the Ted Turners, the Rockefellers, the Kennedys, the Trumps. I think of places like Palm Springs, California, where "simple and unpretentious" homes go for millions of dollars. I think of chief executives officers who earn millions a year. I think of sports and film stars with bloated salaries. These are the rich folks in my book. And I'm certainly not one of them. Or am I?

A visit to a rural church in Central America opened my eyes in new ways. A Christian brother took me to his banana plot a mile up a steep mountain. I counted as we walked. He had over fifty patches on the only pair of trousers he owned. Suddenly I realized I was rich, very rich indeed, with pairs of trousers and shirts to spare. The meaning of "rich" all depends on our social context and point of comparison.

We pity ourselves when we look up the social ladder and compare ourselves with those above us. We certainly aren't rich compared to someone making $50,000 a year more than we do. No, we aren't rich beside the person with a larger house than we have. By looking *up* the ladder, we're *never* rich. Staring up the ladder makes us feel poor. We pity ourselves and the biblical message eludes us. We hope those on the rung above us drop a few leftovers and don't trample our fingers. But that's wishful thinking, because the ones above us are also looking up and feeling poor in contrast to the rich above them. So the feeling of poverty spirals ever upward among the rich because no one can ever have enough.

The upside-down Jubilee perspective reminds us that once we were slaves, once we were captives. This reminder shifts our focus downward, where the biblical spotlight always points. Pagans look up. When we follow the biblical spotlight, we look down and realize we're rich. When we look down, things suddenly appear different and we are moved to compassion. The Jubilee message strikes home.

Few readers of this book are a destitute Lazarus. But Lazaruses *are* in our global community. They search for clean water. They die of HIV/AIDS and other treatable diseases. They hunt for decent housing. They sit by the global curb hungry and malnourished. Even with conservative estimates, about half a billion—that's 500 million—people are gradually starving. *Another* half billion receive enough calories but are short on protein. Some 60,000 people die of hunger-related causes *every* day. About 20,000 of these are children. Nearly 1.3 billion people do not have clean water. From outright starvation to deficient diets, about one fifth of the worldwide village is hungry and malnourished.[8] Compared to them, many readers of this book are rich. Many Christians fight flab. Undisciplined diets send us scampering for weight loss programs.

Ironically the global class structure today looks much like ancient Palestine. A small elite at the top lords it over the vast multitude at the bottom. About one fifth of the world's population gobbles up some 80 percent of our global resources and produces 80 percent of the pollution. The poorer four-fifths of the people in the global village scrap for the remaining 20 percent of the goodies. Nearly *half* of the people of the world live on less than $2 a day— less than what is spent on pets in developed countries.

The average income of Americans is 100 times more than the income of the world's poorest billion. Even when respective standards of living are taken into account and real purchasing power is calculated, the average American enjoys more than 10 times the income of typical people in many countries. Most Christians in western developed countries can only read their Bibles as rich Christians.

Downscaling

Where do we start? We can begin by consuming less. Many of our so-called necessities are status symbols we polish to keep a respectable image among our peers. Incessant shopping has become a sacrificial ritual on the altar of materialism. Curtailing consumption is the beginning of responsible stewardship of God's non-renewable resources.

Our self-image is rooted in how we *think* other people see us. The old social adage is true—I am what I think you think I am. If I think other people think I'm odd, I feel inadequate and unsure of myself. We want others to respect us and think well of us. To gain their acceptance, we display the status symbols of our group—cars, clothing, boats, books, computers, and trinkets. Outdated clothing, small cars, modest housing, and simple vacations violate the rules of middle-class etiquette. To protect and enhance our image, we must ever devour more and more products, few of which are necessities.

Materialism is a dead-end trap. The more we get, the more we want. And the more we get the more we need to maintain what we have. As soon as we catch up with a fad or fashion, someone else moves ahead. Once again, we're behind. Someone else always outdoes us with a bigger model, more accessories, greater speed, superior convenience, or advanced styling. Incessant advertising ever creates new needs and desires. Our socially constructed cravings wrap our lives in artificial trappings and rob our souls of moral integrity. The incessant drive for *more* of everything leaves the rich empty, the poor hungry, and scarce resources wasted. In American society, for example, the average family size shrank in half during the same time that the size of houses doubled.

In the endless race of status escalation, we're always behind.[9] It's tempting to play the game of *conspicuous consumption*—showing off our wares from endless shopping trips—in the hopes of being accepted and applauded by our friends. In sharp contrast, people of the upside-down kingdom engage in *inconspicuous service*—caring for the needy, the ill, the destitute, and the disabled who are often hidden in institutions or living on the edge of society.

To buck the pressures of conspicuous consumption, we need friends for support and affirmation. The social pressures for consumption, conformity, and social status are so strong we can hardly resist them alone. That's why we need Christian friends who also affirm upside-down values and attempt to live them. We're all social beings who depend on others for our sense of worth and value. It's important to select and create circles of friends—supportive networks—that affirm kingdom values. This web of Christian friends needn't have a formal structure, but it can help to reinforce modest lifestyle choices. The loving support of an alternate culture, a Christian enclave, lets us withstand the seductive and demonic forces of materialism.

Curtailing consumption isn't a panacea for world hunger. Buying less steak at the local supermarket won't push more protein into third-world pantries. As Christians, we consume less not because it's always an effective solution to world hunger, but because it's the morally responsible thing to do. We're accountable not for grandiose solutions to world problems but for our personal obedience to our knowledge of the gospel. That, indeed, sums up the parable of the talents.

Consider the size of our ecological footprint. How does our daily lifestyle gobble up natural resources and pollute God's garden? The footprint we leave is determined by things like the goods we trash, the miles we drive, the water we flush, and the electricity we tap. Those and dozens of other daily activities leave their mark not only on the natural resources but on the poor as well.[10]

It's easy to do nothing because we fear our small act won't count. It's true that one more baby, one more luxury car, and one more vacation home won't make a significant difference. However, when several million other people think and act the same way, the *corporate consequences* of our greed are devastating. Five million pieces of plastic litter, 10 million gas-guzzlers, and 20 million babies will make a whopping collective impact—a gigantic ecological footprint. The belief that "my behavior won't make a difference anyway" doesn't excuse us from moral responsibility.

On the other hand, individual acts aren't enough. We also must act together through organizations at local and international levels that make a difference. We need to work to change structures and policies that protect the wealthy and trample the poor. Above all we must nurture a global perspective that makes a difference on the personal and local level.[11]

Consider several simple questions about simplicity and economic justice.

- If everyone throughout the world consumed as many natural resources as I do, what kind of a world would we have?

- How much does my level of consumption drain energy resources and strain the environment? In other words, how big is my ecological footprint?

- Is my lifestyle this year more simplified than it was last year? Or is it more complicated, more consumptive, more stressful?

- In which direction am I drifting?

Practicing Jubilee

Jesus doesn't call us away from the world of commerce and business. He doesn't teach us that managing money and property is wrong. He tells us instead that the reign of God in our lives should shape our acquisition, management, and disposal of wealth.

Many Christians, skilled in managing businesses and understanding economic systems, have made tremendous contributions to the ministry of the church and the needy around the world. The expression of Jubilee takes different forms, depending on our position in a particular economic structure. If we're the rich one in a relationship, it may mean sharing beyond expectation with persons in need.[12]

As employers, we practice Jubilee by paying above-average wages with joy, even when it shrinks our profits. Instead of trying to squeeze the maximum labor from employees at the minimum price, we share profits, provide dignity in work, and encourage stock ownership in the company. This perspective isn't a prescription for bankruptcy or a cavalier view of the bottom line. In fact, the long-term spin off may yield happier employees, working harder to produce more for all. A commitment to the Jubilee perspective calls for distributing wealth fairly among those who help to create it. Funneling all profit into the hands of a few contradicts the Jubilee spirit.

Christian entrepreneurs often struggle with these difficult questions.

- Where does profit come from?

- Where does it go?

- Does its distribution conform to a Jubilee vision? Or does it push a few folks to the top of the economic ladder and hold the rest at the bottom?

Recall the biblical injunction that people and material resources are the Lord's. We're called to value people over things. We're to use possessions, not people. A corporation, following the Jubilee vision, will make special efforts to employ the disadvantaged—the ex-offenders, the deaf, the disabled, and those stigmatized in other ways. For those giving professional services, the Jubilee approach might mean a graduated payment scale tied to client income. Or it might mean charging fees below the prevailing rates. The rich, whom the biblical vision energizes, will share the Jubilee with those around and below them with joy.

Consider an example of modern Jubilee that goes beyond pity. Habitat for Humanity is an international organization that creatively applies biblical economics. Habitat operates in hundreds of locations in dozens of countries around the world. The program builds low-cost, modest homes for those without homes. Prospective homeowners must give hundreds of hours of their own "sweat equity" (volunteer time) to qualify for a house. They also give some of the "sweat equity" to other projects before construction begins on their home. They can pay off mortgages *without* interest over twenty years. Contributors share money, time, supplies, and labor hand-in-hand with the poor. Habitat builds more than homes—it builds relationships and community. Above all, Habitat nurtures dignity, accountability, and responsibility. It is indeed an exemplary model of Jubilee compassion.

Upside-down giving that spills beyond expectation signals our entrance into the kingdom. It's a powerful sign that King Jesus is king of our resources. There are many creative ways to use our resources for the sake of the poor. In one community a pretrial bail association posts property bail so the poor don't need to sit in jail for months before trial. Homeowners provide their properties as bail for this program. In another example, property or savings can be used as collateral for disadvantaged persons lacking credit who want to buy a home or start a business. If we love our neighbors as ourselves, will we sign our neighbor's loan application and risk paying the consequences of default?

The Jubilee spirit can take many expressions. Instead of banging on the boss's office door for our own raise, we might advocate on behalf of those who have less than we do. We might offer to pay beyond the established price for a product or service. We can freely tip beyond expectation. We can add a tithe to the monthly rent or mortgage as a sign of Jubilee. Rather than careless expressions of stewardship, these upside-down signs signal our freedom from economic bondage. Freely sharing in the Jubilee spirit isn't always possible, but as we are able, giving with a generous spirit signals God's love and our release from the demons of mammon.

Upside-Down Giving

There are five signs of upside-down giving. First, we funnel Jubilee sharing toward those crunched by economic disparities. Jesus again and again directs us to give to the poor. In contrast to many religious promoters, Jesus didn't plead for contributions to his cause. His passion was for the poor, not for his religious movement. The most powerful Christian witness comes when our giving is free from the strings of self-interest. Even Christian institutions at times become self-serving and divert funds to their own interests instead of serving the truly needy. Jubilee giving targets genuine need, not self-serving institutions.

Second, Jubilee generosity includes other Christians in the decision-making process. The individualism of western culture assumes that giving is strictly a private, personal matter. Sisters and brothers in the Christian community can help us discern how and where to give. Rather than wheeling and dealing to buy seats of influence and public recognition, Jubilee giving is a collective expression of love from the community, not the individual.

Third, Jubilee giving assumes that one form of giving is not to take money from others in the first place. Taking as much as possible from others to give more contradicts the Jubilee spirit. Jubilee affirms the idea that not taking funds in the first place, even funds that might be rightfully ours, is in itself a form of giving. This in many ways protects the dignity of the individual more than paternalistic gifts.

Fourth, Jubilee giving doesn't send checks to every compassion fund picturing emaciated children. Money addresses only one type of need. Money alone isn't enough. People, time, dignity, and education must also be included in the Jubilee package. Compassion is more than pity and sentimental tidbits. It must be thoughtful, orderly, and humane. It must go beyond Christmas baskets, to jobs, low-interest loans, credit, security, educational projects, and housing.

Fifth, Jubilee giving flows from the story of God's love. It attests to the biblical story of Jubilee—the story of God's compassion embodied by Jesus. Genuine offerings from heart-felt compassion are motivated by God's love and a genuine care for the needy. Without the biblical perspective, financial aid simply pushes others up a hollow economic ladder, where greed begets greed and materialism prevails. Jubilee giving proclaims the good news of forgiveness in Jesus Christ. Charity that doesn't bring a message of spiritual liberation is little more than do-gooder paternalism that may only lead to new ways of worshiping mammon.

8

Impious Piety

Clues to the Crucifixion

Why was Jesus murdered? Why would a preacher of compassion get nailed to a tree? We've already seen some clues to the reason for his death in his critique of the rich. But the message of the new kingdom went far beyond a critique of wealth. What surely sealed the fate of Jesus was his bold challenge to the symbols of Jewish identity. His words and action scorched the flag of Jewish nationalism.

Jesus announced the in-breaking of a new kingdom, a new order, a new day. God's intervention in history brought many surprises that would turn the old things upside-down. Jesus was a Jewish prophet standing firm on the mosaic traditions but saying God was moving beyond them, transforming them in new ways that would more fully fulfill their purpose. The spirit of God would transform sacred symbols—Sabbath observance, purity rituals, sacred boundaries, and yes, even the mighty temple in Jerusalem. Many of the practices surrounding these symbols served to bolster tribal and national identity. The new kingdom would have bigger doors, bigger tables, and a much bigger family. The old ways created tribal identity through separation and exclusion. The new order welcomed everyone.

No one likes to see their symbols seared. No on likes to see their flag on fire. Change, especially religious change, comes hard. Many Christians today would likely have joined the forces defending the tribal flag in Jesus' time. It was the reasonable, rational, natural thing to do in the face of outrageous ideas. In any event, Jesus' critique of pious practices that elevated sacred symbols and religious ritual above human need thickened the plot that led to his cross.

The Oral Tradition

Why did Jesus' ministry bring a head-on clash with religious authorities? Jesus lived in a Hebrew world entrenched in the teachings of Moses. He didn't come to destroy the law or to scorn it. He embraced and fulfilled it. If Jesus affirmed the law, why did he collide with religious leaders? The answer lies partly in his attitude toward the oral law of Judaism. Jesus endorsed the written Torah, the five books of Moses, but he scoffed at parts of the oral law. He saw the oral law as having less authority than the Scriptures. This especially stirred the ire of the Pharisees. Some of the Gospel writers likely underscored the antagonism between Jesus and the Pharisees because the early church faced stiff opposition from them. A brief overview of the oral law helps us grasp the nature of the conflict.

At the time of Jesus there were actually two Torahs, two types of religious law—written and oral. Both Sadducees and Pharisees accepted the written Torah, composed of the five books of Moses, as the holy law of God. It contained the commandments given to Moses on Mt. Sinai. In addition, an unwritten oral Torah passed by word of mouth from generation to generation. The scribes had developed the oral law and by the time of Jesus, the Pharisees followed it to the letter. The oral law evolved through three different stages—*Midrash*, *Mishnah*, and *Talmud*.

The first step, or *Midrash*, emerged after the Jews returned to their homeland from Babylonian captivity five centuries before the birth of Jesus. The Midrash was a verse-by-verse commentary explaining the written Scripture. An interpretation followed each verse. For example, in Leviticus 19:13 the written law says, "You shall not defraud your neighbor; you shall not steal; and you shall not keep for yourself the wages of a laborer until morning." The Midrash commentary following this verse says that

> This applies also to the hire of animals, or of utensils, or of a hired man's wages even if the employee did not come to him to ask for the wages. . . . A wage earner hired for the day must be given pay for the following night; one engaged for the night, for the following day.[1]

In this fashion the Midrash provided a verse-by-verse commentary on the five books of Moses. This vast corpus was preserved *orally*—passed by word of mouth across the generations. It was not written down until *after* the time of Jesus.

A second form of oral interpretation, known as *Mishnah*, emerged in the two centuries before Jesus. Instead of an exact verse commentary, it provided oral interpretations of the Torah applied to many issues not specifically mentioned in holy writ.

Nearly two centuries after the death of Jesus (about 200 C.E.) the oral traditions were gradually written into the *Talmud*. This stirred fierce controversy, since many rabbis considered writing the law the same as burning it. The Talmud, this *final collection* of wisdom and oral law, became the distinctive book of Judaism comparable to Christianity's New Testament.

The oral law or "tradition of the elders" (Mark 7:5) had a noble purpose: to clarify and interpret the written words of Moses. At first the oral tradition was subordinate to the authority of the Scriptures. But over the years the authority of the oral law grew. In time it was said that God had given the oral law to Moses and preserved it by divine providence over the generations. The oral tradition soon assumed equal, if not greater, authority than the written word. The scope and detail of the oral law is astonishing. A written compilation of the Mishnah has some 700 pages of small print![2] The scribes and rabbis memorized it. No wonder a scribe's entire life was devoted to its study and memory.

The Mishnah is organized into six major divisions called *orders*. Each order holds seven to twelve subdivisions called tractates. These are further broken down into some 523 chapters. Finally, each chapter contains about five to ten legal paragraphs.[3] Unwritten at the time of Jesus, the oral version of the Mishnah guided religious practice. The Mishnah covers the whole gamut of questions, which might arise over religious and civil legislation.

Can laborers on top of a tree or wall offer a prayer? Can one open up quarries or wells during a sabbatical year? If one is naked and makes a dough offering from barley in one's house, does that make the offering unclean? Is tying a knot considered work which violates the Sabbath? Can a man divorce his wife for burning a meal? What's the proper death penalty for someone who blasphemes—burning, stoning, beheading, or strangling? Is a man ceremonially unclean if he touches a mouse? If an unclean bird sits on the eggs of a clean bird do the eggs remain ceremonially clean? If a dog eats the flesh of a corpse, then lies at the door of a house, does that make the house unclean?

On and on, the Mishnah spells out the do's and don'ts, the fine lines between sacred and profane. Like a holy snowball, the oral tradition had grown ever heavier over the centuries.

Progressive Pharisees

The Pharisees, unlike the Sadducees, applied the oral law to everyday life. Their intent was good. The Pharisees believed that religious faith should penetrate all aspects of life. By careful examination of the Scriptures, they tried to prescribe proper conduct for every circumstance. They didn't want the Law of Moses to become a sterile book, detached from life. By contrast, the Sadducees affirmed only the authority of the written law. This made it easier not to apply Scripture to new issues of their day. They were able to embrace the Roman presence and accept the influence of alien cultures because the books of Moses seemed irrelevant to these realities.

By adhering only to the written word and some ritual regulations, the Sadducees excused themselves from everyday obedience to the law. Thus they could piously operate the Jerusalem temple even as they flirted with the Romans. The Pharisees, on the other hand, cared about faithful practice. They showed their submission to the Mosaic covenant by obeying the oral law. Carefully they followed the rules of ritual purity and tithing. Scrupulously they observed pious regulations, hoping someday all Jewish people would follow their example.

The Pharisaic vision, in short, was to call forth a holy nation, a nation of priests.[4] Today, the term *Pharisee* carries a negative connotation of hypocrisy and self-righteousness. In the context of their times, however, the Pharisees were sincere progressives! They truly wanted the Mosaic vision to blossom in Judaism's corporate life.

In broad terms, the four religious parties (as noted in chapter three) responded differently to the political situation in Palestine.

The *Essenes* were an out-of-power priestly group. They retreated to separatist communities housed in caves near the Dead Sea. Someday they hoped to displace the Sadducees in Jerusalem and operate the temple. Using the opposite strategy, patriotic *rebels* tried to overthrow the Romans through protest movements and violence. The diplomatic *Sadducees* compromised, working hand-in-glove with the Romans to maintain the status quo for financial gain. In many ways, the Sadducees were the political, economic, and religious conservatives. The *Pharisees*, meanwhile, worked seriously on the Jewish agenda of holiness. They lived in creative tension. They tried to strike a delicate balance between retreat, revolt, and compromise. Amid the tumult they clung stubbornly to their vision of a holy, priestly nation.

Irreverent Jesus

Jesus' irreverence is a fascinating question. Why did he deplore religious ritual? Why did he scorn civil law? He broke the rules of piety by working on the Sabbath, disregarding ritual cleansing, associating with disreputable persons, and purging the temple. We'll explore the meaning of these four provocative acts and then summarize Jesus' verbal critique of the Pharisees.[5]

Jesus' violation of Sabbath norms was most irksome. Surely he knew better! Sabbath rest was one of the Ten Commandments. A symbol of respect and worship of God, it was a distinctive feature of Hebrew faith. It set the Hebrews apart. The Jews carefully preserved the day for sacred worship. Transgressing Sabbath law was a serious matter—offenders received the death penalty. Those who broke a Sabbath ordinance after receiving a warning were stoned. Jesus demolished some of the human *traditions* encrusting the Sabbath but didn't destroy the *principle* of the Sabbath. Indeed, he upheld it.[6]

All four Gospels report Jesus' Sabbath deviance. Matthew and Mark record two violations: harvesting grain and healing (Matt. 12:1-14; Mark 2:23—3:6). Luke notes four controversies (Luke 6:1-11; 13:10-17; 14:1-6). John (5:2-18) reports a Sabbath healing. Matthew, Mark, and Luke show a five-step sequence in harvesting-healing incidents.

First, Jesus defends his disciples for shelling grain on the Sabbath. The offense isn't stealing. Travelers and the poor were allowed to help themselves to grain left standing in the field. There were likely several insults. Jesus and his disciples had probably walked too far on the Sabbath in violation of strict limits. They were working (shelling grain) and perhaps not eating the proper ritual meal on the Sabbath. They were "threshing" the grain in their hand and not preparing a "pure" Sabbath meal. All of these acts violated strict Sabbath regulations.

Second, the Pharisees discuss the violation with Jesus and warn him to follow the law—the religious traditions.

Third, they put him under surveillance (Mark 3:2) to see if they can catch him in a second offense punishable by death.

Fourth, even after a warning, he profanes the Sabbath again, this time by healing. Tension rises. Mark says, "He looked around at them with anger; he was grieved at their hardness of heart" (Mark 3:5).

In the fifth and final step, the Pharisees make plans to destroy him. Jesus suddenly withdraws from the area, apparently fleeing for his life.

Why is Jesus so bold? Why continue this disrespectful behavior? Why play with death? Why does he strike at the oral tradition, risking his very life? The sick person had been ill for many years. Why not politely wait *one* more day until the Sabbath passed? Jesus knows full well the penalties of the law. Despite a second warning, he continues to heal. Why?

Jesus struck at the heart of the oral tradition. Although the Ten Commandments forbade Sabbath work, the oral law encompassed a meticulous system of rules for Sabbath observance. In written form the Mishnah contains some 240 paragraphs on Sabbath behavior. One paragraph lists thirty-nine types of prohibited work: sowing, plowing, baking, spinning, tying a knot, writing or erasing two letters of the alphabet, putting out a fire, lighting a fire, striking with a hammer, and on and on.[7]

Many paragraphs discuss the prohibitions in detail. For instance, camel drivers and sailors couldn't tie knots on the Sabbath. But knots for hairnets, sandals, and belts were permissible. Knots, opened with one hand, were allowed since they weren't considered knots. It was as wrong to untie a knot as to tie one. Territory was divided into four types of space: public, private, neutral, and free. Sabbath rules dictated what material could be moved from one area to another. A person throwing anything from a private to a public space or vice-versa was guilty of a Sabbath infraction.[8]

Ingenious devices were created to bypass Sabbath legislation. The law dictated that people weren't allowed to walk more than 3,000 feet on the Sabbath. However, to circumvent this, they could "establish residence" at the end of their Sabbath day's walk, a day in advance. They established residence by carrying two meals to a place 3,000 feet from their home. One meal they ate there and another they buried—thereby "establishing residence." On the Sabbath day, people could travel the 3,000 feet from their permanent home to their "newly established residence" and then go an additional 3,000 feet. This legal detour doubled the length of Sabbath-day journeys.[9]

The Sabbath, with its complicated ritual, was a central symbol of religious faithfulness and tribal identity. Those who followed the Sabbath recipes were righteous; those who didn't were wicked. The religious leaders had the power to define and enforce Sabbath practice. By violating the Sabbath, Jesus undercut the authority of religious leaders, especially the Pharisees.

Jesus explained his behavior with these words: "The Sabbath was made for humankind, not humankind for the Sabbath; so the Son of man is lord even of the Sabbath" (Mark 2:27-28; Matt. 12:8; Luke 6:5). The point is simple but profound. This act of civil disobedience was not designed to destroy the Sabbath but to clarify its purpose and show who controlled it. The Sabbath was designed to serve people—to refresh us after six days of sweat. It was intended to serve our physical, emotional, and psychological needs. The Sabbath was to be servant, *not* master.

Over the years this principle turned upside-down. As the oral law accumulated, the Sabbath also grew. It soon became a master; it enslaved people. They no longer ruled it. The Sabbath had stopped serving them. People dutifully served it by obeying hundreds of regulations. Instead of rest it provided new things to fret about. Rather than welcoming the Sabbath, people looked forward to workdays, which freed them from Sabbath burdens. This religious practice, once so noble in intention and purpose, had turned oppressor. Then came Jesus, claiming he was Lord of the Sabbath, saying he reigned over religious ritual and tradition. He refused to bow down and worship them. He called those enslaved by custom to serve God and God alone. People dare not, he said, place custom ahead of feeding and healing people. Repeatedly Jesus places human need above religious dogma. He notes ironically that the Pharisees take better care of animals than people. They would pull an ox out of a pit on the Sabbath but prohibit a doctor from touching a sick person. For the Pharisees, religion had become empty ritual. Jesus turned religion upside-down by showing that true worship honors God and serves others.

Dirty Hands

It's hard for us to understand the pious Jew's paranoia of uncleanness. Humans draw lines to separate sacred things from everyday things. We say human life is sacred to separate ourselves from animals. We see praying as a sacred activity sharply separated from playing video games. Societies around the world draw lines between the sacred and the profane. These cultural maps sort people, places, things, and time into sacred and profane boxes. Eating bread in a service of Holy Communion is a sacred activity in a sacred place at a sacred time. Every aspect of eating pizza in a food court at a shopping mall is downright mundane—what scholars call profane.

Not only do we draw lines between the sacred and profane, we get very disturbed if slices of pizza appear on a communion tray. Rules of purity and pollution help us make sure cultural dirt doesn't contaminate clean places. The rules regarding cultural cleanliness apply to people, places, things, and times. We don't, for example, want homeless beggars showing up at wedding receptions. Like other human societies, Israel's purity system had a place for everything and every person—with punishments if dirty things or dirty people fell into clean places.

To worship God, to even approach God, one had to be absolutely clean. Touching the wrong thing, talking with a dirty person, or sitting on a polluted bench would defile one's body and outrage God. The rules and rites that helped to preserve purity were not petty human concoctions. In the eyes of the faithful, they came directly from almighty God, who required absolute and complete purity, a God outraged by blemish and tarnish.

Reflecting these concerns for purity, the law divided objects, persons, places, and animals into two categories—clean and unclean. Camels, badgers, swine, vultures, eagles, and winged insects, to name a few, were all considered unclean. Cemeteries were taboo. Contact with a contaminated person or animal polluted a clean object. The Mishnah devoted 185 pages to laws of defilement and purity. Ceremonial washing before each meal marked conscientious Pharisees. They sanitized themselves without fail, hoping to engender a nation of purified priests.[10] This noble vision drove their obsession with purity.

Jesus irritated the Pharisees by skipping ceremonial washing. Matthew (15:1-20) and Mark (7:1-23) report similar accounts. Pharisees and scribes from Jerusalem walked 60 miles north to Galilee to question Jesus on this issue. Luke (11:37-38) notes that the Pharisee who hosted Jesus for a meal was astonished that he ate without washing. The Pharisees stressed eating with the right people—those who obeyed the purity laws. They also held to the tradition of the elders that required washing hands before eating. The washing sanitized any religious "dirt" accidentally acquired during the day.

Why, the Pharisees wondered, did Jesus neglect the purifying rinse? Jesus answered. "You abandon the commandment of God, and hold to human tradition. . . . You have a fine way of rejecting the commandment of God, to keep your tradition!" (Mark 7:8-9). Quoting Isaiah the prophet, he told them that they worshiped with lips but not heart. They taught human ideas as if they were divine doctrine. In short, the Pharisees had elevated the oral tradition to divine status. They not only served but worshiped oral tradition. They gave it precedence over the Word of God and even used it as an excuse to disobey God's will.

A religious vow called *corban* illustrates how even good things had been perverted (Mark 7:10-13). Through the corban vow, the Pharisees encouraged adult children to consecrate their property to the temple rather than to use it to support their elderly parents. After the property was dedicated to the temple, it could no longer be used to support elderly parents. Cutting off financial support jeopardized the welfare of the elderly. Jesus condemned the corban vow which promoted piety at the expense of human suffering. Human words and traditions superseded the supreme law of loving one's neighbor. The religious system operating in the name of God had ironically, obscured God's law of love.

Jesus was harshly criticizing the purity laws when he said defilement results from things which come out of the mouth, not those that go in. Words of gossip, deceit, false witness, and slander defile a person, not food (Matt. 15:18-20; Mark 7:20-23). In a few words Jesus abolished those aspects of oral tradition that blocked the way to true holiness. Perfect cleansing, he said, comes when acts of charity flow from the heart (Luke 11:41).

Dirty Friends

A third aspect of Jesus' behavior, which peeved the Pharisees, was his fellowship with unclean persons. Tax collectors and sinners who ridiculed the rules of purity were considered filthy. Sinners, meaning the "wicked ones," blatantly spit on the laws of purity, and were considered beyond the sight of God's redemption. The Pharisees, of course, shunned them. Jesus excluded no one. He invited sinners to meals (Luke 15:2) and joined in their parties (Mark 2:15; Matthew 9:10). This infuriated the Pharisees, who mocked him, saying, "Look, a glutton and a drunkard, a friend of tax collectors and sinners" (Matt. 11:19; Luke 7:34). Some scholars contend that Jesus' table fellowship with sinners and outcasts was the distinguishing mark that set him apart from the other religious prophets of his time.[11]

In Palestinian culture, inviting someone to a meal was a sign of honor. Sharing a meal signaled group boundaries—who was in the circle of friends and who was excluded. Dirty and polluted wicked people would never be invited by a Pharisee. The meal signaled peace, trust, intimacy, and forgiveness; sharing a table meant sharing life. In Hebrew culture, table fellowship also symbolized fellowship before God. Breaking bread around a common table brought a corporate blessing to all that joined in the meal. By eating with social rejects—the targets of righteous wrath, Jesus embodies God's compassion for all. Moreover, he signals their inclusion around the heavenly banquet table. He thus welcomes them into the community of salvation.[12]

By supping with Zacchaeus and his sort, Jesus challenged the norms of religious etiquette. His message was clear: people were more important than pious rules. Indeed, he said, he came to save the sick. The healthy don't need a physician (Matt. 9:12-13; Mark 2:17). Ironically, the "sick" leaders who thought they were healthy rejected the Physician. Those who knew they were "sick" and acknowledged their need were invited to the Physician's party.

The rules of religious piety too often become idolatrous and exclusive. They sort people into profane and sacred boxes shielding the "righteous" from the stigmatized. Jesus blurred the fine lines which separated sacred from profane. By embracing the wicked in table fellowship, he made it clear that the new kingdom welcomed *all*, regardless of past sin or piety.

Fumigating the Temple

Defiling the Sabbath, mocking the purity rules, and befriending sinners rankled the Pharisees, guardians of the oral tradition. Jesus' final provocation pricked a different group: the Sadducees. As we saw in chapter three, this political party operated the temple complex—the center of sacrifice and holiness—in Jerusalem. Shortly before his crucifixion, Jesus walked from rural Galilee into the sacred heart of Jewish religion. The clues to why he was executed were becoming clear. The announcement of his new kingdom was challenging the three sacred seats of Jewish faith—Sabbath, purity, and now the very temple itself.

Wealthy Sadducees benefited from income generated by the temple. Jesus' defiance in the temple rebuked the temple hierarchy.[13] The temple was the hub of Hebrew worship. It was one thing to strike against the oral tradition of the Pharisees in upstate Galilee;

it was quite another matter to attack the nerve center of religious, political, and economic power!

The Sadducees enjoyed cozy Roman connections. A cohort of 500-600 Roman soldiers stood by in the fortress Antonia guarding against any ruckus in the temple area. Jesus had left the docile shepherds in Galilee. Now he walked Jerusalem's halls of power. But he came riding on a donkey—overturning all hopes of a military Messiah on a prancing stallion.

All four Gospels report his decisive act in the temple. Fully aware that the Sadducees would charge him with profanity and blasphemy, Jesus moved deftly. He entered the temple and chased out the merchants, then flipped over the tables of money changers and the chairs of those selling pigeons. Moreover, he stopped people from carrying things through the temple. Explaining his dramatic disturbance, he asked, "Is it not written, 'My house shall be called a house of prayer for all the nations'? But you have made it a den of robbers'" (Mark 11:15-17).

The money changers were in the commercial area in the outer Gentile Courts of the temple.[14] Here they exchanged common coins for the "pure" ones required for temple offerings. Animal jockeys sold sheep and goats for sacrifices to pilgrims. The outer plaza, a place of worship, had been turned into a lucrative cattle market and bank. Tables cluttered the area. The stench of animal dung hung in the air. Prayer was not what the setting inspired.

We don't know if Jesus merely chased a few sellers out or if he completely purged the area. A major disturbance would have certainly activated the Roman cohort, stirring his immediate arrest. Regardless of the scope of the purge, in the eyes of the religious leaders, his act was an outrageous profanity in the hallowed courts of God.

Jesus' action did more, however, than open up the plaza so Gentiles could pray.[15] It did more than refocus temple activities on the Holy of Holies. It shut down the temple. By stopping the flow of vessels and animals, Jesus shut the mighty temple down—at least for a few moments. Without animals bought from merchants, without pure coins for offerings, without traffic across the plaza, the sacrificial system came to a screeching halt.

Scholars divide on the exact meaning of Jesus' public act of defiance in the seat of holiness. Perhaps he was trying to reform the economic practices that overcharged poor peasants when they brought their offerings. Or was he a prophet like Jeremiah of old, using symbolic acts to signal the coming destruction of the temple by Roman hands or God's intervention? Or maybe his symbolic shutdown pointed to the end of sacrifice in his new kingdom. Did his challenge of temple restrictions and exclusions open a new age when all peoples, Jew and Gentile, clean and blemished, could worship God without the stain of blood or the smell of sacrifice?

Regardless of the layers of meaning, we have here the Prophet, full of rich symbolism, striking at the nerve center of Jewish religion. In one decisive act, he shuts the temple down.[16] This flagrant act cost Jesus his life.

Mark sandwiches the temple purge between two episodes of a fig tree cursing (Mark 11:12-14; 20-26). Before entering Jerusalem for the dramatic act, Jesus spotted a fig tree. He was hungry and reached for figs. Finding the tree empty, he cursed it. The day after the temple episode, the tree's roots had withered. The fig tree represents the temple, the center of Jewish worship. As the curse shriveled the roots of the tree, so the prophetic purge shriveled the temple's functions.

Jesus' bold move symbolically opened the temple once more for Gentiles and signaled that the new kingdom welcomed *all*—regardless of race or nationality. Jesus is pointing to a new age, a time when a new offering will be made: a body. A permanent sacrifice will be given. Each heart will become a vessel for the Holy Spirit. This is a daring move. But the Prophet is fearless in the face of Roman soldiers and Sadducean authorities. He acts definitively; striking the system that oppressed the poor, shunned the stigmatized, and pushed people away from God with pious rules.

Jesus is not only Lord of the Sabbath and Lord of the oral tradition; he is also Lord of the temple. He ends its sacrificial ritual in preparation for the new kingdom. Jesus finally answers the taunt of the tempter. He does come to the temple! Not in a miraculous parachute, but as Lord of its functions. Jesus himself was performing the temple function—offering forgiveness to all who would listen, without bringing a bloody offering to the altar. His words of forgiveness to sinners, outside the temple plaza, had already rendered it obsolete. In a single dramatic moment he critiques human religion and points to a new age.

The temple purge had sweeping consequences. Flipping over a few tables in a backstreet inn would have been bad enough. But inside the sacred courts, the table turnover looked like a deliberate attack on the Sadducees. Jesus was boldly challenging the authority of the priestly families who ran the temple for lucrative gain. The Sanhedrin—that mighty Jewish supreme court—met a few blocks down the street. Out in rural Galilee a little blasphemy and a little Sabbath naughtiness might slip by. But not here. Not in the sacred temple, not by the doors of the mighty Sanhedrin, not under the very nose of the high priest. The guardians of piety can't permit such irreverence.

In Mark's Gospel the plot to kill Jesus now flares up more openly than any time since the Sabbath clashes in Galilee. Jesus has galvanized the hatred of the chief priests and scribes. They have no choice. They must destroy him. Jerusalem, the place of life and worship, becomes the stage for death and revenge.

Given the danger of anti-Semitism and the fact that Jesus was a Jewish prophet inside Judaism, we need to underscore that what Jesus critiques is finally *human* religion, not *Jewish* religion. Jesus challenges Sabbath practices and the temple operation not because they're Jewish, but because over time, they have perverted true worship. The tendency for religious ritual to turn inward and exclusionary is age-old and worldwide. If Jesus were to return in the flesh today, he would find plenty of tables to overturn in Christian temples.

Pompous Piety

If irreverence wasn't enough, Jesus scolded the religious leaders with a volley of indictments and parables. Many of his barbed stories annoyed pious authorities, but a few accepted or at least befriended him. Some amiable Pharisees warned Jesus that Herod Antipas wanted to kill him (Luke 13:31). The Pharisee Simon entertained Jesus in his house (Luke 7:36). Nicodemus, a Pharisee who perhaps sat on the Sanhedrin, chatted warmly with Jesus one evening (John 3:1). Nevertheless, the synoptic Gospels show Jesus in conflict with the Pharisees. The Gospel writers, reflecting tensions in the early church, may have overemphasized the conflict.[17]

The social glory of the Pharisees was at the root of Jesus' scathing criticism. They offered their sacrifices on the altar of social status. The demands of God mattered little. What counted was how their piety appeared to others. Would their prayers, fasting, and tithes enhance their status in the eyes of their peers? Although he doesn't mention the Pharisees specifically in Matthew (6:1), Jesus debunks their clamor for social applause. "Beware of practicing your piety before others to be seen by them; for then you have no reward from your Father in heaven."

Two kinds of public piety were particularly irksome. Trumpets were blown in streets and synagogues when the religious leaders gave a tithe to "be praised by men." Moreover, the leaders vied for the best seats in the synagogue and wore ostentatious garb. They sewed long fringes on their robes and wanted seats of honor at feasts. They preferred dignified greetings in the streets (Matt. 23:5-7; Luke 11:43; 20:46). Both Mark (12:40) and Luke (20:47) say the scribes made long prayers for the sake of social display. The leaders did all these things, Matthew (23:5) says, for a social audience, "to be seen by others." Luke calls them lovers of money who justify themselves before others (Luke 16:14-15). Such religiosity, oriented toward the applause of others, is an abomination in God's eyes, according to Luke.

John (12:42-43) notes that some of the authorities who believed in Jesus were afraid to admit it because "they loved human glory more than the glory that comes from God." In Matthew's Gospel, Jesus lumps the scribes and Pharisees together in a fiery critique.[18] They are like filthy cups, which appear clean on the outside and like polished tombs, which stink on the inside. "So you also on the outside look righteous to others, but inside you are full of hypocrisy and lawlessness (Matt. 23:28).

In the three synoptic Gospels, Jesus warns his disciples to watch out for the leaven of the Pharisees (Matt. 16:11-12; Mark 8:15; Luke 12:1). Luke calls their cancerous leaven hypocrisy. Although we often associate the word *hypocrisy* with the Pharisees, the issue, as one scholar points out, wasn't really hypocrisy. The Pharisees were actually sincere and devout. The issue was *what* they were sincere about.[19]

The verbal attack on the Pharisees continues. They talk but don't walk, preach but don't practice, theologize but don't obey. Consumed with the details of cleaning pots, they forget the agony of the sick and poor. In a satirical comment, Jesus advised the crowd to "Do whatever they *teach* you and follow it, but do not as they *do*; for they do not practice what they teach" (Matt. 23:3, emphasis added).

Another time, after the elders had questioned Jesus' authority, he made the same point in a biting parable (Matt. 21:28-31). A man had two sons. He asked them to work in the vineyard. The first one said, "No, I won't," but afterward he repented and went. The second son said, "Yes, Dad," but never went. The scribes and Pharisees were like the second son. They smoothly said, "Yes, Dad," but never went to the vineyard.

The religious leaders were like the brothers of the rich man in the Lazarus story. They had Moses and the prophets, yet refused to practice Jubilee. They remembered trivia but forgot justice, mercy, and faith. Foolishly trying to strain a mosquito out of their tea, they overlooked swallowing a camel (Matt. 23:23-24; Luke 11:42). They observed pious regulations but foreclosed on widows' houses (Luke 20:47; Mark 12:40). With the vow of corban they thwarted the law of love by pushing the elderly into poverty (Mark 7:9-12). Their verbiage produced no action and their sweet God-talk camouflaged economic injustice as they merrily went on their way tithing herbs. Nevertheless, their intentions were good. They sincerely thought their rituals of purity would eventually make the whole nation a nation of priests.

How Great Thou Art

Careful observance of religious dogma breeds pride. The Pharisees were like a person singing "How Great Thou Art" in front of the mirror each morning. In a pithy little parable, Jesus condemns their arrogance.[20] A Pharisee walks to the temple to offer his prayers

(Luke 18:9-14). The devout one finds his prominent place and offers a prayer of thanks. He thanks God that he's not a cheat; that he's not unjust; that he doesn't lust after women. Peeking out of the corner of his eye, he sees a tax collector, who surprisingly also came to pray. The Pharisee ends his prayer with a special thanks that he's not contaminated like this tax collector who robs the poor.

The Pharisee offers his righteous deeds to God. Although the law calls for an annual fast on the Day of Atonement, he reminds God that he voluntarily adds a fast every Monday and Thursday. He gives tithes on everything he buys from the shopkeepers. If the grower has previously paid a tithe of the products, the Pharisee tithes again to make sure everything he uses is holy. This man represents the epitome of Hebrew orthodoxy. He stands atop the religious ladder of piety.

The tax collector, ostracized by decent people, is considered a robber with no civil rights. He can barely reach the ladder's bottom rung. He stays at the edge of the temple plaza, not venturing to a prominent spot. In contrast to the proud Pharisee, the tax collector is embarrassed to even lift his hands heavenward. Instead he pounds his chest, a sign of deep contrition. He cries out to God in despair, overwhelmed by the gulf of separation. Repentance, for this man, doesn't mean pleasant smiles. It means leaving his profession and starting over. It means repaying fivefold all the people he has cheated. He doesn't even know how many he has swindled. This is an impossible situation, so he cries for mercy.

Three stark contrasts frame this story: attitude, identity, and location. The opposing attitudes are obvious in the text. What is less clear is the contrast between identities. The Pharisee represents the sacred role of ritual devotion. The tax collector symbolizes the wicked who are not even on the grid of holiness. The two locations—temple and household—also paint a sharp distinction. The wicked one who comes to God in humility, without any offering or fast, goes *down to his house* justified. Even on the high sacred temple mount, the Pharisee finds no salvation. But the humble of heart finds God's welcome in his home—without altar, sacrifice, or tithe.

Unexpectedly, the upside-down moment strikes. In a surprising reversal, the penitent tax collector is commended. This social bandit, this betrayer of the nation, has found favor with God. The Almighty has accepted the tax collector's sacrifice of a broken and contrite heart. Meanwhile, the arrogant Pharisee misses the blessing.

This story surely sounded upside-down to Jesus' audience. Those who arrogantly trust in themselves and despise others have rejected God despite all their religious motions. Self-centered worship sneers at others rather than taking personal inventory. It derives false piety from social comparison. The barbs of the parable stung the haughty Pharisees.

Keep Out

Condescending pride turns churches into exclusive clubs. Shunning outsiders and mocking their ignorance wasn't the Pharisees' only fault. They used a barricade of trivial rules to bar sinners from the table of salvation. Jesus detested this exclusive spirit of the Pharisees.

> They tie up heavy burdens, hard to bear, and lay them on the shoulders of others; but they themselves are unwilling to lift a finger to move them. . . . But woe to you, scribes and Pharisees, hypocrites! For you lock people out of the kingdom of heaven; for you do not go in yourselves, and when others are going in, you stop them." (Matt. 23:4, 13-15; Luke 11:45-52)

In contrast to the burden of rules which crushed devout Jews, Jesus offered a light load. "For my yoke is easy, and my burden is light" (Matt. 11:30). In their attempt to translate the five books of Moses into daily practice, the Pharisees had mistakenly thrown away the key to the kingdom. They had locked themselves inside the synagogue of their own ritual and sealed others out. Ceremonial religion not only accents ritual; it also creates a gap between insiders and outsiders.

The Last Will Be First

Many of Jesus' parables are a defense of the Gospels. His acceptance of sinners embodied the good news. Religious leaders were indignant that Jesus welcomed the wicked—swindlers and adulterers—into the kingdom. "Sinners" were customarily deprived of civil rights—office holding and serving as a witness in court. The list included tax collectors, shepherds, peddlers, tanners, pigeon racers, and others in tarnished jobs.[21] Jesus' message in numerous parables is clear. The religious establishment may toss these people from the kingdom, but God still loves them. Jesus offers such love in table fellowship in homes despite the scorn of leading Pharisees. Adding insult to injury, Jesus says the Pharisees' smug rejection of "unclean" people is no flippant matter. Things just might turn upside-down. The religious leaders might find themselves outside the banquet door while repentant sinners feast inside with the prophets.

Yes, says Jesus, God cares for these social outcasts. In four stories he shows how God's forgiving compassion welcomes rebellious sinners and outsiders.

Jesus compares God to a father who waited day after day for his rebellious son to return home. When he does return, the father hugs and kisses him and even throws a party in his honor (Luke 15:11-24). God is like a woman who sweeps every crack of her house searching for a lost coin (Luke 15:8). God can even be compared to a shepherd trudging over hilly country looking for a weak lamb snared in the thorns of thickets (Luke 15:3-5). Or imagine God as a farmer who cared so much for his laborers that he gave some of them a full day's wage for only one hour of work (Matt. 20:1-16).

The parables sizzle into the minds of the religious heavyweights: Your attitude is just the opposite of God's. You're like the elder son who grumbles at the sight of a party thrown for his own brother (Luke 15:25-32). You're like the farmhands who work all day, receive their promised wage, then gripe because the latecomers received the same (Matt. 20:11-16). Like the tenants of a vineyard, you refused to give the owner wine from his own vineyard. You kill the servants he sends and finally you even have the audacity to kill his only son (Luke 20:9-16). Suddenly the tables turn and the owner gives that vineyard to others.

The biting stories continue. Like the guests invited to a banquet you refuse to come when the feast begins (Luke 14:15-24; Matt. 22:1-10). Because of your stubbornness God invites others to replace you at the table. God welcomes the poor, the leper, the maimed, the blind, and the lame from city streets. God even goes to the countryside searching for spit-upon outcasts to fill the banquet table. The moment of judgment strikes! None of those invited guests who refuse to come will enjoy the banquet" (Luke 14:24).

Jesus clarifies the upside-down reversal in another picture of impending crisis. The judgment will surprise even the staunchest defenders of the faith. Some will say, "Lord, we ate and drank with you and taught in our streets," but the judge will reply,

> 'Go away from me, all you evildoers!' There will be weeping and gnashing of teeth when you see Abraham and Isaac and Jacob and all the prophets in the kingdom of God, and you yourselves thrown out. Then people will come from east and west, from north and south, and will eat in the kingdom of God. Indeed, some are last who will be first, and some are first who will be last." (Luke 13:27-30)

Speaking to the Pharisees, Jesus ends the parable of the two sons in the vineyard with these terse words: "Truly, I tell you, the tax collectors and the prostitutes are going into the kingdom of God ahead of you" (Matt. 21:31). After blasting the scribes for devouring widows' houses and making long prayers as a pretense, Jesus says they face not only exclusion from the kingdom, but "they will receive the greater condemnation" (Mark 12:40; Luke 20:47).

The stalwarts of the faith had access to Moses and the prophets. The leaders were given a talent—knowledge of God's law—but so buried it in oral tradition that sinners missed God's call. The pious human traditions, in fact, repulsed the outcasts and drove them far from God. Jesus restores the day of grace. His table fellowship with the stigmatized signals the dawn of God's salvation. The impious, social castaways, unlike the Pharisees, readily embrace God's welcome.

This is tragically upside-down. The ones who worked so hard to apply the Torah to everyday life are left behind. Their fervor and enthusiasm for ceremonial piety thwarts God's law of love. Those who fought so hard for religion are in jeopardy. The newcomers, meanwhile, are a motley-looking crew, but their righteousness exceeds that of the Pharisees (Matt. 5:20). Indeed, the wicked are welcoming God's reign. One of their crowd, Zacchaeus, returns the goods he stole. A prostitute who anointed Jesus repents and is forgiven much. The tax collector at the temple penitently beats his breast. A runaway son returns home.

In contrast to the religious elite, these sinners are truly sorry for their sins. They walk the kingdom's red carpet. The tragic message finally penetrates the skulls of the haughty. "When the chief priests and the Pharisees heard his parables, they realized that he was speaking about them. They tried to arrest him, but they feared the crowds, because they regarded him as a prophet" (Matt. 21:45-46; Mark 12:12; Luke 20:19).

Brittle Skins and New Patches

What does all this mean for us today? How do kingdom and church intersect? Jesus described the in-breaking of the kingdom with two stories (Mark 2:21-22). Always wash a patch before sewing it on an old garment. Otherwise the patch will shrink after the first laundering and rip the old cloth worse than ever. Moreover, store new, fermenting wine in new and pliable wineskins. Bubbling wine poured into brittle old skins will crack them open and drain away.

In picturesque words, Jesus pinpoints the tension between the new wine of the kingdom and older religious structures. New skins, soft and pliable, are needed for new wine. As the wine ferments the skins expand and contract. The kingdom wine of the Jesus Movement was cracking the brittle skins of the Sadducees, Pharisees, and scribes. The skins of the oral law were too hard to hold the ferment of the new wine. The wicked could no longer smell the wine. All they could see were the callous, old skins. The wine of the upside-down kingdom requires new skins—flexible institutional structures.

How do we distinguish between the kingdom and the institutionalized church?[22] Is the kingdom the same as the church? The biblical shift from "kingdom" to "church" between the Gospels and the epistles reflects a shift from Jewish to Greek culture.[23] One of the difficulties in distinguishing between kingdom and church today lies in words that we often use loosely—church, denomination, institution, and people of God.

A careful distinction among four realities—*kingdom*, *church*, *culture*, and *structure*—can clarify the conceptual waters.

The kingdom Jesus announced points us to something greater than our own structures and ourselves. We've already said that the *kingdom* refers to the rule of God in our hearts and relationships. God was "at hand" in Jesus, living amid people and calling them to obedience. Today God rules through the Holy Spirit's presence. The Spirit points us in kingdom directions. The wine in the parable symbolizes God's dynamic power infiltrating our lives. Like fresh wine in ferment, the kingdom embodies the dynamic and creative power of God's Spirit. It takes on visible expression in new and exciting ways as people submit their lives to God's rule.

The kingdom entails a new *vision*, a new set of *values*, and a new *openness* to yield to the ways of God. Past and present, now and future, the kingdom is the reign of God in the lives of believers. It becomes visible in form and practice as persons yield to God's dynamic rule.

The *church* is the assembly of people who have welcomed God's reign in their hearts and relationships. The church consists of the citizens of the kingdom. It's the body of Christ composed of obedient disciples following in the way of Jesus. We can also envision the church as the community of believers—the collective gathering of the people of God. The church isn't a building, a sanctuary, or a program. It's the visible community of those who live by kingdom values.

Culture entails the values and practices of a particular body of believers. What views, habits, and practices do they prize? Which ones do they reject? The ideas and values of the kingdom take on different cultural expressions in different settings. Believers in Honduras will have different practices and patterns than those in Japan. The key question however is this: How do kingdom values shape cultural practices irrespective of country?[24] Kingdom people, in other words, should create their own cultural practices based on kingdom values. They may share many practices with their host culture, but their life should reflect kingdom values, which sometimes may diverge from mainstream culture.

Finally come the *structures*. The people of God need social vehicles—institutions and programs—to meet their own needs and the needs of others. The church creates social vehicles and servant structures to accomplish its mission. Servant structures include the whole gamut of organized church bodies and programs. They encompass denominations, schools, liturgical traditions, mission agencies, publishing ventures, camps, and, of course, committees, commissions, traditions, and programs galore. These are the social skins, the servant structures the church creates to do its work. They are *not*, however, the church or the kingdom.

The kingdom transcends the church in two ways. It existed before the beginning of the church and will be God's kingly domain throughout eternity. The kingdom is also larger than the church. It represents the ultimate lordship of Christ over all peoples, principalities, and powers. The church, the body of believers, embraces the rule of God. The culture and structure of the church, designed to express kingdom ways, can become brittle and leak the precious wine. These cultural expressions and organized structures, these human creations, need periodic overhaul to assure they remain servants of the kingdom.

This fourfold distinction of kingdom, church, culture, and structure highlights their different features. The church began and existed alongside the kingdom as persons accepted the rule of God in their lives. The kingdom has visible social and political characteristics both in the body of believers who declare Jesus as King, and in the cultures and structures they create to accomplish their mission.

A focus on the culture—the values and practices—of the body of believers raises the question of their origin. Is the culture of the church driven by the larger society or by kingdom values and priorities? Furthermore, if we view church programs and structures as human creations, not the kingdom itself, we less easily sacralize them. The moment church structures become identical with the kingdom, they rise to sacred heights. The structures of the church reflect and embody the kingdom but are neither the kingdom nor the church itself.

Expressing the vision of *one* kingdom, the structures we create will take on *diverse* forms in different cultures. They should, however, not be mere reflections of their culture. Their diverse skins should be culturally relevant but not culturally determined. The kingdom message, anchored in the biblical story, should shape the social architecture of the churchly programs. When cultural rather than kingdom values craft the church's institutional forms, the salt loses its savor.

Sacred Cows or Servant Structures?

The vision of the kingdom breaks in upon us in fresh ways through the ministry of the Holy Spirit. It takes shape in new buildings, new projects, new programs, and new committees. These social structures, however, soon solidify. First-generation participants enthusiastically welcome the new programs. But spontaneous patterns soon gel and become routine. Gradually they're taken for granted. They become "the way things are." They exude a sense of "rightness." No longer are they seen as one of many ways of meeting a need. The second generation sees them as the *only* way. They have, in short, become sacred cows. Structures once created seek their own legitimization. They perpetuate themselves, often with the blessing of religious language.

The Pharisee temptation is always with us. The one-time spontaneous expression of love solidifies as an organization grows in size and age. The constitution gets longer. The red tape grows thicker. The symbols are idolized. Procedures rigidify. Evangelism yields to ethnicity. Openness to new needs gives way to preserving the status quo. In-group words and symbols emerge and exclude others. Outsiders feel left out. Policies and structures can smother the way of love. When the structures calcify, it's time for new skins.

The genius of the Gospels is its seed of self-criticism or self-reformation. Each generation of Christians, like the Pharisees, is tempted to sacralize its programs and freeze its routines. Jesus showed us that humanly created structures aren't sacred. There are no sacred places, organizations, times, objects, doctrines, or social positions, except in the sense that all good things are finally sacred.

The altar in a church building is no closer to God's heart than a rest room. The unfortunate use of the term *sanctuary* encourages us to view the church building as a sacred place deserving special reverence. Religious buildings often witness to our rigidity, pride, and social status. When Jesus purged the temple, he declared once and for all that even the most sacred of buildings don't deserve our worship. They can be dedicated as one of many tools for proclaiming and celebrating the good news of the kingdom, but they are only human creations. They should always be subservient to the assembly of believers.

The same loving irreverence must apply to doctrine, objects, social positions, and programs of the church. The creed, which molds a denomination's unique identity, can supersede biblical authority. The chair of the board of elders may offer wise counsel but holds no sacred position. The pastor may offer special insight and understanding but is not a hero set above the saints we're all called to be. Symbols of faith—the cross, the pulpit, the altar, the basin—are as mundane as other everyday objects. They *do* point us to spiritual meanings. But they aren't sacred *in and of themselves*.[25]

White Elephant Sabbaticals

The institutional programs of the church sometimes become sacred cows—or should we say white elephants. Organizations, traditions, and programs designed as servants, can over time rise up and master us. Their original purpose met real needs and communicated the Gospel effectively. But over the years they turn brittle. Routine practices related to worship services, youth programs, mission boards, educational agencies, and service organizations easily become coercive because they are the "Lord's work."

Organizations are necessary and useful to funnel human activity in effective ways. We need social institutions and will always have them. We are not only producers of them, but also their products. We have been shaped and nurtured by schools, and many church-related organizations. It's important, however, that we periodically evaluate their role and purpose. Perhaps institutional sabbaticals—periodic times when we review programs and projects—would help us rejuvenate our structures. If they no longer serve their original intent, we ought to nudge them back toward servant roles, or even bury them.

The seventh or sabbatical year in the Hebrew calendar provided time not only for rest but also for reflection. Would it be fitting, every seventh year, to call a sabbatical rest for the committees, commissions, and programs that make up much of institutional religion today? During this seventh year, extensive study and evaluation could assess the effectiveness of these programs. Some might need a major retrofit. Others might continue in their present form. Still others might need a funeral. Seven-year intervals allow enough time to test a program and reflect on its contribution.

Too often religious white elephants plod on and on. Since they involve the "Lord's work," no one dares tamper with them. Service to others and edification of the faith community is the benchmark for evaluation. When pastors have to urge, cajole, and beg parishioners to participate in a particular program or attend a certain service, it may no longer be serving a real need. It may be time for a funeral. When structures serve the true needs of members, participation is joyous and spontaneous.

Jesus is Lord of the "Sabbaths," those religious structures we create. Human creations, structures have an uncanny way of taking charge and becoming the masters of their own creators. The Spirit of Jesus and the perspectives of his kingdom critique our social skins. The lordship of Christ over organizational structures prevents them from perverting the Gospels and enslaving the faithful. Too often we forget that Jesus is Lord of the Sabbath. We too easily equate our own structures with the kingdom. One-time servant structures, in time, sometimes rise up and beckon us to serve them.

How do we evaluate servant structures? The following questions may help assess their servant posture.

- What are the specific needs this program addresses?

- Would people create this project anew if it were terminated?

- Does it express the spirit and mission of the Gospels?

- Is this structure designed to serve in the Spirit of Jesus?

- Does it promote an exclusive self-righteous posture?

- Do people enjoy participating in it?

- Is flexibility built into its nature?

- Has a time been designated to evaluate its functions?

- Is there a decision-making process to declare a "funeral" if necessary?

- Is it clear that the people of God, led by God's Spirit, have the authority to declare its moratorium?

The church is always caught in the tension between the traditional solutions of the past and the fermenting wine of an ever-new kingdom. It's a tension between form and love, structure and Gospel, organization and vision. The symbols of the past threaten to become idolatrous. The old rituals assert themselves as absolute. The Spirit of the Jesus who violated Sabbath rules, avoided purity rituals, ate with sinners, and purged the temple is Lord of our structures also. He judges them, critiques them, and makes them pliable for the new wine.

Hidden in the excruciating pain of judgment is the germ of renewal. Kingdom values form fresh, elastic skins for the kingdom's ferment. In this sometimes painful process, the church reforms itself across the generations.

9

Lovable Enemies

The Foolish Father

Jesus' criticism of wealth and religion may sound harsh to our ears, but it flows from a heart of love. Indeed, the very foundation of Jesus' new kingdom rests on love. What kind of love is it? What does it look like? We explore these questions in chapter nine.

Violence is obsolete in the new kingdom. *Agape* love becomes the new mode of governing. The Greek word, agape, means unconditional love. Wholly unselfish, agape surpasses passion, friendship, and benevolence. It supersedes self-interest. Agape is more than unselfish feeling. It acts. It loves unlovables, even enemies. Compassion, generosity, forgiveness, mercy—these are the essence of agape.[1]

Agape flows from the king of the kingdom, who is like a loving parent. The ruler's subjects aren't slaves but children. They don't say, "Yes, your Majesty" but fondly call him *abba,* or "Daddy." Citizens in this new order love generously because a gracious Parent has overwhelmed them. Divine love stirs their own. What kind of Parent triggers such love?

Responding to complaints from scribes and Pharisees that he was eating with sinners, Jesus told a story to clarify God's love. God, sinners, and Pharisees are portrayed in the story by a father, a runaway son, and a complaining brother (Luke 15:11-32).[2] What is God like? That is the parable's central question. Jesus suggests that God is like a foolish father.

According to Jewish custom, the younger of two sons was entitled to one third of his father's property. Wealth could be passed on in two ways: by a will at the father's death or as a gift during the father's lifetime. In contrast to Western culture, if the son received the property as a gift, he did not have the right to dispose of it until

167

after the father's death. To dispose of it while the father was living was treating the father like a corpse. Jewish custom expected children to honor their parents by obeying and supporting them financially.

The young upstart violates several cultural customs. First, he demands his share of the property long before his father dies. He deserved a flogging for simply making such an arrogant request. Indeed, the son's gross disrespect for his father is as sinful as his vice in a foreign country. He leaves his father and squanders funds that can never support the father again. He treats his father like he's already dead! It was the rudest thing a son could do to a father.

Piling insult upon cultural insult, the son ends up tending swine. Such work was prohibited in Jewish culture, which considered pigs not only unclean but the very abode of devils. The son not only does degrading work but also identifies with the pigs by hungering for their food. Symbolically, he has fallen below the bottom of the cultural pit.

Imagine the father's embarrassment. The scribes in the village surely sneered at him. Why did he foolishly give property to his son at such a young age in the first place? Neighbors must have scorned the old man with laughter until they cried. The son had shattered his father's reputation, esteem, and honor. What a shame! Such a father would never be fit again for synagogue leadership.

To vindicate himself, a good father would at least publicly deplore such behavior. A wise father wouldn't just look the other way and quietly approve of rank disobedience. He would legally disown the son.

But not this father. He doesn't defend himself. He doesn't retaliate to protect his social status. He doesn't run after the son with a search party. He gives his son the freedom to go. His love for his son is stronger than his own need for social approval. Moreover, he patiently waits for his son to return. He never forgets him. He walks out the lane every day—waiting, watching, hoping, expecting.

Finally the son "comes to himself." In the Aramaic, this phrase suggests repentance. He finally realizes the stupidity of his ways and turns around. He returns home expecting the worst. He knows how harshly fathers react when publicly disgraced. So he comes confessing, begging his father to accept him as a mere servant.

We might expect several responses from a Jewish father who sees his son walking home splattered with dung. A reasonable father might slam the door in his face and declare him an alien. He might ask his son to wash before he launches into a tirade about disobedience. He might investigate the details of the deviance and then render punishment. Justice would certainly prescribe punishment to teach the boy a lesson. A whipping was perhaps in order. Maybe the runaway should serve time as a slave. Let him prove that he is really sincere.

The father rejects all these fair and common sense solutions. Seeing his son, he is moved to compassion. In upside-down fashion, he foolishly welcomes the scoundrel home, rolling out, in effect, eight red carpets.

- He doesn't wait for the son to knock. His compassion compels him to run. It was considered undignified for an older person to run. The father had no idea what the son would say. Running to him would surely signal endorsement of his vices.

- Then the father hugs the boy, breaking another rule of social etiquette. Embracing was disgraceful for an aged person. He was welcoming a rebellious son covered with dung.

- A kiss—the biblical symbol of forgiveness—follows. The father wipes the slate clean. He welcomes the son back from the pigpen, not as slave, not as hired servant—but as a son.

- In fact, the next sign of welcome heralds the son as an honored guest. The best robe swirls around him. This fine garment was a mark of high distinction. It was reserved for royal guests, not disobedient sons.

- The son receives a signet ring symbolizing authority. He returns not as a stigmatized parolee but as one worthy of power and prestige.

- The shoes the servants place on his feet also signal his high status. Free men wore shoes. Slaves went barefoot. This reclaimed son would return as a free person. The servants would serve him.

- A fat calf was killed. Steak was reserved for special occasions. The son, who only yesterday ate with pigs, dines today on steak.

- No whips crack. Instead music soars and dancers twirl. It's time to celebrate a dead son's resurrection. A sinner has come home. Let the party roll!

The noise of the party surprises the older son when he returns from fieldwork that evening. The father's foolish forgiveness outrages him. He demands justice and fairness. Where is the punishment due his rebel brother who squandered his father's security?

Moreover, where is the elder son's long, overdue party? Who is celebrating his years of faithful labor in the fields? Contemptuously, the elder son calls his own brother "this son of yours."

But the loving father responds with "My dear child."

The older son, consumed by rage, never enters the house. Like the scribes and Pharisees, he refuses to join the party. And now he is lost, at the very moment his brother is found.

God is like an upside-down parent. God forgives generously as we repent. God is like a Jewish father who rewards his pork-eating son with steak. Instead of spanking the son who brings disgrace, he elevates him to the high post "of most honored guest." God is like a parent who asks no questions, even when treated as dead. This is limitless, unconditional love with no strings attached. This story takes us to the very heart of God and exposes God's nature—agape.

Such a Parent propels us to act. Like the man who found a treasure in the field, such stunning forgiveness sweeps us off our feet. This overwhelming love energizes a chain reaction. The children of such love want to pass it on. Like their Parent, they become merciful. They love as God loved. Because God has forgiven them, they too can forgive.

Grateful response to God is the motive for action in the upside-down kingdom. Deeds of loving kindness, stirred by God's goodness, embody God's caring hug for this world. Triggered by God's love, these deeds are a sweet offering on the altar of worship.

Another layer of meaning underlies the story. The prodigal also represents Israel in exile that now is being restored in the ministry of Jesus. The elder son typifies the scribes and Pharisees who are resisting the in-breaking of the new kingdom in their midst. The party celebrating the return of the runaway also points to Jesus' table fellowship with sinners who are welcomed in the new kingdom. In this deeper sense, the story captures the meaning of Jesus' announcement of the kingdom.[3]

Get Off Your Donkey

How does agape act in daily life? If God's compassion looks foolish, do God's children look foolish as well? Jesus clarified the essence of agape with a story. It spells out the radical nature of upside-down love in his new kingdom (Luke 10:25-37).[4] The story is Jesus' answer to a lawyer's question—the big question about how to obtain eternal life.

It begins in a believable fashion. A man walks along the winding, desolate road from Jerusalem to Jericho. The audience assumes the walker is a fellow Jew. Bandits living in caves infested the barren hillsides along the winding road to Jericho. A robbery came as no surprise.

Priests and Levites living in outlying areas returned on this road after performing their duties in the Jerusalem temple. Everyone knew that priests and Levites, who followed the purity laws with obsession, would be contaminated if so much as their shadow touched a corpse. The traveler in Jesus' story, stripped and beaten, appeared nearly dead. A conscientious priest would avoid him at all costs.

The audience expects the story to end with a scathing criticism of the religious elite. Like many of Jesus' other parables, this one will criticize callous leaders who lack compassion. The crowd expects a common farmer will turn hero by rescuing a fellow Jew. Such an ending will prick the priests and Levites. A Jewish peasant shows more compassion than religious leaders! Once again, Jesus nails the heavyweights with a stinging story.

Suddenly, Jesus flips their expectations upside-down. A *Samaritan*, not a Jew, pops up as hero. The audience is appalled. How can this be? Why a Samaritan? Their symbolic world turns on end.

Why is a Samaritan so shocking? Bitter tension divided Jews and Samaritans. Samaria, to the north of Jerusalem, was sandwiched between Judea and Galilee. The Samaritans emerged about 400 B.C.E. from mixed marriages between Jews and Gentiles. The Jews regarded them as half-breed bastards. They had their own version of the books of Moses. They had constructed their own temple on Mt. Gerizim north of Jerusalem. They even claimed their temple was the true place of worship. Samaritan priests traced their bloodlines back to the royal priestly line in Hebrew history.

To the Jewish mind, the Samaritans were worse than pagans, because they at least knew better. Samaritans, hated and despised by Jews, were at the bottom of the social ladder.[5] The Scripture attests to the belligerent racism between the two groups. John (4:9) reports that Jews have no dealings with Samaritans. When some Samaritans refuse to give Jesus lodging, James and John are so angry they beg Jesus to scorch the village with fire (Luke 9:51-56). Jewish leaders call Jesus a "Samaritan," a derogatory nickname for the demon-possessed (John 8:48).

When Jesus was about twelve years old, Samaritans sneaked into the Jerusalem temple at night and scattered human bones over the sanctuary. This outrageous act inflamed Jewish passions. Jews would not eat unleavened bread made by a Samaritan, nor an animal killed by a Samaritan. One rabbi said, "He who eats the bread of a Samaritan is like one that eats the flesh of swine."[6]

Intermarriage was taboo. Jews considered Samaritan women perpetual menstruants from the cradle and their husbands perpetually unclean. The saliva of a Samaritan woman was unclean. A whole village was declared contaminated if a Samaritan woman stayed there. Any place a Samaritan slept was considered unclean, as was any food or drink which touched the place. Another rabbi said the Samaritans, "have no law or even the remains of a law and therefore, they are contemptible and corrupt."[7] Samaritans frequently attacked Galilean Jews walking to Jerusalem. To devout Jews, Samaritans were worse than the Romans because the half-breeds mocked Jewish faith by practicing a rival religion amid God's Holy Land. Samaritans, in short, were not even on the purity grid—they were fully polluted.

Back to our story. Jesus shocked Jewish minds when he said a Samaritan merchant, a despicable enemy, stopped to aid the victim. If Jesus merely wanted to teach about neighborly love, the hero of the story could have been another Jew. Better yet, why not tell a story where a Jew rescued a Samaritan? That would have stroked tribal egos—by showing good guy helps bad guy.

But to turn a rascal into a hero? Unthinkable! Jesus flips the crowd's social world upside-down. The good guys—the priests and Levites—turn bad. The villain turns hero. Jesus ties together two unthinkable words: *good* and *Samaritan*. An equivalent mix in our world might be *good* and *terrorist*.

What an earthquake! It shakes the crowd's assumptions. Fault lines gape in cultural maps. Dogmatic judgments, established conclusions, and conventional assumptions suddenly collapse.[8] Contradictory facts collide. Jewish leaders act without compassion. A vile Samaritan behaves like a loving neighbor. The enemy is moved by compassion, by the same force that overcame the foolish father. The priest and Levite, representing the Jewish temple, refuse to help because of religious regulations. The Samaritan, flying the flag of a rival temple, defies ceremonial prescriptions and offers tenderness.

Oil and wine were often used as a crude ointment and antiseptic. But they were contaminated if touched by a Samaritan. The Jerusalem temple held sacred oil and wine, stored in holy places, for special sacrificial occasions. Only officiating priests could touch the sacred oil and wine. Now, a stranger, a Samaritan, pollutes the sacred emblems with his touch, then uses them to heal his Jewish enemy. This is true worship, true forgiveness, genuine sacrament without an animal sacrifice, far away from the Holy of Holies!

The Samaritan lavishly pours the sacred elements on his opponent, not even tithing them according to proper Jewish procedure. Like God's love, the oil and wine aren't restricted to special people in holy places. They are shared freely, even with enemies. In a few short lines this story not only redefines love, it destroys the necessity for the temple and its sacrificial altar.

Only twice in the Gospels is Jesus asked how to gain eternal life. The first time, Jesus directs the rich young ruler to sell out to the poor and follow him. The second time Jesus tells the story of the Good Samaritan to explain kingdom love to a Jewish lawyer, a student of the Torah. This upside-down story reveals the shocking answer to the lawyer's questions, "How do I inherit eternal life?" and "Who is my neighbor?"

The Torah defined the tribal boundaries of the people of Israel. Loving one's neighbor would surely refer to those inside the Jewish tribe. In a few short words, Jesus smashes the old ethnic borders and shows that the walls of the new kingdom go far beyond Israel. This is not merely a story about new borders and a good act. It is also a story about a *good* person, a story that shows the goodness in even an enemy. In so doing, it stretches the umbrella of the new kingdom over all humankind. In one short story, Jesus demolishes our labels of neighbor and enemy, insider and outsider.[9]

The story clarifies kingdom values and agape love in several ways. (1) Agape is *indiscriminate*. Kingdom love mocks the labels underlying the lawyer's question, "Who is my neighbor?" The lawyer wants to sort people into boxes of neighbors and enemies. Jesus' disciples love indiscriminately; their love stretches beyond neighbors. Agents of agape don't draw lines of responsibility and exclusion. The answer to the lawyer's question is clear. If even enemies are defined as neighbors, then certainly anyone less hostile deserves the grace of agape.

In other words, the question, "Who is my neighbor?" is moot. The story defines *everyone*, even my enemy, as my neighbor. Our "neighbor" becomes all-inclusive in the upside-down kingdom. In a broad call for human solidarity, the categories of friend and enemy dissolve since everyone is a neighbor. We treat as neighbor even those to whom we have no obligation to act neighborly—even enemies we could rightfully hate. Agape love responds to persons, not to social categories. Jesus reverses things by asking the lawyer, in essence, "Are you acting like a neighbor to everyone?"

(2) Agape is *bold*. Religious custom doesn't stymie it. Compassion suspends social norms which might justify callous disinterest. Unlike the priest who feared his shadow might touch a corpse, agape values people over religious rules. Agape penetrates the social barricades which hide people in prisons, hospitals, addiction centers, and ghettos of all sorts.

(3) Agape is *inconvenient*. The priest and Levite "saw and passed by on the other side." The Samaritan had compassion and got off his donkey. He placed the victim on his donkey and walked alongside. It's often inconvenient to get off the donkeys which carry us to places of comfortable security. The agape of the kingdom calls us to such inconvenience.

(4) Agape is *risky*. The whole scene of this story might have been a frame-up. Perhaps the robbers were hiding nearby waiting to pounce on anyone who offered help. By walking with the victim instead of riding, the Samaritan made himself vulnerable to more attacks after the rescue. Nevertheless, this good enemy takes a risk for the sake of the victim.

(5) Agape *takes time*. The rescue disrupts the Samaritan merchant's schedule. Stopping and bandaging the victim, walking alongside him, and stopping at the inn surely delayed the merchant's trip. Compassion requires action which requires time.

(6) Agape is *expensive*. The Samaritan paid the innkeeper the equivalent of twenty-four days of lodging and offered a "blank check" for any additional costs. If Jew were helping Jew, a civil court would have likely repaid the helper. But a Jewish court would never reimburse a Samaritan. The enemy freely lends finances without hope of return. This is precisely what Jesus says in a formal instruction: "Lend, expecting nothing in return" (Luke 6:35).

(7) Agape *jeopardizes social status*. What happened when word got back to the Samaritan's hometown that he was aiding Jews? He likely was labeled a traitor to the Samaritan cause. His reputation and social status were tarnished. He surely faced ridicule from his own people.

This upside-down story leaves no doubt about the courageous nature of agape. Compassion involves more than warm fuzzy feelings. It's more than good attitudes toward others. It doesn't stop with sweet smiles. This foolish love is assertive. It's costly, both socially and economically.

Although the story shows the shape of agape, it doesn't answer all of our questions. What if the Samaritan had found the robbers beating the victim? How would agape have responded? Should force be used to stop the atrocity? Does agape only apply Band-Aids to the wounded? Did the Samaritan ever get to the root of the problem by going back to the caves and searching for the robbers? If he had found them, what did he have done with them? What if one sees many battered victims? Which ones receive priority? These questions, unanswered in the incident, often beg for answers in our world today.

The One-Leg Law

The Gospels herald agape love as the single sacrament of the upside-down kingdom. After the great commandment to love God with all our being comes the revolutionary instruction. Love your neighbor in the *same* manner that you love yourself. All three synoptic writers underscore this Christian manifesto (Matt. 22:37-40; Mark 12:28-31; Luke 10:25-27).

The simple phrase is packed with meaning. First, it assumes self-love is appropriate. There is a place for personal respect and dignity. It's all right to have personal aspirations. But there's a catch. The revolutionary phrase calls us to care for our neighbor as intensely as we care for ourselves. We should work as hard to help our neighbors achieve their goals as we work for our own.

The invitation to love our neighbor as ourself collides with selfish individualism. The wise admonition balances the pursuit of self-interest with the needs of others. It celebrates personal needs and desires, but then restrains them by calling for equal attention to others. Selfish individualism is abolished in the upside-down kingdom. Here equal doses of self-love and neighbor love flow from our ultimate love—our devotion to God. Such love eradicates pride. Caring for our neighbor's welfare with the same intensity as we care for our own eliminates greedy egoism.

For Jesus, the norm of agape love summed up the *entire* law and the message of the prophets (Matt. 7:12). Although agape was the key to Hebrew righteousness, Jesus called it a new commandment. We're to love others as God loved us. Our practice of love is the sign that we are indeed disciples of Jesus (John 13:34-35).

Jesus added new dimensions to the meaning of love. A skeptical Gentile once told a rabbi he would accept the Jewish faith if the rabbi could summarize the Jewish law while the Gentile stood on one leg. The rabbi replied, "Do not do to another what would be hurtful to you." Jesus flipped the negative rule upside-down and turned it into a directive for action. "As you wish that men would do to you, do so to them" (Luke 6:31; Matthew 7:12).

Jesus modeled agape. He embodied it by being an advocate for the poor. He violated civil and religious laws to serve human need. His words and deeds insulted the rich and powerful. He championed the downtrodden, the outcasts, and the oppressed even when his behavior created a ruckus.

Although agape willingly suffers, it understands that a firm "no" is also an expression of loving care. The young child, the emotionally disturbed, the adolescent with a character disorder, and the irresponsible adult may need a *"no"* rather than a sweet smile. Kind but firm confrontation can be a deep expression of agape. True love confronts even when confrontation is painful. In fact, gentle confrontation expresses agape more than avoidance or implicit approval of irresponsible behavior. Saying that agape can be firm and confrontive dare not, however, excuse the use of violent means, even for good ends.

Suggesting that agape is the single ordinance of the kingdom sounds nice. But it's no panacea. How does one respond when the needs of three or four different "neighbors" clash? Caring for one neighbor may harm the interests of another one. In an age of aggressive competition, how does a Christian enterprise embody agape in the face of strident competitors? Are corporate competitors also "neighbors"? How do we love our neighbor when the neighbor's goals clash with Christian values? Although such questions beg for answers, the agape view offers new perspectives. It tilts us away from arrogant individualism and prods us to ask the right questions about neighborly love.

Beyond Tit for Tat

Agape love revises a widespread social rule—the norm of reciprocity. Throughout the world, reciprocity shapes our expectations for giving and receiving favors—both verbal and material. If I buy you a cup of coffee, you are obligated to say "thank you" and return the favor sometime. The exchange needn't be equal in value or form. A candy bar might be an acceptable thank you for a cup of coffee. The underlying rule, however, is simple: we should appreciate and return favors.

The norm of reciprocity assumes that people should help—and certainly not injure—those who have helped them. Reciprocity maintains a balance of obligations in social relationships. We feel awkward if we can't reciprocate a gift. We consider rude those who break the rules of reciprocity. Gift giving and card exchanges at holidays illustrate the norm. Gifts need to be of similar value so things don't get skewed. Giving a $2.00 gift in exchange for a $25.00 one makes us uncomfortable. We send holiday cards to those who we think will send one back. Our relationships tip out of balance when a holiday gift or greeting is not returned.

This rule isn't just a seasonal thing. It pervades all aspects of human relations. The little "thank you's" we say and do throughout the day are governed by reciprocity. So is the exchange of labor for wages and fees for service. We can manipulate relationships for personal gain by building up indebtedness with others. This happens when salespersons "wine and dine" prospective customers—thereby obligating the prospects to return the favor by making a purchase. If we want to ask a favor of others, we may take them out to lunch, thus obligating them to help us.

The subtle flip side of this norm is often unspoken but pervasive and powerful. While we're expected to help those inside our web of reciprocity, we're not obligated to go out of our way to do favors for strangers. We have no obligations to outsiders. That's why random acts of kindness to strangers are so surprising. We have no debts with those who have done nothing for us. We can ignore strangers without feeling guilt. But when it comes to enemies, it's a different story. We have a duty to hate them.

Jesus slices through the norm of reciprocity: "If you love those who love you, what credit is that to you? For even sinners love those who love them. . . . And if you lend to those from whom you hope to receive, what credit is that to you? Even sinners lend to sinners, to receive as much again" (Luke 6:32-34).

Jesus presses the point by asking, "For if you love those who love you, what reward do you have? Do not even the tax collectors do the same? And if you greet only your brothers and sisters, what more are you doing than others?" (Matt. 5:46-47). In other words, agape love stretches far beyond simple reciprocity.

Don't be tricked, says Jesus, into thinking agape love is the same as the norm of reciprocity. Agape isn't about returning smiles for smiles or favors for favors. Even sinners play by that rule. Pharisees and tax collectors smile back when people smile at them. Pagans return favors to persons who favor them. Gentiles politely conform to these rules of social etiquette. It's no big deal if you simply play by the rules of reciprocity. That's not kingdom love.

Agape is a norm of *excess*. It goes beyond reciprocity. The foolish father didn't play by reciprocity when he welcomed his stinking son home. The Samaritan crossbreed didn't play by reciprocity when he got off his donkey. Your heavenly Parent doesn't play by that rule either. God sends sun and rain on the unjust as well the just (Matt. 5:45). God models the norm of excess. We should be merciful as God is merciful (Luke 6:36). "You received without payment, give without payment" (Matt. 10:8).

God injects a divine dimension into the old "tit for tat" formula. God enters the equation of social relationships. God has taken the initiative by doing us a favor. God loved the world so much that God became a human person. God redeems and saves us through Jesus Christ. God acts first and initiates a chain reaction. We've been graciously forgiven. How do we repay? By sharing God's love initiative with others. In this network of social relations there are three actors. *God* takes the initiative by extending unconditional love like the foolish father. *We* reciprocate our indebtedness to God by spreading the loving initiative to *others*.

We erase our indebtedness to God by loving others. Paul spells out the workings of this "love debt" succinctly: "Owe no one anything, except to love one another; for the one who loves another has fulfilled the law" (Rom. 13:8). Jesus spells it out as clearly when he says: "Truly, I tell you, as you did it to one of the least of these, who are members of my family, my brethren, you did it to me" (Matt. 25:40). In this context he describes acts of love to the most destitute: the hungry, the thirsty, the sick, the prisoners, the strangers, and the naked. As you love even the least of these—

hanging on the bottom rung of the social ladder—you have repaid me!

The transaction is complete. A new chain reaction begins. The least of these who experience God's care now pass it on. The Jubilee refrain rings in our ears again. As I have liberated you, so liberate others! This isn't a cold, calculating exchange where we seek to "repay" God in some legalistic way. It's impossible to fully repay our enormous debt. This is a joyous Jubilee response—spontaneous gratitude for God's marvelous grace.

Agape love exceeds the norm of reciprocity in three ways. First, the initiative is now ours. Instead of waiting to return a favor, we make the first move because God has already favored us.

Second, agape serves others regardless of their status. It doesn't focus on friends or peers to whom we must "be nice." As the story of the Samaritan suggests, under the reign of agape, strangers, foes, and outcasts are cared for as well as close friends.

Third, agape love doesn't expect a return. Since God has taken the initiative, we've already been paid. In typical upside-down fashion, agape urges others to pass the love on, offering the favor to someone else instead of returning it.

Jesus articulates this clearly. "When you give a luncheon or a dinner, do not invite your friends or your brothers or your relatives or rich neighbors, in case they may invite you in return, and you would be repaid. But when you give a banquet, invite the poor, the crippled, the lame, the blind. And you will be blessed, because they cannot repay you, for you will be repaid at the resurrection of the righteous" (Luke 14:12-14).[10]

Jesus' disciples don't love for personal gain, nor do they expect a return. After mocking those who pride themselves for following the norm of reciprocity, Jesus spells out the boundless nature of agape. "But love your enemies, do good, and lend, expecting nothing in return. Your reward will be great, and you will be children of the Most High; for he is kind to the ungrateful and the wicked" (Luke 6:35).

The disciples of Jesus are upside-down deviants. They exceed conventional expectations. They take the initiative. They don't discriminate between enemies and neighbors. They expect no return.

When we expect payback, we turn the recipients of our gift into clients. When we expect no return, we free them from debt.[11]

It's often difficult to accept a gift. We hate to feel indebted. We worry about how to reciprocate. Our gifts to others may make them feel awkward as well. The agape posture alleviates the awkwardness. When someone gives us a gift and says, "Just pass the favor on," it relieves our indebtedness. It also protects our dignity since we can reciprocate in due time through someone else. Passing on the kindness, also, of course, enlarges the circle of redeeming love.

A Slap for a Slap?

We've looked at the positive side of the norm of reciprocity—do good to those who do good to you. The downside, however, allows us to harm someone who has harmed us. It's fair play to retaliate if someone has deliberately hurt us. In fact, we can go beyond an eye for an eye. If someone pokes out one of our eyes, we may poke out both of theirs. This norm of negative reciprocity undergirds the spectrum of human behavior from sibling pinches to international war. In brief, if people injure me, I may injure them.

If someone files a suit against me, I may counterfile. If someone swindles me, I have license to cheat them back. If another nation launches missiles against us, we may counter-launch. In fact, even if we *think* they're about to launch, we have the right to launch first. The negative side of reciprocity not only permits self-defense, it legitimates a spiraling cycle of endless retaliation. The revenge may exceed the original insult to "teach" the aggressor "a lesson." We reflect this when we say, "She had it coming to her," "He got what he deserved," or "It serves them right."

In upside-down fashion, Jesus overturns the negative rule of reciprocity. His words and actions are forthright. There can be no question. Jesus suspends the negative as well as the positive side of the norm.

> You have heard that it was said, "An eye for an eye and a tooth for a tooth." But I say to you, do not resist an evildoer. But if anyone strikes you on the *right* cheek, turn the other also; and if anyone wants to sue you and take your coat, give your cloak as well; and if anyone forces you to go one mile, go also the

second mile. Give to everyone who begs from you, and do not refuse anyone who wants to borrow from you. (Matt. 5:38-44, emphasis added)

Christians have largely ignored these surprising instructions or have used them as recipes for not resisting evil. Is Jesus calling us to be sponges that absorb any insult or injury? To the contrary, one scholar shows that Jesus was likely calling his disciples to resist evil with these symbolic acts of nonviolence.[12] Some cultural context helps to shed light on the meaning of the text.

First, Jesus is not talking about fistfights or schoolyard brawls. A slap to the *right* cheek was often given with the backside of the right hand by a master who wanted to reprimand or humiliate a servant. Second, this culture made a big distinction between right hands and left ones. The left hand was used for unclean tasks, but never the right. A blow to the right cheek symbolized ultimate contempt. If someone got angry and hit an equal on the right cheek with a fist, they were fined a day's wage. If they gave a humiliating slap with the back of their hand, the fine multiplied a hundred times. The fines, however, only applied to equals, not to servants. A master could slap a slave and not be fined.

Thus Jesus is talking about insults, not fistfights. More importantly, he is pinpointing unequal power relations between masters and slaves, landlords and stewards, husbands and wives. Jesus is speaking to his disciples and to others who had been humiliated with backslaps by higher ups—masters, soldiers, husbands—in positions of power. If insulted by a slap, a slave basically had two choices: hit back or cower in humiliation. Most servants would cower down because to slap back would give the master excuse for beating the slave. Why would Jesus tell these already humiliated people to turn the other cheek?

Jesus proposes not a retaliatory blow or dropping to the ground in submission—but a third way. Offer the other cheek and rob the aggressor of the power to humiliate. By offering the other cheek, the left one, the slave is saying, "Try again. I refuse to be humiliated." Such nonviolent resistance exposes the evil act and shames the aggressor. It does not compliantly accept injury but resists it, not with violence, but with love. Jesus' examples of giving one's last garment and walking the second mile illustrate the same principle of nonviolent resistance.[13]

Symbolic forms of resistance that humiliate and shame oppressors must be balanced by Jesus' command to love the enemy. To love the enemy requires respect and appreciation of his/her human dignity. Symbolic acts of resistance should never vilify or demean the evildoer. Indeed, any resistance must be guided by love because Jesus calls us to love our enemy.

"You have heard that it was said," continues Jesus, "'You shall love your neighbor and hate your enemy.' But I say to you, Love your enemies and pray for those who persecute you" (Matt. 5:38-44).

Love our enemies? They're the one category of people that the norm of reciprocity *urges* us to hate.[14] Love for enemies is the ultimate flip-flop, for it demolishes the norm of reciprocity. Enemy love, however, flows not just from this text but from the entire spirit of Jesus' stories and ministry.

In Luke's Gospel Jesus offers upside-down responses to seven types of aggressors (Luke 6:27-30). How should Christians respond when someone makes an evil move? What treatment does the old norm of reciprocity prescribe for aggressors? An item-by-item contrast between a typical response and an upside-down kingdom response is sketched below. The proposed kingdom reactions seem utterly unfair according to the norm of reciprocity.

Type of Person	Typical Response	Kingdom Response
Enemies	Kill	Love
Haters	Hate	Do good
Cursers	Curse	Bless
Abusers	Exploit	Pray
Strikers	Slug	Offer other cheek
Beggars	Avoid	Give
Thieves	Prosecute	Do not request goods

In calling for enemy love, Jesus clashes with the Essenes, the rebels, and the Pharisees. The patriotic rebels, as we've seen, didn't hesitate to kill enemies. The Essenes, living in isolated Dead Sea communities, thought it was their righteous duty to hate sinners. Jewish law, taught by the Pharisees, said it wasn't necessary to love an enemy. Jesus reverses these typical solutions to evil. Revenge and retaliation are obsolete in the new kingdom.

As assertive love supersedes reciprocity, so forgiveness obliterates the tit-for-tat of revenge. Forgiveness is the startling mark of Jesus' disciples. They forgive 490 times a day (Matt. 18:22; Luke 17:3-4). Jesus isn't setting legal limits. With a twinkle in his eye, he suggests that forgiveness is the perpetual mark of kingdom citizenship. If 490 sounded humorous to some, it surely outraged religious leaders who thought forgiveness could only come in the temple with a bloody sacrifice. Jesus' disciples can forgive here and now because they were so graciously forgiven.

Moreover, those who don't forgive, jeopardize their own forgiveness. "If you do not forgive others, neither will your Father forgive your trespasses" (Matt. 6:15). Jesus models this bountiful forgiveness when he tells the woman caught in adultery to go and sin no more. According to Jewish law, she could have been stoned on the spot. Forgiveness replaces retaliation. It's the distinguishing mark of the upside-down way.

Jesus models the way of forgiveness even on the cross. If retaliation is ever in order, this is the time. If violent self-defense is ever justified, this is the moment. But in a startling reversal, amid bloody torture, Jesus pleads on behalf of his enemies, "Father, forgive them" (Luke 23:34). He urges us to "love one another as I have loved you. No one has greater love than this, to lay down one's life for one's friends" (John 15:12-13).

In the new kingdom we treat enemies as friends. This kind of forgiveness, however, is risky. It brought Jesus to the cross. Nevertheless, he also invites us to forgive abundantly even at the risk of our lives. There is no witness, no redemption, no love if we play by the old rule of retaliation. The willingness to suffer amid injustice witnesses to the power of divine love. In front of the cross Jesus rejects self-defense. "All who take the sword will perish by the sword" (Matt. 26:52). "If my kingdom were from this world, my followers would be fighting, to keep me from being handed over to the Jews" (John 18:36).

In the face of brutal torture, Jesus offers this sweeping rejection of violent retaliation. His agonizing prayer in Gethsemane, "Not my will, but yours, be done" (Luke 22:42), wasn't mere submission to a divine order of events. It was Jesus' commitment to embody forgiving love even in the shadow of doom. God practices patient forgiveness amid hatred. Even Jesus found that difficult as he struggled with the prospect of death in the garden of Gethsemane.

When faced with conflict, our natural impulse is fight or flight. We want to whip out the guns or vanish to the hills. Jesus offers a third way—agape love in the face of evil. Abhorring both violence and passivity, Jesus models both resistance and nonresistance. To focus only on one distorts his message. Resistance and nonresistance must hang in healthy tension.[15]

We have already seen the resistant side of Jesus. Many of his stories and acts were direct forms of resistance. He taught us, however, not to resist evil with evil, but with goodness. He implores us to use nonviolent means to resist evil—not violent ones. The moment we succumb to violence, we mirror the very heart of evil itself. Ironically, we become what we hate.[16]

The image of a passive, spineless Jesus—a wimp on the cross— blurs the fact that Jesus' active ministry triggered his death. It was precisely *because* of his assertive love that the cross came about in the first place. Jesus acted decisively and forcefully, eating with sinners, healing on the Sabbath, and challenging religious leaders. Jesus confronted injustice. To face evil serenely isn't to be forever mild and passive. Jesus doesn't call us to be passive peace*keepers* who merely preserve the status quo. His blessing falls on the active peace*makers* (Matt. 5:9).

But there is also a nonresistant side to Jesus. He carries his own cross, the instrument of torture. He doesn't run away, fight, or resist. When the evil powers react to his criticism of injustice, he demonstrates God's patient grace. He offers forgiveness. He loves his enemies who literally torture him. He practices God's patient nonresistant love. And it is a courageous nonresistant love that has the power to transform enemies into friends and convert villains into humans with a force more powerful than any other. It is the powerful force of God's patient forgiving love—God's nonresistant love that can absorb the painful prongs of evil. Resisting—challenging evil—must always be checked by God's nonresistant agape.

The message of Jesus is clear. The use of violence, whether physical or emotional, is not God's way. Jesus shows us how to absorb suffering, not inflict it. By refusing to cheer on the revolutionary rebels, Jesus even rejects violent resistance to protect the suffering. Jesus modeled God's new way—the power of patient grace and forgiving love.

Detours Around Agape

Many scholars agree that nonviolence is central to Jesus' teachings and to the message of the New Testament.[17] The early church practiced nonviolence for nearly three centuries after Jesus' death. Nevertheless, the call to love enemies has baffled human logic over the centuries. Even the church has condoned the use of violent means in various ways.[18]

Christians have evaded the message of the Prince of Peace through several detours. One tempting excuse arises from warfare in the Old Testament. Didn't God send Israel into battle? At first glance this looks like a license to fight. Modern warfare, however, doesn't follow Old Testament strategies. When Yahweh commanded Israel to engage in military action, it was clear that Yahweh was the head warrior who would triumph. Thus military force was deliberately scaled *down* so any victory would be a miraculous one that would applaud Yahweh's divine intervention. If we took the ancient biblical model of warfare seriously, our modern armies would dramatically *reduce* their size and firepower and rely on God's miraculous intervention for victory!

Beyond this key difference, and more importantly, Jesus introduced a new norm, the Torah of love. As God's full and definitive revelation, Jesus is the key for interpreting all of Scripture. He is the supreme authority. As the final word in God's progressive revelation, Jesus offers a new way that transforms, and goes beyond, the old tit-for-tat patterns.

A second detour emerged in the eleventh to thirteenth centuries when Christian crusades, supposedly under the banner of God's blessing, slaughtered Muslims who had conquered Christian holy areas in the Middle East. In this sad and tragic moment, Christians deceived themselves into believing that God was on their side, blessing their use of violence. The temptation to think that God blesses and fights for particular nations, as Yaweh did in ancient Israel, continues even today.

The seductive power of nationalism seeks to wrap God's blessing around national destinies that have nothing to do with Christian faith. Some Christians still prostitute the gospel by justifying military crusades under the flag of God's blessing. For example, singing "God Bless America" while marching off to war, turns God into a tribal deity that favors pet nations. This distortion of the gospel imagines that God smiles warmly on the military endeavors of some countries, but not on others. The use of God-talk to justify militarism spans many centuries—from holy crusades to modern versions—with claims that God "blesses" military action. Coins inscribed with "In God We Trust" are a mockery when a nation spends billions of dollars for defense. Americans obviously trust weapons, not God.

A third detour, the idea of a "just war," emerged in Christian thinking in the third century, as the church melted more into Roman society and sought ways to justify its defense. Although based on the premise that war should only be a last resort, the just war doctrine put a divine blessing on the use of violence for self-defense and the protection of innocent victims. Just war guidelines specified *when* a war was justifiable and proper rules for *how* it could be fought.

Over the centuries, the just war approach enabled political leaders to receive a blessing from the church when using violence. This also made it acceptable for Christians to participate in various roles in military operations. Ironically, however, enemies in the same conflict often called their cause "just," leading both sides to claim God's blessing. One Christian scholar has argued that instead of trying to justify war, we should develop specific policies and steps for just peacemaking.[19]

A fourth detour suggests that Jesus only calls us to love personal enemies. Jesus' words, in this view, apply only to interpersonal relationships. Because God institutes governments, we're obligated to obey the call of conscription and defend the country. We should love our personal enemies, yes, but not national ones. Making this distinction strikes a line between personal morality and one's obligation to the state. This view elevates national allegiance *above* kingdom loyalty.

The classic Christian text that calls for submission to government (Rom. 13:1-7) is sandwiched between two ardent pleas by the apostle Paul for suffering love. In addition there is a big difference between obeying government and submitting to its authority without resorting to violence when we disagree. Furthermore, this passage will sound very different in the context of a democratic government versus a tyrannical one. Often interpreting out of context, we use this passage to place national loyalties above kingdom values, thus negating allegiance to Jesus and bowing down to tribal deities.[20]

We take a fifth detour when churches affirm the way of peace in public statements but view it as an appendage to the gospel. Instead of seeing forgiveness and its social implications as the core of salvation, we see it as marginal. Nonviolence is merely seen as an accessory that's nice when it works. Furthermore, we deem peacemaking a question of "individual conscience," not a gospel mandate. We can take it or leave it. Likewise military service is a matter of individual conscience, we conclude. What is at stake here is our ultimate allegiance. National loyalty often rises above our allegiance to Jesus.

Nagging Questions

Despite Jesus' clear call to peacemaking, many thorny questions lurk in our minds. May violence be used for self-protection? Is it ever God's will for Christians to use violence to further justice? For example, may violence be used to protect innocent victims? Jesus does not speak directly to the issue, but based on his teaching and ministry, his likely response is neither flight nor fight, but nonviolent resistance. His own actions suggest this. He was not a passive bystander in the face of Roman oppression, but neither did he lead an armed revolt. In fact, it may take more courage to engage in non-violent resistance than to pull a trigger or press a button to launch a missile.

The issues of peacemaking and violence in our world stir many difficult ethical questions. I am fully persuaded that Jesus rejected the use of violence to confront evil, but I realize there are many nagging questions. In a short survey I cannot explore these issues in depth but do want to note some of the questions with which Christians of good faith struggle as they seek to practice the non-violent way of Jesus amid a world of evil.[21]

Is there a difference between using force and lethal violence? Governments use force to restrain violent criminals. Is the use of non-lethal force acceptable to restrain evil? Is it morally okay to shoot to cripple belligerent bullies as long as we don't kill them?

Are police-keeping actions to maintain order within a society different than using military means for national self-defense? May Christians participate in police actions to keep civic order?

Can a moral line be drawn between private acts of aggression and the use of lethal force by military units of legitimate governments? Is there a difference between murder and state-sanctioned killing? Or is all killing murder?

Is there an ethical difference between using violence for self-aggression, for self-defense, or for protecting innocent victims? Can Christians in good faith use violent force to defend innocent people against tyrants who might kill them? Is it acceptable to shoot a bully wounding or threatening smaller kids in a schoolyard? A bully in an international conflict?

Do Jesus' instructions on peacemaking apply only to his followers or to others as well? Should Christians expect and urge governments to practice nonviolence? In other words, are the ethics of nonviolence applicable to international relations?

Even though we know violence is not the way of Jesus, is it ever necessary to knowingly sin (engage in violence) to protect others and restrain evil?

These are difficult questions without easy or simple answers. Despite their moral complexity, Jesus' call to love the enemy slices through the issues with simplicity and clarity. We are easily trapped into thinking that violence is the most effective way to solve problems. Jesus calls us to faithfulness; to faithfully embody God's loving forgiveness. Many times, such love may, in the long run, be more effective than resorting to violence. Nevertheless, it's hard to discard our belief that violence is the ultimate answer to many problems.

The Myth of Redemptive Violence

We live in a violent world. As technology races ahead, our potential means of destruction grow. The great twentieth century of "progress," left some 140 million dead from dozens of wars—likely over ninety percent of people ever killed in war. Trillions of dollars were invested in weapons of mass destruction that could have destroyed entire societies as well as all of humankind. Evil is well and alive, but not only "out there"; it also stalks the depths of all our hearts. Again and again, we are tempted to think that violence will help us fix things and make them better.

The myth of redemptive violence thrives whenever we assume violence is the most effective way to solve a problem. Terrible as it is, we are tempted to believe violence can bring good things out of a bad scene. Indeed, violence assumes a virtuous character whenever we expect it to save us from evil. The myth of redemptive violence fills video games, movies, and typical interpretations of national and global history.

If we believe that violence works, that it redeems bad things, then we readily turn to it when we face a fight. When we want to fix things that have gone awry, we reach for guns, bombs, and missiles. But sadly, when we try to redeem things through violent means, we may actually become the very evil we hate.[22]

Talk of lovable enemies is hard to hear in a world loaded with weapons of mass destruction. Superpower nations have the capacity to pulverize each other many times over. A single submarine *alone* has the capacity to destroy some 400 separate cities each with a blast five times stronger than the bomb used on Hiroshima. Weapon after weapon, system after system—the overkill capacity is mind-boggling. Preparations for war rob the world's poor of basic necessities, such as food, shelter, and healthcare. Building stockpiles of weapons of mass destruction is an immoral waste of resources when one fourth of the world community lives in squalor. When we believe violence redeems, the upward spiral of violence never ends. Threats beget more threats. Acts of violence trigger more violence. Wars against terrorism breed more terror and birth more terrorists. Amid wars and acts of terror, the Carpenter's appeal to love our enemies suddenly sounds like good advice. Isn't it more reasonable to learn to live with our enemies and to seek diplomatic solutions, than to use weapons that not only destroy, but also fuel the fires of hatred? Christians in every land must insist that war in the name of peace is really death in disguise. Imagine the global impact if Christians in every country were willing to pledge that they will never kill another human being.

A Vision of Shalom

We often think of peace as the absence of conflict. *Shalom*, the Hebrew word for peace, is closely connected with ideas of justice, righteousness, salvation, and well-being. It suggests a complete sense of well-being in personal, social, economic, and political spheres.[23] There is no peace when greedy systems oppress the poor. Peace vanishes when the stigmatized find no justice in the courts. The "peace" which hangs on a precarious balance of nuclear warheads isn't shalom. An individualism, which cares only about number one also destroys the harmony of community.

The church is called to nonviolence because it reflects the very nature of God. We are called to practice nonviolence in all areas of life not because it is always effective, but because it witnesses to the love and character of God. Consider three of many nonviolent approaches that spurn the myth of redemptive violence and strive for shalom: nonviolent social change, nonviolent witness, and restorative justice. These positive initiatives illustrate some possible ways of interrupting the deadly cycle of violence.

Over the centuries, many Christians and various movements have witnessed the power of nonviolence in the face of conflict and aggression. Some of these movements have used nonviolent resistance to press for social justice for the poor. Others have used nonviolent tactics to stop military campaigns and to overthrow military dictators. Scholars and historians have described literally hundreds of examples of effective nonviolent interventions in a variety of struggles in many countries.[24]

Nonviolent strategies, for example, propelled the civil rights movement in the United States, dismantled racial tyranny in South Africa, and aided the sudden collapse of dictators in communist Eastern Europe. Social change in all these areas would have been much more bloody without the nonviolent interventions of thousands of people.

Practical applications of nonviolence range from bully prevention programs in elementary schools to international peace-building programs—to tame larger bullies. Conflict mediation and transformation programs seek to resolve hostilities in nonviolent ways in family disputes, church fights, corporate conflicts, and international showdowns. Christian Peacemaker Teams, an ecumenical church-based program, dispatches volunteers to international hot spots, where they intervene in violent confrontations. Risking their lives, these volunteers witness to the love of a God without enemies. They straddle enemy lines and embody such love even amid hate. Their credible witness contends that Christian peacemakers must be willing to die for the peaceable kingdom like soldiers die for their country.[25]

The restorative justice movement offers a shalom approach within the criminal justice system. Retaliation and revenge often flourish when criminals are punished. Many times "justice" looks more like revenge than true justice. The standard "lock'em up and toss the key" approach of *retributive* justice underscores broken laws, damaged property, guilt, punishment, and revenge.

By contrast, *restorative* justice emphasizes rebuilding relationships, reconciliation, and reparations. Moreover, offenders often have to face their victims and acknowledge the injury they caused. A variety of Victim Offender Reconciliation Programs that are part of this movement bring victims and offenders together for face-to-face accountability. Restorative justice is but one example of a peacemaking initiative within and along side the criminal justice system in several countries.[26]

Shalom arises when right relationships flower among people in all realms of life. The Scriptures tell us that peace is God's gift.

Through Jesus Christ we have peace with God and our neighbors. Shalom is God's design for the created order. God is a God of peace. Jesus is the Prince of peace. The Holy Spirit is the Spirit of peace. The kingdom of God pivots on justice, peace, and joy. The children of God are peacemakers. The gospel is the good news of peace. Shalom is the core, not the caboose, of God's salvation.

10

Inside Outsiders

Flying with Similar Birds

Chapter nine explored Jesus' teaching on agape. Now we consider how agape translates into social interaction. What kind of people join God's kingdom? A sage once noted that "Birds of a feather flock together." Like-minded people do in fact cluster together. We enjoy those with whom we share things in common. We feel awkward in new settings with people from strange places. We like those who think as we do. And we begin to think like the people we respect. But don't opposites attract? Perhaps on an emotional level they do, but when it comes to beliefs, opposites repel and birds of a feather fly together.

Many social factors bind humans together—income, education, occupation, race, religion, politics, lifestyle, family, ethnic background, and national heritage. We migrate toward similar people and feel most comfortable with those. It's easier to talk with people in similar occupations. We're attracted to those whose social views mirror ours. We seek friends who reinforce our ideas. Without objective yardsticks to confirm the truth of our beliefs, we find security and support among like-minded friends. Strange ideas may threaten our beliefs and force us to rethink our convictions. We might even need to change!

The "birds of a feather" principle not only governs personal relationships, it also shapes group interaction. People with similar educational backgrounds and jobs often live in the same area. If we know a person lives on "the hill," in "the ward," or on "the lower side," we can often predict their race, income, and social prestige. We can venture safe estimates of lifestyles, political views, and educational levels of people who reside in "Walnut Hill Estate" or "Executive Manor." Congregations and parishes often attract similar people as well. There are, of course, exceptions to these patterns. But the glitches don't erase the fact that in most places, most of the time, most people flock with birds of a common feather.

Playing Social Checkers

Human communities draw lines. They create boundaries that separate good from evil, clean from dirty, stigma from respect, insiders from outsiders. A checkerboard helps us visualize the lines that organize social interaction. Each square on the board represents different types of people. Lines around the boxes define patterns of social interaction. Groups as well as individuals occupy boxes on the board. We play, ski, dine, travel, and swim with folks from our own or nearby squares. It's a rare occasion indeed to relate intimately with someone in a box on the other side of the board. We treat "inbox" members as friends and neighbors. We invite people from similar boxes to our home. These familiar habits eliminate worries about dealing with weird people from distant squares. Human clustering within social squares orders life and makes it predictable.

Most people occupy several boxes. I'm a father, husband, teacher, neighbor, and writer. Some of our boxes—race, sex, and country of origin—we inherit without choice. We usually have more sway over our occupation, religion, politics, and education. Each box includes certain rights, privileges, and obligations. The social definition of a box determines to a large extent how we perceive ourselves and how we expect others to treat us. The labels on boxes tell everyone how to relate to the boxholder. Take a police uniform, for example. It reminds officers to behave appropriately when on duty. But the officers also expect citizens to show them respect when they're wearing a badge. The labels on social boxes shape our patterns of social interaction for good or bad.

We carry social checkerboards around in our minds. As we meet people we sort them into social bins. Lacking detailed information, we simply toss them into boxes based on their external appearance. They're white, oriental, sloppy, preppy, a nurse, or a trucker. Additional snatches of information may allow us to tag them: fundamentalist, Buddhist, charismatic, peacenik, redneck, drug addict, or gay.

In addition to labeling people, we generalize about everyone in a particular bin. In other words, we stereotype. We *assume* a particular person behaves according to our view of everyone in that box. We assume charismatics try to get people to speak in tongues. Theological liberals, of course, don't believe in the virgin birth. Puerto Ricans are lazy. Asians are smart. Fundamentalists care not a whit for social justice. Republicans are fiscally conservative. Democrats are soft on national defense. Jews are tight. Wealthy folks are indifferent and callous. Salespersons are tricky. Women are emotional. Teenagers are irresponsible. And parents are rigid. On and on the stereotypes roll.

Playing social checkers is dangerous and deadly. We easily place people in the wrong box. Our labels often flow from myth rather than fact. Even if a stereotype is partly true, it may not fit a particular person. Boxing not only injures others, it restrains our behavior. We relate to others by labels instead of encountering them as real people. We may avoid folks because their tag says deaf, ex-con, democrat, disabled, prostitute, rich, homosexual, or white. Boxing people isn't entirely harmful, however. It helps to stabilize social life, making it orderly and predictable.

Jesus plays a new game of social checkers. He models creative ways of penetrating boxes. He crosses lines. He walks over borders and deals with real people. He walks through social barricades. Wandering across the checkerboard of his time, he disregards the "No Trespassing" and "Stay Out" signs hanging around the necks of many.

Jesus ignores the social norms that spell out the who, when, and where of social interaction. In fact, when the Herodians and Pharisees try to trap him on the question of taxes, they preface their tricky question with some flattery: "You are sincere and show *deference* to no one; for you do not regard people with *partiality*, but teach the way of God" . . . (Mark 12:14, emphasis added). In other words, Jesus ignored social boxes. He ignored the cultural labels and invaded the social boxes.

Purebred Pedigrees

In modern societies personal identity is largely shaped by individual accomplishment and choices. Occupations, lifestyles, and hobbies reflect and define individual identity. In ancient society, personal identity was completely wrapped up in tribe, family, and group. Individualism, as known in the modern world, simply didn't exist. One's tribe, one's people were all that mattered. For example, all the members of a thief's family could expect revenge from the community, not just the thief. Group identity completely overshadowed personal identity. Moreover, some groups were pure and others, according to religious standards, were dirty.

One of the boxes Jesus shattered was ethnic purity. Racial purity was crucial in Palestinian culture.[1] People were careful not to contaminate family lines by marrying a person with bad blood. Purebred pedigrees weren't just a genealogical hobby. They determined one's civil rights in Hebrew culture. A clean pedigree was required to participate in court and to hold a public office. In short, a pure family tree was a ticket to power and influence.

The thoroughbreds—priests, Levites, and others who could prove their pure lineage—lived at the top of the checkerboard. In a box below were the slightly blemished Jews, often illegitimate descendants of priests and proselytes. Much lower were those gravely blemished—the bastards, eunuchs, and persons without known fathers. Gentile slaves were exiled to a box by themselves. Although circumcised, they weren't part of the Jewish community. Dumped in the worst box—below the checkerboard—were Samaritans. These rigid social rankings shaped daily interaction in ancient Palestine.

Breaking Gentile Boxes

On top of the smaller boxes were two large ones—Jew and Gentile. Jews treated Gentiles with the same contempt and animosity as they did Samaritans. The Gentiles were unclean outsiders. They were pagans who contaminated the purity of ceremonial ritual. Jews avoided Gentiles, whom they called "wild dogs." They were careful not to let Gentiles tarnish them in everyday life. Early Hebrew Scriptures envision Abraham's blessing touching all nations. In the first pages of the books of Moses, Gentiles receive the divine blessing. By the time of Jesus, however, that vision had vanished. To most Jews, Gentiles were pagan dogs who polluted racial purity.

We left a riddle dangling in chapter five when Jesus announced his kingdom in the synagogue. Luke reports that after Jesus' inaugural speech, "All in the synagogue were filled with rage. They got up and drove him out of the town, and led him to the brow of the hill on which their town was built, so that they might hurl him off the cliff" (Luke 4:28-29). Why did the crowd explode with anger?

Reminding them prophets are not welcome in their own country, Jesus told two stories. There were many widows in Israel in the days of Elijah, he said. But in the time of famine, Elijah didn't visit a pedigreed Jewish widow. He was sent to a Gentile widow in the land of Sidon for help. The second story has the same opening and punch line. There were many lepers in Israel at the time of Elisha the prophet. But it was Naaman, a Gentile Syrian, who was cleansed.

The message sliced through Jewish pride. It stirred rage because belonging to Israel gave no one a special right to healing. Having a pure pedigree offers no perks in God's kingdom. Jubilee news is good news for all. In two swift strokes, Jesus cut through the crowd's ethnicity. He shattered their tribal pride. He demolished national identity.

The original Jubilee vision applied only to Hebrews. Gentile slaves and debts weren't released in the seventh year. Hebrews could charge Gentiles interest on loans. Jews expected God's vengeance to fall on Gentiles. Now in a split second, Jesus puts the Gentile community on par with Israel.[2]

Exclusive membership cards, it turns out, are unthinkable in the upside-down kingdom. God's favorable year, the day of salvation, applies to *all*. Jesus shreds the patriotism of the synagogue audience. His words sting. They smash ethnic pride. Outraged, the crowd tries to shove him over a cliff to his death.[3]

The implications are clear. The new kingdom stretches beyond the Jewish nation. Again in Mark's Gospel, Jesus includes unclean Gentiles in the kingdom. Couched between Mark 6:30 and 8:30 are symbolic signs of Gentile inclusion in the kingdom.[4] The sequence begins with Jesus feeding the five thousand. Later that night, he walks on the water and announces, "It is I." The Messiah is here. The water-walking feat astonishes the disciples. But they miss the spiritual meaning of the bread and the picnic.

Next the Pharisees quarrel with Jesus for refusing to wash before eating. Then Jesus enters Gentile territory. A widow rebuffs him when he refuses to heal her child. In her reply she calls him Lord. Amazed that she recognizes his lordship, he casts the demon out of her child.

Now a new sequence begins. Jesus moves to a Gentile region on the east side of Lake Galilee and heals a deaf mute. Another feeding of 4,000, another controversy with the Pharisees over a sign, and another discussion with the disciples about bread ensue. Jesus asks his disciples if they understand the significance of the numbers. A blind man receives sight after two touches from Jesus. This is followed by Peter's declaration: Jesus is the Christ!

The incidents in these chapters come in twos. Two feedings. Two sides of the lake. Two boat rides. Two discussions of bread. Two controversies with the Pharisees. Two healings. Two touches. Two sets of numbers with two feedings. What do the numbers mean?

The first feeding of five thousand involves five loaves. Twelve baskets are left over. It's on the western side of the lake—the Jewish side. There are five books of Moses and twelve tribes of Israel. This is the Jewish feeding. Everyday bread is broken for the hungry five thousand. Yet the bread's significance is profound. It's prophetic bread. The Messiah's own life is about to be broken for the life of his own Jewish people. After this feeding Jesus announces on the water, "It is I" (Mark 6:50). The same utterance appears in Exodus 3:14 when God declares, "I AM WHO I AM." According to Mark, Jesus is telling the disciples that Almighty God is in their midst. The Messiah is among them here and now! Had they understood the symbolic feeding, the water-walking Messiah wouldn't have shocked them. But they missed the signals.

More Signs and Surprises

The next episode finds the Pharisees quarreling with Jesus about his improper ceremonial cleansing. They reject this prophet who mocks their rites and rituals. So Jesus moves on to Gentile turf in the land of Tyre and Sidon (Mark 7:24-30; Matt. 15:21-28). He tries to evade the public eye, but a courageous woman begs him to exorcise a demon from her daughter. She pleads with Jesus to heal her child. He stalls and turns away. She persists.

Finally Jesus defends his hesitation with a Jewish proverb, "It is not fair to take the children's food and throw it to the dogs," meaning the Gentiles. Jesus tells her it's unwise to share the Jewish Messiah with Gentiles. But she courageously uses his own proverb to argue back: "Sir, even the dogs under the table eat the children's crumbs" (Mark 7:28). She acknowledges his authority, and Jesus heals her child.

The upside-down moment, once more filled with irony and paradox, arrives. A Gentile woman, of all people, receives healing for her daughter. In the feeding of the five thousand, Jesus symbolically announced his messianic mission. But both the disciples and the Pharisees were blind and deaf to the good news. Yet here on Gentile turf a pagan woman calls him Messiah. She sees and hears!

Then Jesus pushes eastward to the Decapolis, a circle of ten Gentile cities. Here he heals a deaf mute, another sign that the Gentiles hear. This miracle leads to the second feeding.

The new feeding involves a new set of numbers—seven loaves, seven baskets of leftovers, and four thousand people. Is it just another feeding? In contrast to the first one, this luncheon is on the eastern side of the lake—the Gentile side. Seven is the biblical symbol for wholeness, completeness, and perfection. Seven completes the Jubilee cycle. Four represents the four corners of the earth. It signifies the time when people from east, west, north, and south will come to eat the salvation banquet. In the second feeding the messianic bread is broken for all humankind. This complete and perfect messianic meal includes the Gentiles and all other peoples.

Irony visits again. After the picnic the Pharisees come to Jesus begging for a sign, for a symbol. Amid all these symbols, they don't see; neither do they hear! After breaking Jewish bread for the five thousand, the Pharisees pester Jesus about washing before eating. And now, after the Gentile feeding, they come asking for a sign! The disciples are in the same boat. Like the Pharisees, they too are deaf and blind to the symbolic meaning of the numbers (Mark 8:17-21).

Jesus tries again when a blind man cries out for healing. Jesus touches him and asks, "Do you see anything?" The man replies, "I can see people, but they look like trees, walking" (Mark 8:24). Jesus touches him again. Now he sees everything clearly. Two touches: one yields fog, the other sight. The Pharisees and the disciples had foggy eyes and plugged-up ears. They weren't hearing and seeing the messianic announcement.

Ironically, things had been perfectly clear to the Gentile woman, even before the second feeding. Suddenly, now even Peter begins to hear and see. The numbers start to click, the fog clears. "You—" he stammers in amazement. "You are the Messiah!" (Mark 8:29).

In the rich symbolism of these passages, Mark points us to Jesus' embrace of the Gentiles. Parts of the message arise from Jesus' own words and parts flow from Mark's editorial work. But the message is plain. Jesus has shattered the social boxes. Jews and Gentiles march arm-in-arm into the new kingdom.

In another instance a Roman centurion—commander of 100 men—asks Jesus to heal his servant (Matt. 8:5-13, Luke 7:1-10). The centurion doesn't speak to Jesus directly in Luke's account. But he makes clear he believes Jesus can heal his assistant from a distance. The commander's faith impresses Jesus. Without going to the man's home, Jesus cures the subordinate and exclaims, "Truly, I tell you, in no one in Israel have I found such faith" (Matt. 8:10).

A Gentile army officer displays greater faith than the religious leaders of Israel. This is upside down indeed! At the end of the incident Matthew reports Jesus saying, "I tell you, many will come from east and west and will eat with Abraham, Isaac, and Jacob in the kingdom of heaven, while the heirs of the kingdom will be thrown into the outer darkness; where there will be weeping and gnashing of teeth" (Matt. 8:11-12). In the upside-down kingdom Gentiles come from the four corners of the earth while some sons and daughters of Abraham are barred from the banquet.

Jesus meets another Gentile, the chain-snapping demoniac. He roamed in the country of the Gerasenes, Gentile turf east of the Sea of Galilee. Mark says the demoniac worshiped Jesus and called him "Son of the Most High God." After Jesus exorcises the demons, he tells the man, "Go home to your friends, and tell them how much the Lord has done for you" (Mark 5:19). This contrasts with Jewish healings, where Jesus warns the healed to hush up and tell no one!

So we see Jesus engaging three Gentiles: the Syrophoenician woman, the Roman centurion, and the Gerasene demoniac. Not only were they Gentiles; gender, politics, and illness stigmatized them. We hear two of them, the woman and the demoniac, confessing Jesus as the Messiah. The centurion receives the "Great Faith" award, and Jesus urges the demoniac to spread the good news. The upside-down movement is growing. The kingdom is breaking in among the Gentiles!

The Gentile vision flashes through the Gospels in other places as well. Jesus sends out seventy missionaries, a number symbolizing the wholeness and completeness of his mission (Luke 10:1). He instructs the disciples to be light and salt, not just within Judaism but in the whole world (Matt. 5:13-14). He chases the money changers from the temple's outer court so it can be a house of prayer for *all* nations (Mark 11:17). Jesus' earthly sojourn begins and ends in "Galilee of the Gentiles" where his disciples receive a final mandate to go and make disciples of all nations (Matt. 28:19).

Others also witness to the multiethnic vision of the kingdom. Matthew sees Jesus' ministry fulfilling the words of Isaiah: "I will put my Spirit upon him, and he shall proclaim justice to the Gentiles. . . . And in his name will the Gentiles hope (Matt. 12:18, 21).[5] Devout Simeon, seeing the babe in the temple, says this salvation was "prepared in the presence of *all* peoples, a light for revelation to the Gentiles" (Luke 2:31-32, emphasis added). John the Baptist prepared the way in the wilderness so that "*all* flesh shall see the salvation of God" (Luke 3:6, emphasis added).

There can be no doubt. The new kingdom transcends Hebrew boxes. This is clear in the Acts of the apostles as well. Paul's concept of justification involves social reconciliation of Jew and Gentile in the community of faith.[6] The social barricades between Jew and Gentile crumble in the presence of Jesus, the Messiah, and they continue to crack in the early church.

Shattering Samaritan Boxes

We've already noted the barrier between Jews and Samaritans. Jesus shatters this ethnic wall as well. Striking at Jewish pride in the story of the Good Samaritan, Jesus holds up a Samaritan, not a Jew, as the supreme example of agape love. This was earthshaking because Samaritans were, by social definition, "bad." Another Samaritan, whom Jesus called a foreigner, was *the* only one of ten lepers to return and give thanks for a healing. This thankful half-breed was the sole recipient of Jesus' blessing (Luke 17:16-19).

The last place a Jewish rabbi wanted to be found was in a Samaritan village. But on his way to Jerusalem, Jesus, the upside-down rabbi, entered Samaritan turf. With daring irreverence for social boxes, he struck up a conversation with a sleazy Samaritan woman (John 4:7). In a related incident, some Samaritans incensed the disciples by denying them and Jesus lodging. The box-conscious Samaritans couldn't permit a Jew in their backyard, especially not one headed for the rival temple in Jerusalem. So they kicked him out. Undisturbed, Jesus refused to comply when some of his disciples, "the Sons of Thunder," asked him to torch the Samaritan village with fire from heaven (Luke 9:55).

The record is clear. Jesus doesn't bypass Samaritans just because of their name tags. He boldly walks on their turf. He engages them. He loves them.

Welcoming Women

It's difficult to grasp the dismal status of women in Hebrew culture. They were stashed at the bottom with slaves and children. Male and female boxes were different as day and night.[7] One of the six major divisions of the Mishnah is devoted entirely to rules about women. None of the divisions, of course, deal exclusively with men. The Mishnah section on uncleanness has seventy-nine legal paragraphs on the ritual contamination caused by menstruation!

Women were excluded from public life. They belonged at home. When walking outside the house, they covered themselves with two veils to conceal their identity. A chief priest in Jerusalem didn't even recognize his own mother when he accused her of adultery. Strict women covered themselves at home so even the rafters wouldn't see a hair of their head! Even in public places they were to remain unseen. Social custom prohibited men from being alone with women outside the home. Men dared not look at married women or even greet them in the street. A woman could be divorced for simply talking to a man in public. Public life belonged to men.

Young girls were engaged around twelve years of age and married a year later. A father could sell his daughter into slavery or force her to marry anyone of his choice before she was twelve. After this age she couldn't be married against her will. The father of the bride typically received a considerable gift of money from his new son-in-law. Because of this, daughters were considered a source of cheap labor and profit.

In the house, the woman was confined to domestic chores. She was virtually a slave to her husband, washing his face, hands, and feet. Considered the same as a Gentile slave, a wife was obligated to obey her husband as she would a master. If death threatened, the husband's life must be saved first. Under Jewish law, the husband alone had the right to divorce.

The wife's most important function was making male babies. Her womb was the temporary garden where the husband planted *his* seed. The absence of children was considered divine punishment. There was joy in the home at the birth of a boy. Sorrow greeted a baby girl. A daily prayer repeated by men intoned, "Blessed be God that hath not made me a woman."[8] A woman was subject to many taboos in the Torah. Girls couldn't study the Holy Law—the Torah. Women couldn't approach the Holy of Holies in the temple. In the temple plaza, they couldn't enter the Court of Israelites—the exclusive domain of men. During their monthly purification from menstruation, they were excluded from even the Women's Court on the temple plaza.

Women were forbidden to teach. They couldn't pronounce the benediction after a meal. They were barred as witnesses in court for they were generally considered liars. Even linguistic structure reflected the low status of females. The Hebrew adjectives for "pious," "just," and "holy" do not have a feminine form in the Hebrew Scriptures.

In this context, Jesus knowingly overturns social custom when he allows women to follow him in public.[9] His interaction with women shows he views them as equal with men before God. In a stunning, outrageous upheaval, he declares that female harlots may enter the kingdom of God before religious male leaders (Matt. 21:31). The prominence of women in the Gospels as well as Jesus' interaction with them shows his irreverence for sexual boxes. Without hesitation, he violates social norms to elevate women to a new dignity and a higher status.

Consider a few examples of Jesus' upside-down attitude toward women. The most striking is his talk with the Samaritan woman at Jacob's well (John 4:1-42). Samaria was sandwiched between two Jewish areas: Galilee to the north and Judea to the south. Jews moving between these areas often bypassed Samaria to avoid attack.

In this instance, Jesus takes the shortcut and walks through Samaria. He waits alone, by a well, while the disciples buy food in a nearby village. A person approaches with three stigmas hanging around her neck: woman, Samaritan, flirt. Jesus asks her for a drink. In a split second he shatters all the rules designed to prevent such behavior. Jesus isn't merely being polite. His simple request slices through six social norms.

In the first place, Jesus violates turf rules. He has no business being here. Samaria is outside the Jewish box. Jesus has wandered into enemy territory controlled by a rival religion.

Second, she's a woman. Men weren't to even look at women in public, much less talk with them. The rabbis said, "A man should hold no conversation with a woman in the street, not even with his own wife, still less with any other woman, lest men should gossip."[10] Woman she may be, but Jesus addresses her. This makes him vulnerable. Anyone approaching the well and seeing the conversation could ruin his reputation. He doesn't care. He cares more for the person than his reputation.

Third, this isn't just another woman. She's having her sixth affair. She's a promiscuous flirt. Everyone in town knows her number. Rabbis and holy men scurry from such women. Jesus doesn't run. He takes a risk; he puts his career on the line by asking for her help.

Fourth, she's not only promiscuous, she's a Samaritan. Jewish rabbis said Samaritan women were menstruants from the cradle and thus perpetually unclean. Jewish social norms were clear: look the other way. Avoid her. Act as though you don't see her. Jesus boldly shatters the social barricades.

Fifth, he addresses her. He initiates the conversation. Things would be less obnoxious if he had responded to a plea from her. But he is the beggar. He obligates himself by asking something of her.

Finally, and worst of all, he *deliberately* defiles himself. As a supposed menstruant from the cradle, she was unclean. Anything she touches becomes unclean. A whole Jewish village was declared unclean if a Samaritan woman entered it. By asking for dirty water, which she has touched, Jesus is intentionally polluting himself. The religious rule was clear: "Stay as far away as possible from unclean things." His brief request mocks the norms of purity.

Jesus was completely out of place in every way—doing the wrong thing with the wrong person in the wrong place. Yes, merely saying, "Give me a drink," shattered six social norms regulating gender, religion, purity, and ethnicity.

Such unprecedented behavior startled the woman and the disciples. She stammered, "How is it that you, a Jew, ask a drink of me, a woman of Samaria?" When the disciples returned, they were also shocked and "astonished that he was speaking with a woman" (John 4:9, 27). His simple request cut the social trappings that separate people and bind them in their boxes.

It all began with water—the one element of life all humans need, regardless of their box. When it comes to water we're all equals. As the living water, Jesus provides life for all. No other person in the Gospels received Jesus' private disclosure of his messianic identity. Jesus reveals himself not to the chief priests in Jerusalem, not to the members of the Sanhedrin, nor to the scribes—but to this promiscuous half-breed. She asks about the Messiah. And Jesus tersely responds, "I am he."

How upside down! A defiled woman from a rival religion receives the highest honor—hearing the Messianic confession in first person. Jesus not only cuts through social red tape to ask for a drink, he lifts this defiled woman up to the privileged holy of holies and whispers, "I am the Messiah." God is with you. What a flip-flop!

This miracle moves Samaritan villagers to beg Jesus to stay with them. Beyond all dreams the unheard-of happens. Enemies fellowship and eat together. Many believe. They switch temples, not from

Mount Gerizim to Jerusalem, but to the living temple of spirit and truth. And it is this new church of Samaritan half-breeds that then declares, "This is truly the Savior of the world" (John 4:42). Not the Savior of the Jews, but the Savior of *all*. The despised, the outlaws, the enemies—Jesus pulls them from their boxes and elevates them to authentic personhood and dignity in his kingdom of surprises.

In another meeting with a woman already noted in chapter seven, we find things upside down again. A prostitute anoints Jesus at a Pharisee luncheon (Luke 7:36-39). The term *Messiah* means "The Anointed One." Jesus, the Messiah, is anointed by a woman— a prostitute. The woman, overwhelmed by his forgiving love, takes the tainted perfume of her trade (worth a year's wages) and anoints him. Perfume was used to prepare bodies for burial. This outcast simultaneously anoints the Messiah and signals his death. A woman has the honor of anointing the Messiah! Religious boxes shatter again!

On another occasion, a woman with a twelve-year hemorrhage (Mark 5:25-34) touches Jesus. Mark reports she suffered under many physicians, had spent all her money, and was getting worse. Such a person was considered filthy and ceremonially unclean. Leviticus purity laws viewed her as a perpetual menstruant (Lev. 15:26-27). Her touch infected others. Moreover, anyone touching what she touched became polluted. The contamination could only be removed by ceremonial washing. She finds a different attitude in Jesus. In a daring move, she touches the edge of his coat and is healed.

The typical rabbi would have cursed the filthy woman and scampered for ceremonial cleansing. Jesus invites her to come forward not for a rebuke but for a blessing. "Daughter, your faith has made you well; go in peace, and be healed of your disease" (Mark 5:34). Jesus understands her agony. Despite her stigma, he loves her.

In another episode, Luke reports Jesus' compassion for a widow as he comes upon a funeral. The dead man is the widow's only son. When a man died, his property went to the eldest son, not the wife. If there were no sons, the youngest brother of the dead husband often married the widow; but he had the right to refuse.

In that case the widow became an object of charity with no means of support. The death of this widow's only son means financial uncertainty for her—possibly poverty. Jesus, moved with compassion, raises her son to life.

Luke, who seems to have a special interest in Jesus' relationship with women, tells another story (Luke 10:38-42). Jesus is about to dine with Martha and Mary. Like a good Jewish domestic, Martha is engulfed in kitchen duties. Women were household servants; they were forbidden to study the Torah or to converse with rabbis. Mary breaks from her culturally prescribed role. She forgets the kitchen. She enjoys Jesus' teaching. This peeves Martha. Perhaps both Mary's impropriety and the extra work in the kitchen anger her.

In a few words, Jesus redefines the role of Jewish women. He chides Martha for fretting about Mary's deviance. Mary, he says, has chosen the "better part." She is fully human, entitled to think, able to engage in intellectual discourse. The message is clear: women belong in the human box. They're more than domestic servants.

Some women accompanied Jesus' band of disciples. As he preached the good news of the kingdom, Mary Magdalene, Joanna, and Susanna were among the many who accompanied him. Luke notes that these women helped support the disciple's band financially (Luke 8:1-3). The Greek wording of this passage suggests the women were deaconesses.

By permitting women to travel with him in public and listen to his teaching, Jesus was overturning other social boulders. Esteemed tradition said women were only to walk in public if they had domestic errands. They weren't to wander in the countryside. They had no business studying and discussing religious matters.

Moreover, to travel in a mixed group made them sexually suspect. The other great rabbis never permitted women to follow them or listen to their teaching. One teacher said it was better to burn the law than to let a woman study it. By permitting women to join his disciple band, Jesus upset social and religious protocol. Gender boxes were crumbling with the arrival of the kingdom.

Surprisingly the Gospels portray women as the most loyal disciples. Tough Peter swore he'd never chicken out. But under pressure, he ran for cover—denying any association with Jesus as the rooster crowed. The male disciples fell asleep or slipped away when crunch time came in Gethsemane (Mark 14:50). The women, courageously, persisted to the bitter end. All four Gospels note that the women, who followed from Galilee, watched the bloody crucifixion (Matt. 27:55; Mark 15:40; Luke 23:49; John 19:25). They didn't abandon Jesus in the moment of crisis and they soon had their reward. The resurrection was first announced to them—to women. Mary Magdalene was honored as the first person to see Jesus after the crucifixion (John 20:11-18). When the disciples heard the women's tale of Jesus' resurrection, Luke notes they scoffed because the "words seemed to them an idle tale, and they did not believe them" (Luke 24:11).

The upside-down moment strikes again. Women, barred from Jewish courts because they were considered liars, are first witnesses of the resurrection. These so-called "liars" certify the spectacular moment. They have the distinctive honor of announcing the victory. Untrustworthy women become the heralds of the upside-down kingdom. Meanwhile the men refuse to believe the story.

Beyond his face-to-face encounters with women, Jesus also includes them in his teaching. In an earlier chapter we saw him highlight a widow as a model giver. He uses female imagery to describe his compassion for Jerusalem. "How often have I wanted to gather your children together as a hen gathers her brood under her wings, and you were not willing!" (Matt. 23:37). In another instance Jesus compares God to a woman looking for a coin (Luke 15:8-10). Male interpreters have overemphasized the lostness of the coin. But there's another side to this penny. God is like a woman who diligently searches—who doesn't give up looking until she finds it. She embodies divine compassion.

By word and by deed Jesus confers a new dignity on women. One confesses him as Lord (Matt. 15:22-28). He spills his messianic secret to another (John 4:26). A woman is the only person to anoint him as Messiah (Luke 7:38). And women, of all people, are chosen to certify the resurrection. In a male-dominated culture, amid patriarchy blessed by religion, these were shocking signs that women had a new status in the upside-down kingdom.

Inviting Outsiders and Nobodies

The calling of the twelve apostles offers a fascinating instance of unboxing. In this motley crew we find Matthew, a tax collector. Jewish tax collectors, working for the Romans, were considered outright traitors—especially by patriotic rebels. Matthew apparently stopped collecting taxes to follow Jesus, for Luke says he left all (Luke 5:28). Another disciple was Simon the Zealot (Luke 6:15). It's possible that other disciples were former rebels or at least shared their sympathies. James and John, "Sons of Thunder," Judas Iscariot, and Simon Peter are likely prospects with rebel connections.

In any event, Simon the Zealot, a political rebel, would have eagerly overthrown the Romans before he met Jesus. Joining the disciple band required repentance and a change of loyalties. Matthew the tax collector and Simon the Zealot came from opposite ends of the political checkerboard. Simon likely had harassed his share of tax collectors.

Now, political opponents are walking and sleeping together. Unheard of!! What a mighty witness to the unboxing that occurs when Jesus is Lord. Old labels and tags are torn off. Former enemies stand together as friends in a new kingdom, under new lordship.

Political adversaries also come together at the cross of Jesus. One of the bandits hanging beside Jesus is moved by his forgiving love. This rebel confesses his faith and asks Jesus to remember him. That very day, Jesus assures him, he will be in paradise (Luke 23:43). The crucifixion also overwhelms the Roman centurion, exterminator of Jewish rebels. He is terrified and exclaims: "Truly this man was God's Son!" (Matt. 27:54). Bandits and centurion, lawbreaker and law keeper, find themselves face-to-face with Jesus in between.

The boxes of occupation, power, and wealth often overlap. Jesus moves around the Palestinian checkerboard with little care for social labels. He converses with Nicodemus, a ruler of the Pharisees. Joseph of Arimathea, a rich, silent sympathizer, donates a tomb. The daughter of Jairus, ruler of a synagogue, is healed. The Roman centurion's request is honored. Rich Zacchaeus has a surprise guest for lunch. Doctors of the law debate with him. The rich young ruler challenges him. Magi, astrologers from afar, visit the manger. People of wealth, prestige, and influence seek him out. They perceive an unusual openness. Jesus accepts them, regardless of the tag on their box. These folks live in the big boxes at the top, but Jesus goes beyond the high and mighty.

Jesus goes to the bottom and interacts with the lowly. Shepherds as well as wise men visit the manger. Herding sheep was a dirty and despised occupation. The wealthy living in Jerusalem hired shepherds to watch their flocks in the countryside. But shepherds were suspect. They were considered dishonest for several reasons. Sometimes they led their flocks on other people's land. Sometimes they sold milk and young animals on the sly and pocketed the cash. Indeed it was forbidden to buy wool, milk, and kids from shepherds because they often embezzled the money. Some rabbis called herding the *most* disreputable occupation.[11]

By now surprises should no longer surprise us. Angels sang the good news of God's incarnation not to priests in the golden temple but to scoundrel shepherds in a Bethlehem field. From beginning to end, from start to finish, the thread of inversion and irony weaves its ways through the gospel. Mary believes the angel but Zechariah, the patriarch, doubts the angel's message. Shepherds hear the good news first. In parabolic form Jesus compares God to a shepherd who wiggles through thorny thickets to find a lost lamb. Jesus even calls himself a *Good* Shepherd, underscoring their negative reputation. Women certify the resurrection. Stigmatized occupations receive honor in the upside-down kingdom. Again and again, at every turn, Jesus upends our social boxes.

Jesus accompanies fishermen who enjoy moderate prestige. He pounds nails himself as a carpenter. But he spends most of his time with the masses—the poor and the sick. Although he relates to all sorts of people, the Gospels show Jesus' special care for those branded with stigma. His network includes the demoniacs, the blind, the deaf, the lame, the ill, the paralyzed, prostitutes, tax collectors, sinners, adulterers, widows, lepers, Samaritans, women, and Gentiles. In short, a big band of nobodies from nowhere.[12]

Although he spans the entire checkerboard, Jesus spends much of his time with outcasts. These were the throwaways—dumped on the social trash pile. Instead of spitting on them, as most people do, Jesus touches them, loves them, and names them God's people. Table fellowship in Palestine involved ritual meals that reflected the boxes and ladders of status and stigma. The meals marked social boundaries—they included some and excluded others. Jesus' fellowship with social outcasts turned the rules of table fellowship upside-down. Everyone was welcome at his table!

Jesus' words underscore his commitment. Again and again he recites the same catalog of people: the poor, the blind, the lame, the oppressed. They pop up in his inaugural sermon. He mentions them when John's disciples probe his messianic identity. He welcomes them at the banquet when the invited guests refuse to come. He tells us to invite them, instead of friends, to our meals.

In the final judgment scene they reappear again. People are rewarded or damned for their response to the hungry, the thirsty, the naked, the stranger, the prisoner, and the sick (Matt. 25:31-46). In the East these words stir images of the dead.[13] These are folks without hope. These are people overwhelmed with suffering. Life for them is too miserable to be called life. Jesus brings life to these who are as good as dead. He brings healing, hearing, walking, talking, sanity, purity, and freedom. These images of transformation signal the age of salvation. The Messiah is here. Restoration is complete. *Now* is the favorable year of the Lord.

The spirit of Jesus penetrates social boxes. Barricades of suspicion, mistrust, stigma, and hate crumble in his presence. He also invites us to see human beings behind the labels of stigma. His kingdom transcends all boundaries. He welcomes people from all boxes. God's love overpowers the social customs which divide, separate, and isolate. All are invited to the table in the new kingdom. None are pushed aside or excluded. Jesus' broad welcome lies at the heart of the gospel. Reconciliation forms its core. This good news melts spiritual barriers between humans and God and dismantles walls between people. The agape of Jesus reaches out to boxed-up people, tells them God's love washes away their stigma, and welcomes them into a new community.[14]

The Dog and the Checkerboard Tail

Once again a dog-and-tail question faces us. How does the dog of faith relate to the tail of social interaction? Does our faith make a difference in our social relationships? Or do customary social patterns wag our theology? Does Christian faith nudge us toward boxes marked "Keep Out" and "Undesirable"? Or do we play social checkers like everybody else—interacting with those who are like us and politely obeying the "No Trespassing" signs hanging on the necks of weirdos? Do our pious slogans keep us from others—"To each his own" or "Never trust a stranger"? When this happens, the tail of social custom wags the dog of faith.

God has created us as social beings. Boxing and labeling others are natural social processes. They organize social life and make it predictable. But these social routines can demean and dehumanize. God's Spirit can redeem our attitudes and enable us to see the people behind the labels. In this way God transforms our social interaction. This doesn't mean we'll live without boxes. However, it does mean we won't allow social labels to block our love and care for others.

How do the people of God relate to each other? How do our social relations transform? Do we label others like everyone else? Many of the labels we learn in society we bring along to church. We often relate to other members of the body of Christ on the basis of their social tags. We see them as doctors, secretaries, professors, Mexicans, students, Republicans, Democrats, or females rather than as siblings in the family of God. These external tags often shape our interaction even in the church.

Informal networks in the church form around common occupational, educational, and theological interests. Charismatics cling to each other. Members of the local country club huddle and chat after the worship service. The college crowd sticks together. The elderly sit near each other in the pews. The snowmobilers and waterskiers flock together. "Committed" members, involved in the leadership of church, interact with each other. Clusters and cliques emerge. The number and type of subgroups vary from parish to parish, but careful observers can detect them in every religious setting. Beneath the surface, these informal networks regulate the flow of congregational life.

Subgroup formation isn't all bad. Even mature birds with common feathers need to flock together. We gain security in circles of commonality. But we also need to transform our social clusters. They offer us needed security, but they can also fragment congregational life. They can become exclusive cliques—divisive ghettos of gossip. Controversies related to pastoral leadership, buildings, theology, educational curriculum, and the like often stem from subgroup loyalties.

Several steps can hasten the redemption of social clusters. First, we need to openly recognize their inevitability. We do need them and they can nurture our faith as long as they don't become exclusive and divisive.

Second, teaching and preaching ministries ought to call people to a common faith in Jesus Christ that transcends social ties. Is our common bond of unity in Christ stronger than the social glue that holds small cliques together? This is precisely the genius of the gospel—diverse people from all sorts of boxes joining together in Jesus Christ.

This doesn't mean people jump completely out of their boxes. It does mean that in the new kingdom social boxes should mesh in a complementary way. Fellow Christians need each other. The intellectuals need the charismatics. The fundamentalists need the social activists. The young need the old. The complementary nature of the different clusters builds up the whole community so the *entire* body matures in Jesus Christ. The apostle Paul's analogy of the body applies to subgroups as well as to individuals. Social clusters need each other to keep things in balance.

Third, we can as individuals seek ways to crisscross established boundaries. We can venture beyond our boxes. We can sit in different pews in the worship service. We can invite people from other boxes to our homes. We can join in churchwide activities. We can visit folks with labels different than our own.

Finally, we can alter patterns of congregational life to open our boxes. Time for social interaction is necessary to pull off masks and peel off labels. Weekend or daylong congregational retreats in a different setting help to shake up old patterns and build new relationships. More unboxing can happen in a three-day retreat than in fifty-two Sundays of bench warming. Work projects, involving a variety of ages, are great community builders that can also serve the needs of others.

In an age of specialization the church has developed unique activities for those with special needs—the elderly, teens, adoptive parents, singles, disabled, professionals, and the like. Although these are helpful, we also need times when folks of all stripes mix together in congregational life.

One congregation upset the routine in their church school this way. One quarter of each year, classes formed around common birthdays. All the October babies, for example, met together for twelve Sundays. In this way young and old, male and female, Democrat, Republican, and others studied together. The rest of the year they returned to their typical classes. Such creative ventures break down walls, build understanding, and embellish the common life of the body.

Although we must unlatch the doors that shut us off from others, we do need social boxes for our emotional well-being. We need caring networks of others who listen to our frustrations, doubts, and hassles. We may find the warmest acceptance among those most like us. They understand and care best because they identify with our problems. Although Jesus straddled the social checkerboard of his day, he also had an inner circle of three. Peter, James, and John witnessed the transfiguration and huddled closely with Jesus in Gethsemane. We too need the close fellowship of similar others as we use our special gifts to minister to the whole body. We need a healthy tension between our natural tendency to snuggle up to similar others and the inclusive spirit of Jesus' that accepts others regardless of social status.

Church Boxes and Welcome Mats

Churches as well as people carry labels. Denominations carve out unique historical identities. Songs, practices, and creeds articulate a denominations' history and identity. Religious schools, publications, and conferences sharpen the consciousness of a people and shape a denominational identity. Catholics act so and so. A good Presbyterian thinks so and so.

Specialized words in a denominational culture acquire secret meanings, known only to the insiders—"confirmation," "second work of grace," "friendship evangelism," "discipleship," "missional." Such words can become codes that stir the passions of insiders who know their secret meanings but leave outsiders cold.

It's natural for churches to cultivate a sense of common solidarity and identity. A common social glue sharpens members' sense of belonging. They know who they are, where they're from, and where they're going. Members have a place, a group—a people. Traditions and identities however good, can also create problems. They can become idolatrous, demanding more respect than the Scriptures themselves. Thick ethnicity can cloud the centrality of Jesus Christ. The biblical Jesus can easily become a denominational Jesus—a Baptist Savior, a Mennonite Lord, and an Episcopal Creator. Denominational glue can clog the free exchange of love and cooperation among denominations.

Most seriously, denominational traditions can barricade others from the kingdom. We've already heard Jesus' indictment of the Pharisees. Too much denominational glue frightens others away. Strange words, odd rites, and obsolete traditions obscure the welcome sign. A sharp theological identity and distinctive practices are essential for a vigorous church, but they must be balanced with programs that welcome newcomers.

One of the dilemmas faced by growing churches is that birds of a common feather do flock together. Lower-class folk feel at home in congregations with those of kindred class. Upscale congregations attract the well heeled from upper-class backgrounds. Hispanics feel most at home when worship springs from Hispanic culture. Professionals migrate toward congregations which enjoy endless heady talk.

Should congregations focus their efforts on homogeneous neighborhoods that match the congregation's own racial, social, and economic profile? This may be a sound strategy if the only goal is a surge in attendance. Although the easiest route to growth often involves attracting similar people, the message of social reconciliation can easily be lost. Simply getting the same kind of people together is no real great feat. It happens all the time in all sorts of organizations and service clubs. If the gospel transforms social relationships, if the church is to be more than just another Rotary Club, then spiritual and social reconciliation need to spearhead its ministry.

In the genius of the gospel, when people declare Jesus as Lord, they experience a new unity that transcends social boxes. True church growth uses the best insights from social science to call *different* kinds of people together under a common Lord. A gospel which only attracts similar people blurs the good news that bonds Jew and Gentile, male and female, black and white.

This doesn't mean we ignore social characteristics. Just the opposite. We take them seriously as real ingredients in congregational life, but we also search for a delicate balance between sameness and difference. Our natural tendency is to flock toward other birds like ourselves. The good news of Jesus Christ, however, welcomes all, regardless of their feathers.

11

Low Is High

The Social Ladder

In the last chapter we viewed human interaction on a social checkerboard. Social life, however, isn't flat. People and groups rank themselves from low to high. We can capture this vertical dimension of life with the image of a social ladder. People aren't equal. Some are more important and distinguished than others. Inequality, in one form or another, pervades all societies. Pecking orders are deeply embedded in human experience throughout the world. This chapter explores Jesus' views on power, status, and inequality.

Some folks prefer to smile sweetly and think that, after all, everyone is equal. But think again. Society has layers. A mother with a daughter who graduates from law school bubbles with pride when she talks with friends about her daughter's achievement. The same mother is embarrassed to report that another child has dropped out of high school.

Let's face it—the chair of a committee has more power than rank-and-file members. Episcopalians are higher on the ladder of denominations than Pentecostals. Pastors of large congregations outrank those of small churches. Hispanics, becoming the largest ethnic group in America, wield more political influence on American politics than the Amish. Cities, churches, ethnic groups, occupations, and people are ranked and layered in our minds. Superpower nations tower over small underdeveloped countries.

Social ranking shrinks the value of some people and expands the worth of others. We value folks for their ability to perform a certain job. Presidents, doctors, and managers are typically considered more valuable than shoe shiners, dishwashers, and typists.

Our weekly paychecks underscore this harsh fact. We're paid according to socially determined values. Our paycheck reminds us how much we're worth. It's difficult to sort out the difference between one's personal and financial value. Our view of others leans heavily on their financial value as a wage earner. We can tell people they're important, but if we turn around and pay them half as much as others, they know jolly well what we think.

One sociologist noted cryptically that we should choose our mothers carefully.[1] Our birth determines our rung on the ladder of life and shapes our opportunities and barriers. Being born rich or poor makes a world of difference. A gigantic gap stretches between the opportunities enjoyed by a child born to a million-dollar mother and one born to an impoverished drug addict. Our birth rung influences whether we'll experience malnutrition, infant mortality, college, prison, and mental torture. Our quality of life, our medical care, education, work, shelter, and how long we live, to a great degree, rest on our rung of birth.

Social Muscle

Social power rises and falls with the rungs on the ladder. In a broad sense, power is the ability to affect social life. It's the capacity to "make things happen." To make things happen we need resources. We need knowledge, money, and position. Those who own and control these resources can make things happen more easily than those who don't.

Four major types of power flow from our resources.

(1) *Financial power* is rooted in economic resources. Money makes things happen. It's one of the most important sources of power.

(2) *Expert power* stems from extensive knowledge and special information. Doctors and lawyers for example, exercise expert power because they have aquired and hold special knowledge in medicine and law.

(3) *Organizational power* arises from a person's position within an organization. An executive vice-president has more power than a janitor, because the executive has a higher position in the organizational flow chart.

(4) *Personal power* emerges from personal appearance and personality traits. Certain people attract us because of their pleasant

interpersonal style and manner. Their charm appeals to us and shapes our opinions.

When individuals or institutions have access to all four types of power, they wield enormous clout. To be president, personable, wealthy, and smart yields enormous power! Social muscle isn't necessarily good or bad. All of us exercise some power every day. It is a natural part of social life. We do, however, need to grapple with how we use and disburse it. What are the proper ways to flex power from a Christian perspective?

Joe Down and Doc Up

An example from the academic world sharpens the inequalities produced by social status. We'll compare Dr. Up, a full professor on a university campus, with Joe Down, a janitor who cleans Dr. Up's office. Consider some of their differences.

Joe and Doc share opposite ends of the campus hierarchy. Doc is near the top of the "professional" community. Joe is part of the lowly maintenance crew. The status difference is present in their titles. Dr. Up is often called "Prof" or "Doctor." Students are very careful to call him by title. Dr. Up's name and title hang on a nameplate outside his office. Joe doesn't have a title. He's simply "Joe." He has no office or nameplate.

Clothing also signals their status differences. Joe wears old jeans, T-shirts, and tattered sneakers. Dr. Up wears a tie and coat. He checks his tie and hair frequently with a mirror in the private closet of his office. Joe, of course, has no private closet or mirror.

Joe and Doc also part ways when it comes to power. Doc can ask Joe to work for him in the office—hanging pictures, rearranging furniture, and moving boxes. If the central air conditioner is turned up too high, Doc asks Joe to turn it down. If Doc forgets the key to his door, he calls for Joe to open it. Joe even makes the coffee for Dr. Up and his colleagues. If Joe makes mistakes, Dr. Up sends a memo to Joe's supervisor and bingo, that's the end of any raise.

Joe has no control over Doc. He might ask Doc for a favor, but Joe has no real power. He certainly can't reward or punish. Doctor Up knows the university president personally and sometimes asks for special favors. The president doesn't even know Joe's name, let alone hand out favors to "some old janitor."

When it comes to prestige, there's also a wide gulf. When Doc strides down the hall students greet him with smiles and choruses of "Hi, Doc." They politely step out of his way if he's in a hurry. The university president shakes Doc's hand and smiles warmly. When students bring their parents on campus they drop by Doc's office for introductions. Doc has a website so students and people around the world can track his important work. Doc likes telling friends in the community that he's a college professor. It's a respectable job.

When Joe comes down the hall, the most he gets is a nod or a "Hi" from a few folks who know him. He rarely gets warm smiles from the president or introductions to parents. He doesn't have a computer, let alone a website. Few people on campus know what he does, let alone the world. And he really doesn't like to tell people what he does. He knows it's the kind of thing any old Tom, Dick, or Sally could do.

In terms of privilege, things are also quite different. Salary is Doc's obvious advantage. He makes three times as much as Joe for only eight months of work. Joe, on the other hand, gets one week of vacation, several personal days, and one third of Doc's salary. Doc's fringe benefits far exceed Joe's because they are pegged to his salary. Doc's retirement perks also soar higher because they're tied to a percentage of his salary.

Doc has a desk and private office all his own. Doc controls his schedule. He arrives in the morning when he feels like it and leaves when he needs to. If something important turns up, Doc can cancel his classes for the day and simply post an "out of town" note. As long as he doesn't miss classes, Doc can take off for medical appointments or a snack with an out-of-state friend without informing anyone. He goes downtown for coffee breaks.

For Joe, things are different. Morning and evening he punches the time clock. He must schedule vacation days at least two months in advance. Coffee breaks stay on campus. About the only privilege Joe has is the opportunity to read everyone's junk mail as he empties trashcans.

Despite all their differences, Doc Up and Joe Down pay the same price for bread, gas, and household utilities. Two human beings, they interact daily, yet with very different status and resources.

A U.S. Senator describes the prestige and privilege which accompany his status:

> My every move through the Senate perpetuates this ego message. When I leave my office to go to the Senate floor, an elevator comes immediately at senatorial command, reversing its direction if necessary and bypassing the floors of the other bewildered passengers aboard to get me to the basement. As I walk down the corridor, a policeman notices me coming and rings for a subway car to wait for my arrival and take me to the Capitol Building. The elevator operator, the Capitol policeman, and the subway drivers all deferentially greet me. On the subway car I may take the front seat, which is reserved for Senators who may ride alone; tourists already seated there are removed by a policeman unless I insist otherwise. At the Capitol another elevator marked FOR SENATORS ONLY takes me to the Senate floor. There at the raising of an eyebrow a page comes to give me a glass of water, deliver a message, or get whatever I need. Aides scurry about telling me when votes will occur on which bills, although no one bothers me with all the details unless I ask.[2]

Ladders of power and prestige stand everywhere—in families, clubs, work places and churches. The two most basic social processes involve comparison and domination. We continually compare ourselves with others, and our group with other groups. We incessantly check who's ahead or behind, who's up or down, who won or lost, and who's climbing on the charts or slipping to the bottom. From sports teams to stock markets, from music charts to politics, we're constantly tracking who's up and who's down and how we compare with them—personally and our group.

The vertical system rests on power and domination. Those at the top dominate the lower rungs. From office suites to international politics to church committees, the higher ups influence and control those below. Domination doesn't need to lead to abuse, but it is a basic social process that penetrates all groups and all societies.[3]

Says Who?

Social ranking language peppers the Gospels. The angel told Mary that Jesus would be called son of the Most High and the power of the Most High would overshadow her (Luke 1:32, 35). Zechariah expected his son John to be a prophet of the Most High (Luke 1:76). Jesus said those who love enemies, do good, and lend without expecting a return, will be children of the Most High (Luke 6:35). A demoniac called Jesus son of the "Most High God" (Mark 5:7). Most High is used in the Scriptures as another name for God, suggesting that God tops the highest ladder.

The word *authority* frequently appears in the gospel stories. Luke begins with Jesus rejecting the "authority" and the "glory" of the kingdoms of the world (Luke 4:6). Later in the same chapter, Jesus expels a demon and the people are amazed. They ask, "What is this word? For with authority and power he commands the unclean spirits, and they come out" (Luke 4:36).

Jesus turned his back on the legal right to rule by political authority, but he didn't reject authority outright. His right to rule comes not from coercive political force but from the Most High. He doesn't command armies, but he does command demons. Although his authority doesn't come from white horses, chariots, and military victories, the people recognize its authenticity. "Now when Jesus had finished saying these things, the crowds were astonished at his teaching, for he taught them as one having authority, and not as their scribes" (Matt. 7:28-29; Mark 1:22).

Ironically, Jesus comes to the people without the traditional trappings of authority. He doesn't have any political clout nor the training of a scribe. After hearing one of his lessons, "The Jews were astonished at it, saying, 'How does this man have such learning, when he has never been taught?'" (John 7:15). Without a scribe's license he's not merely teaching, but teaching in a compelling way. His words earn their own authority. The audience certifies his authority, not a board of theological experts in Jerusalem.

The crowds aren't the only ones who ratify his authority. When the centurion approaches Jesus to request healing for his servant, Jesus turns toward the centurion's home. But the centurion hedges, saying he isn't worthy to have Jesus enter his house. "Only speak the word, and my servant will be healed. For I also am a man under authority, with soldiers under me; and I say to one, 'Go,' and he goes, and to another, 'Come,' and he comes, and to my slave, 'Do this,' and the slave does it" (Matt. 8:8-9). When Jesus hears this he marvels and heals the servant. The soldiers and slaves under the centurion jump at his words. The centurion, in turn, recognizes Jesus' spiritual authority.

Why does Jesus marvel when the officer describes his powerful position? Is he threatening Jesus—heal my servant or else? Rather, the centurion is comparing Jesus' authority to his own. This Gentile understands that Jesus, like himself, is a man of authority. This is a Gentile confession of faith, not a military threat. He acknowledges that Jesus has the power to heal his servant even from a distance. Jesus marvels that this Gentile has such a full understanding of God's authority and power.

Ironically, the peasants and the centurion understood the nature of Jesus' authority while the religious authorities remained perplexed. One day the chief priests and elders interrupted his teaching and asked, "By what authority are you doing these things, and who gave you this authority?" (Matt. 21:23 and Mark 11:28). In other words, who said so? Who gave Jesus the right to teach? Who signed his ordination papers?

Jesus answered by posing a question. Where did John's baptism come from? The heavyweights were in a jam. If they said John's authority came from heaven, then why had they refused to listen to John? If they said John's authority merely came from his personal powers of persuasion, the crowd would be angry because they thought John was a prophet. Jesus didn't answer their question because they couldn't answer his. But in asking the question about the Baptist, he aligned himself with John. The questions and answers about the authority of John's ministry also fit his own. The Pharisees had earlier charged that Jesus' authority came from Beelzebub. Now the chief priests were faced with two options. Either Jesus had the endorsement of the Most High, or he was an astute crowd charmer.

In John's Gospel, Jesus clarifies the source of his authority

I can do nothing on my own . . . I seek to do not my own will, but the will of him who sent me. (John 5:30)

The Father . . . has granted the Son . . . authority to execute judgment. (John 5:26-27)

My teaching is not mine, but his who sent me. (John 7:16)

I do nothing on my own, but I speak these things as the Father instructed me. (John 8:28)

For I have not spoken on my own, but the Father who sent me has himself given me a commandment about what to say and what to speak. (John 12:49)

Again and again, according to John, Jesus underscores the root of his authority. It's not his own. He is steward of God's authority. He has the power of attorney. He acts on God's behalf. His Parent has given him the "right" to speak about the kingdom. The one who speaks on behalf of another directs people to the other. Self-appointed leaders who speak on their own authority point others back to themselves. Jesus understands this well when he says, "Those who speak on their own seek their own glory" (John 7:18). After Jesus healed the paralytic, the crowds "were afraid, and they glorified God, who had given such authority to human beings" (Matt. 9:8). Jesus uses his authority in a way that clearly points to God. He's not a self-acclaimed prophet basking in the crowd's applause.

In summary, several themes lace Jesus' understanding of authority.

(1) There is no question that he saw himself as a steward of God's power. It was God who gave him the right to speak.

(2) He was careful to use his authority in a way that didn't bring personal prestige. His words and acts reflected God's desires.

(3) He used his authority to serve and help others. They were the beneficiaries of his power.

(4) Although his ordination wasn't certified through proper channels, the crowds felt the authenticity of his message and gave it grass-roots accreditation.[4]

Stop Climbing

Jesus rebukes the ladder-climbing leaders throughout the synoptic Gospels. He pinpoints three ways religious leaders polished their eminent rungs on the Jewish ladder. First, ostentatious clothing charmed them. In the words of Jesus, they made long robes, sewed broad phylacteries, and added fringes to their robes (Matt. 23:5; Mark 12:38; Luke 20:46). The Pharisees used extravagant clothing to remind people of their superior niche in the social system.

Second, the synagogue held a special place for prominent dignitaries. A scribe would sit on the seat of Moses at the front of the room, facing the people. Everyone could see him and admire his special seat. Jesus derides the scribes for seeking prestigious seats in the house of worship (Matt. 23:6; Mark 12:39; Luke 20:46). The scribes also scrambled for the best seats at feasts—the distinguished positions on the right-hand side of the host. Jesus made it clear such maneuverings in public meetings don't fit in the upside-down kingdom.

Third, the scribes used language to polish their prestige. They insisted on being called rabbi (Matt. 23:8). Since a greeting represented a communication of peace, strict ceremonial rules governed to whom and how a greeting was given.[5] Jesus knew that titles reinforce social ranking by calling attention to status. They remind us everyone isn't equal.

In one stroke Jesus erases titles. "You are not to be called rabbi, for you have one teacher, and you are all students. And call no one your father on earth, for you have one Father—the one in heaven. Nor are you to be called instructors, for you have one instructor, the Messiah" (Matt. 23:8-10). Tagging each other with titles has no place in the upside-down kingdom where everyone stands on equal ground. In his critique of those hankering after prestige, Jesus debunks the desire for status which drives and energizes many people.

Growing Down

Clamoring up the ladder wasn't only a Pharisee problem. It also snared the disciples. One day they began arguing about who was the greatest (Mark 9:33-34). Peter felt he deserved to be number one because he was the first to realize Jesus was the Messiah. James and John, however, thought they should be first because they had seen the transfiguration. James and John were so eager to be on top that they pulled Jesus aside and pleaded, "Do for us whatever we ask of you" (Mark 10:35). They wanted to sit in the best seats, on the right- and left-hand side of Jesus, in his kingdom.

Matthew even reports that their mother encouraged their plea (Matt. 20:20-21). In any event, we find the old dictatorial spirit of "do this and do that" amid the disciples. The bossing mentality ranks people from greatest to least. Jesus rebuked their status striving by taking a child in his arms. "Whoever welcomes one such child in my name welcomes me; and whoever welcomes me, welcomes not me but the one who sent me" (Mark 9:37).

A few days later, as the disciples were screening visitors, they pushed aside children who tried to touch Jesus. He was furious with this power play (Mark 10:13-14).[6] To the disciples, these children were social nobodies. They held no prominent positions. They wouldn't help the cause. Jesus should spend his time with the movers and shakers. Playing with children would divert Jesus from his mission.

The disciples still hadn't grasped the upside-down logic. To Jesus, children were as important as adults. He not only spent time with these little ones, he held them up as model citizens in the new kingdom. "For it is to such as these that the kingdom of God belongs. Truly, I tell you, whoever does not receive the kingdom of God as a little child will never enter it" (Mark 10:14, 15). Never enter it? Adults will never enter it *unless* they become like children?[7]

As the disciples vied for status and pushed toddlers away, Jesus used a child to symbolize kingdom values. Typically we tell people to grow up and "act their age." Jesus reverses the logic. He invites us to grow down and regress to childlike behavior. Why? How can children instruct kingdom learners? Why go to the very bottom of the social ladder to model kingdom citizenship?

Children rank low in status and power. Totally dependent on others, they're economic liabilities. Small children make few social distinctions. They don't put others in boxes. They haven't learned to play by adult social rules. They befriend strangers without fear.

They haven't yet learned racial and ethnic slurs. Color, nationality, title, and sexual boxes mean little to the young. They have no sense of bureaucratic structures and hierarchies.

The use and manipulation of power is foreign to a baby. Its cry certainly makes things happen. Parents do come running. Cries, however, are a response to biological needs, not a cunning move to manipulate others. Children learn the tactics of power as they grow older. In early years they exhibit trusting confidence. A child of good parents trusts them completely.

Jesus invites kingdom citizens to babyhood in all these areas. Instead of pursuing the number one spot, he prods us to ignore hierarchy as children do. He tells us to become blind to status differences and, like infants, see *all* others as equally significant despite their social rank. Instead of clamoring for more and more power, we followers of Jesus happily share it. We welcome interdependence. Rather than claiming self-sufficiency, we acknowledge our need for community and dependence on others. Blind to social distinctions, dependent on others, we live as children, for of such is God's kingdom.

Bottom Up

The disciples remain baffled. As they sit around the table during the Last Supper, an argument about greatness breaks out. After all the teaching on babyhood, amid this culminating sacred event, the disciples bicker about who is the greatest. Like typical human beings, they wonder how they stack up with each other.

Jesus tries again. He revamps the meaning of *greatness*.

> "The kings of the Gentiles lord it over them; and those in authority over them are called benefactors. But not so with you; rather the greatest among you must become like the youngest, and the leader like one who serves. For who is greater, the one who is at table, or one who serves? Is it not the one at the table? But I am among you as one who serves." (Luke 22:25-27)

Again Jesus flips our social worlds upside-down. He reverses our assumptions and expectations. He radically redefines greatness.

These words strike at the root of domination in all societies—big and small. Our typical assumptions about greatness flow together in this equation:

Greatness = Top, powerful, master, first, ruler, adult.

Jesus radically inverts the equation:

Greatness = Bottom, servant, slave, last, child.

There can be no misunderstanding here. Jesus turns our conventional definition of greatness upside-down. Pagans lord it over their subjects. They develop hierarchies of power. "Not so among you," whispers Jesus. In the upside-down kingdom greatness isn't measured by how much power we exercise over others. Upside-down prestige isn't calculated by the height of our rung on the social ladder. In God's inverted kingdom, greatness is signified by our willingness to serve. Service to others becomes the yardstick of stature in the new kingdom.

Jesus poses a profound question. Who is greater, the chief executive officer of a Fortune 500 company seated in the executive dining hall? Or the waiter who serves her? The president of the country flying in a private jet? Or the stewardess who serves him? The executive and the president are more important, of course. They were selected by a massive and expensive search process. Waitresses and waiters are a dime a dozen. Anyone can do their work. The chief executive has years of special training and experience. Any nitwit knows an executive is more important than a server.

Not in my kingdom, says Jesus. I am a servant Messiah. I am among you as a waiter, a slave, a servant, not a boss. Instead of giving orders and directives down the hierarchy, Jesus is asking how he can serve. The Jesus way looks up from the bottom, not down from the top. Such a posture flies in the face of egotistic individualism, which strives for personal rights and privileges over all else. Jesus invites humble servanthood, not assertive individualism. Rather than asking how we can get ahead, fulfill our needs, and soar to the top, disciples ask how we can best serve others.

Contemporary talk of "service" often falls short of Jesus' way. Sometimes we use service slogans not so much to serve others as to seduce them into buying products or "services" they really don't need. When this happens, the so-called servant turns artful manipulator. She or he becomes an ad agent, using the language of service to promote selfish interests. Some professionals high on the status ladder look at their clients from a "top down" perspective. They'll "serve" their clients as long as their service pays well in dollars and prestige. But when client needs run counter to the professional's interests, the "service" abruptly ends. Such self-serving "service" was not on Jesus' mind.

In contrast, the servanthood of Jesus ended on the cross. He was willing to serve the needs of the sick on the Sabbath even at the risk of his life. He forgave sins, not in the temple, but on dusty, rural roads, where such words were sheer blasphemy. Jesus' style of service brought neither financial gain nor social prestige. Quite the opposite. His service outraged authorities and triggered a violent death. For Jesus, serving didn't mean catering to the well-to-do, who could pay high prices. He cared about those with genuine needs regardless of status.

Jesus served the "least of these," those at the bottom. The least of the least can't pay back. Serving them may tarnish a professional's reputation in the professional community. After all, only incompetent lawyers, doctors, and teachers serve the stigmatized. And they do it only if they can't develop a profitable practice among the respectable. The disciples of Jesus don't worry about this. They generously give "a cup of cold water to one of these little ones" who have little power or social prestige (Matt. 10:42).

In a few sweeping stories, Jesus has redefined greatness. But what does he mean? How are the least among us the greatest in the kingdom? He understands that social greatness rises with access to power. We consider great those with authority over others. The president, the chief executive officer, the department head are applauded—by society at large, if not necessarily by their subordinates.

Is Jesus suggesting that janitors, day laborers, part timers, the weak, the poor, and the stigmatized automatically soar to the top of his kingdom? Is he calling for a complete flip-flop where the top rungers of this world fall to the bottom rung in the kingdom of God? Surely not. Instead of turning the old hierarchy upside-down and making a new one, Jesus questions the need for it. He declares hierarchy unconstitutional for his people. Moreover he proposes new criteria for evaluating greatness.

Describing John the Baptist, Jesus says, "I tell you, among those born of women no one is greater than John; yet the least in the kingdom of God is greater than he" (Luke 7:28). What do these baffling words mean? Among persons born in the flesh, none is greater than John. He is the greatest, the last of the prophets.

But in the kingdom, among those born of the Spirit, even the least is greater than John. If the least of kingdom citizens is greater than John, the rest are obviously also greater. Jesus isn't mocking John's significance. He's merely saying that everyone born of the Spirit is as great as the greatest prophet. His eyes twinkle. He's arguing that in the upside-down kingdom, everyone is the greatest! There are, in short, *no* little people in this kingdom.

Jesus is spoofing the language of "greatest and least." That kind of talk has no place in kingdom conversations. Rather than exchanging a new hierarchy for an old one, Jesus flattens hierarchies.[8] He understands that hierarchies too easily begin to act like deities. Humans bow down, worship, and obey them. Jesus once and for all disarms the authority of hierarchies to act like gods. He calls us to participate in a flat kingdom where everyone is the greatest. In this kingdom the values of service and compassion replace dominance and command. In this flat family, the greatest are those who teach and do the commandments of God (Matt. 5:19). They love God and others as much as themselves.

Do not misunderstand. Jesus is not calling for social anarchy— for tossing out all the rules of social organization. His is not a recipe for disorder and confusion. Social roles and rules are needed and necessary for happy human living. Clear lines of communication and coordination are necessary in social organizations from families to large corporations. Different people have different gifts, different jobs, and different levels of authority and responsibility. Nevertheless, amid these webs of responsibility, kingdom people treat others and their contributions with dignity, equality, and respect—recognizing that in God's eyes there are no small people. Everyone counts in a big way.

Looking Down

Arrogance rides with power and prestige. Some who make it to the top of worldly kingdoms pride themselves in their successes. They bask in the limelight of celebrity sun. Not so in the new kingdom.

Jesus tells the story of a man at a feast who carefully inspects the prestige of all the seats. He picks a distinguished one to display his status. The seats fill up. An eminent guest arrives a few minutes late after all the top seats are full. The toastmaster asks the earlier guest to take a lowly seat away from the head table. Embarrassed by his downgrade he slips away.

It's better, Jesus says, to select the bottom seat unless the master of ceremonies motions you to a higher one. Inversion visits again. "For all who exalt themselves will be humbled, and those who humble themselves will be exalted" (Luke 14:11). This rule of thumb appears after the parable of the breast-beating tax collector and haughty Pharisee (Luke 18:14) and after Jesus rebukes the Pharisees for seeking status with clothing and titles (Matt. 23:12).

What does this riddle on humility mean? Jesus isn't teaching dining etiquette. He's unpacking bigger things. Our normal tendency is to pursue positions of honor. Enjoying the oh's and ah's of special approval, we take it for granted that upward is better. Rather than endorsing such upward flight, Jesus calls us to downward mobility. He asks us to take the seats at the bottom. His disciples defer to others, happily yielding up the good seats. They're so busy waiting on tables, in fact, that they have little time to sit. Serving, not jockeying for seats, is their occupation. Those who exalt themselves will have a backseat in God's reign. Those who confess their pride and quietly serve others are exalted in the upside-down kingdom.

Contrary to kingdom thinking, we typically look down the social ladder and scorn those below us. We mutter, "If I did it, they can do it too. If the poor would just work a little harder and be more responsible they could pull themselves up by their bootstraps, too." Proud top rungers often assume their hard work and motivation *alone* pushed them to the top. We like to think our hard work is the sole factor behind our success. In reality, at least seven factors in one way or another place us on a particular rung of social life. We control some of them, but many are beyond our reach. A unique mix of factors—culture, context, providence, place, and people—carves out our special niche.

What are these formative factors?

(1) *Biological constraints* shape our place in life. Physical traits, intelligence, energy levels, skin color, sex, and some diseases are obviously inherited. We don't control them. A retarded child doesn't choose to be stigmatized. These genetic handcuffs limit some and favor others.

(2) *Cultural values* also condition our experience. In some cultures, children are taught to work hard. They even enjoy it. In others, hard work is ridiculed. Hard workers can hardly thank themselves if they happened to be born into a culture which taught them to enjoy hard work.

(3) *Personal motivation* often has both biological and cultural roots. The amount of personal gumption, drive, and sheer persistence mediates the impact of other factors. Personal motivation may help us overcome certain barriers. Or lack of it may lead to despair in the face of obstacles.

(4) *Community assets* also make a difference. The cards of life favor children born into upper-class communities with topnotch jobs, schools, and hospitals. No matter how hard they work, children plunked into destitute neighborhoods face enormous hurdles.

(5) *Family stability* also shapes a child's emotional makeup. Lifelong insecurity may nag the children of dysfunctional homes. Happy children have a head start in the race of life.

(6) *Financial inheritance* can boost a child into prominence. Some people are simply born rich. Inheriting a business, fortune, or political name propels many into powerful positions they probably could never attain on their own.

(7) *Chance* also carves our niche in life. Some make it rich because real estate prices in their region happen to triple overnight. Others lose everything through social or financial catastrophe. Being in the right place with the right people at the right time may make all the difference without any help from hard work or intelligence.

The influence and mix of these factors varies greatly. Obviously we don't choose our parents, our birthright, our communities, or our cultures. Many factors that mold our place in life are simply beyond our control. This doesn't mean we're mere robots or puppets yanked up and down by mysterious forces. Choices and decisions do shape our destinies. Personal motivation does make a difference. Hard work matters, but it's one of many factors.

Contrary to the myth of triumphant individualism, ambition isn't the only factor that explains success. Individualism breeds unfounded pride in *personal* achievements and contempt for others on lower rungs who often land there for reasons beyond their control. Only arrogance can lead people to assume that they "made it" just because of their hard work. Haughty individualism takes personal credit for all achievement, neglecting the role of social shackles and silver spoons. To use another image, everyone doesn't begin the race of life at the starting line. Some get a lengthy jump-start and others run only on one leg.

Skin color, for example, can be an insidious source of status or stigma. In many societies light is better. Light-skinned people have special privileges just because of their color. They don't have to worry about obstacles to jobs, houses, or advancement because of their pigmentation. By contrast, the harsh court of social opinion holds darker-skinned babies back from the moment of birth. These nasty judgments and practices, called racism, stigmatize people by the color of their skin and place extra hurdles on the track of life.

Those who fare well in the race often like to cite God's blessing on their life. A spirit of gratitude appropriately reflects sincere thanksgiving for what has come our way. But to carelessly assume that everything on our platter is a sign of God's blessing implies that those with empty platters have no heavenly blessing. Jesus was very clear about this. God's rain falls on the just and unjust. God's sun shines on everyone each day—on the evil and the good (Matt. 5:45). And as we have already seen, the woes and blessings handed out by Jesus surprised almost everyone.

Looking down the social ladder moves the followers of Jesus to compassion. Humility fills their spirit. They understand that they stand where they do because of many different factors. They also realize that not sloth, but capricious social or genetic factors may have stranded many of those below them. This doesn't erase the importance of personal initiative. But it does put personal initiative in perspective as *one* of the many streams that influence our destiny. A realistic grasp of how we arrive at different rungs on the social ladder wipes away arrogance and propels the people of God toward compassion and empathetic understanding.

Upside-Down Power

Jesus wasn't a typical king. He didn't bark orders to his generals nor threaten his subjects. He didn't command a religious or political dynasty. On the organizational charts, he was powerless. He commanded no armies. For heroes he holds up the young, the last, and the least. He acclaims the child, the servant, and the slave as model citizens. He describes himself as gentle and lowly in heart, saying his yoke is easy and his burden light (Matt. 11:29-30). He reveals his truth to babes rather than to wise intellectuals (Matt. 11:25).

Was he, in the end, a spineless, wishy-washy wimp? No. Jesus didn't run from power. In fact he exercised a great deal of it. Had he stayed in the desert and quietly taught his disciples in a cave, he wouldn't have threatened the ruling powers. Although he held no formal seat of power, he certainly wasn't powerless. Far from it. Jesus was so powerful, able to make things happen so quickly, that he was killed. His power unnerved the religious and political authorities.

Why did Jesus become a threat? His very life and message menaced political and religious authorities. Designating himself a waiter, he criticized the scribes' pursuit of prestige. He condemned the rich for dominating the poor. By challenging the oral law and purging the temple, he assaulted the citadel of religious power. His appeal to servanthood offered an alternate model of power. He hardly was a politician, but the kingdom he announced had political implications. It was a political movement that promised to reorder social and religious life.[9]

The in-breaking reign of God in the life of Jesus cut the muscles of the reigning powers.[10] The authorities killed him because they couldn't cope with political instability. Indeed, they had to be careful how they removed him. He not only had a small band of devoted followers but drew large crowds. His clout over the masses was so strong the authorities feared revolution. If they didn't remove him carefully, they would have had a revolt on their hands (Luke 22:2). Indeed, they arrested Jesus under the cover of darkness to prevent a tumult.

Jesus had power, but he didn't exploit it. Did he hide his messianic identity to prevent the crowd from declaring him king? When he thought they might crown him king by force he escaped to the hills (John 6:15). His power over the crowd didn't flow from formal positions or credentials. The masses followed him because he had genuine authority authenticated by his power to perform miracles and promise of a new kingdom.

Jesus exhibited both expert and personal power. His knowledge of the law and his penetrating spiritual insights were the base of his expert power. He knew the secrets of the kingdom. Jesus' personal power came not from physical charm but from his notable compassion for all. He had no financial or organizational power. He exercised power through influence, not coercion and control. He wasn't an irrational demagogue. He told provocative stories that stirred imaginations and flipped social worlds upside-down. Even here he gained respect through rational influence, not emotional manipulation.[11]

Jesus had no access to soldiers. He didn't command an army. Nor could he use pay raises to prod his followers. He simply spoke the truth and allowed individuals to make free choices. He described himself as the Good Shepherd. He didn't chase or drive his sheep, he called them. Those who recognized his voice followed (John 10:4).

Jesus added mighty acts to his potent word. By breaking social norms—Sabbath healings, eating with sinners, talking with women, purging the temple—he heralded a new set of values in a new kingdom.[12] Here was a man with the wisdom of a prophet who violated social custom when it oppressed people and kept them low. Here was a man whose power rested not on coercive threats but in radical obedience to God's reign. Such allegiance pushed all other gods aside. Jesus wasn't about to salute another king. It was this utter abandon to the reign of God, even in the face of a cross, that scared the authorities.

The hallmark of Jesus' upside-down power was his willingness to spurn what was rightfully his. Instead of mimicking a typical king, Jesus worked from the bottom up. Rather than demanding service, he served. Rather than dominating, he invited. As servant, waiter, and janitor, he ministered to those strewn on the city dumps. The powerful weren't amused. They were jittery and they responded with their kind of power—a violent cross.

Jesus wasn't powerless. But he rejected domination and hierarchy in social governance. Two factors undergird his use of power.

(1) Influence, not control, was his primary mode. He beckons individuals to follow him. His words and acts create a crisis and invite us to make a choice, a voluntary decision.

(2) He used power and mobilized resources to serve the needs of the hurting and the stigmatized. Jesus didn't use power for self-gain or glory.

In these ways he willingly suspended his own rights and served at the bottom of the ladder. Defying social custom, he redefined social *rights* and *expectations* in the new order of God's kingdom.

From There to Here

What can we learn from Jesus' understanding of power? For the sake of discussion, consider several suggestions.

We should use power to empower others.[13] This is the opposite of what normally happens. Power usually snowballs. Powerful persons and institutions seek more and more power, often at the expense of others. The powerful use their power to protect and perpetuate it. The powerful use their power to gain more muscle. Consequently, the exercise of power often increases power inequities. The upside-down perspective uses power to empower others. It seeks to provide others with the resources for self-determination. This does not mean that power is bad or must be discarded. Rather, it should be used to serve and empower others.

We should distribute power as widely as possible. Power tends to gravitate to the hands of a few. Those in the hub of an organization have more clout than those on the margins. There will always be power differentials. Christians, however, will work to share and decentralize power as much as possible.

Kingdom people will also strive to minimize hierarchy in social governance. As organizations grow, the number of rungs on social ladders multiply. Although some rungs are necessary, we should shorten ladders as much as possible. As this happens, coordination replaces domination. Collapsing ladders is another way of diffusing power.

Followers should freely give authority for leadership. Leadership should be neither self-appointed nor imposed on a group by an outside agency. Leadership is only worthy of allegiance when the led freely grant it to the leader in response to the leader's servant posture.

The Christian perspective looks down the ladder. We often want to scramble up ladders as fast as possible. The disciples of Jesus work to serve the powerless at the bottom. This may happen through direct forms of ministry or by remodeling social structures. As we model the posture of Jesus, we become more concerned about the plight of those at the bottom than about advancing our own position.

Historically the Christian church has sometimes perpetuated systems of hierarchy and stratification. Within church life, we occasionally sanctify with pious language, chains of command and layers of domination. Although our human inclinations build pyramids of power, Jesus doesn't bless them, even in the church.

One thing bears repeating. This is not a call for anarchy, disorder, or confusion. Power is not inherently wrong or evil. The issue here is how we use it. Do we build self-serving empires? Do we abuse others with our social muscles, or do we marshal our resources to truly serve others? The Spirit of God brings orderliness to the life of God's people. But the search for order doesn't require blind adoption of secular structures. The form and shape of the church's corporate life, if patterned on kingdom principles, will likely take a different twist from typical bureaucratic models.

We will use consensus whenever possible to confirm decisions. This encourages participation and collective ownership. All members should have the opportunity to debate and ratify actions proposed by servant leaders. Consensus may not be possible, but dissenting voices deserve respect. However, to the extent a corporate body is just (otherwise prophetic witness may be needed), individuals need to yield their vested interests to the welfare of the corporate body as a whole.

Large size is the friend of bureaucracy and hierarchy. Decision-making that involves all members happens best in groups of less than 150 persons. Large congregations need smaller units to permit fuller participation in their corporate life, rather than allowing bureaucratic structures to spiral.

Firm and decisive leadership is critical for the health and well-being of a robust group. But firm and decisive servants can lead without dictating goals and policies. They help the accomplishment of common goals by proposing directions and projects for broader review. Rather than declaring "I think this and I think that," servant leaders ask, "Where do *we* want to go?" "What are *we* saying?" "What are *we* sensing?" and "How can *we* be faithful to the way of Jesus?" Servant leaders will use their power to help members discern the Spirit's will for the group.

The Holy Spirit endows each of us with unique gifts and abilities. We use these gifts in various ways to build up and minister to the total body. We should equally esteem each contribution, whether preaching, washing windows, caring for children, managing projects, or setting up chairs. In a flat kingdom, each job makes an important contribution. If all jobs are important, should they have different rates of pay? What do we say about the worth of people if we make a sharp distinction in their pay?

Titles are foreign to the body of Christ. Terms like Doctor and Reverend perpetuate status differences unbefitting the spirit of Christ. Titles pay tribute to position, degree, and status rather than to personhood. Members of flat kingdoms call each other, as the sign of highest personal respect, by our first names.

Kingdom members involved in business, education, and other kinds of public life will use their influence to nudge organizations in flat directions. Christians in upper-level management and in professional roles will seek to express power through servanthood, not domination. The bottom-up perspective doesn't mean teachers will sweep floors and lawyers will shine shoes. There's a beauty in finding the proper fit between personal abilities and vocational slots. Good matches bring personal fulfillment and honor God's reign.

Perhaps the key question is how we pursue a particular vocation or passion. A medical doctor can practice in a plush suburban area with an excess of physicians. Or she can defy the tug of upward mobility and work in a poor community for a bare-bone salary. A truck driver can take high pay and cross-country runs which tear the family apart. Or he can accept local hauls and spend more time with his family. A business executive can build a new plant in a community with dependable labor and low unemployment, or she can construct the new plant in an area which desperately needs new jobs, but has less skilled labor.

Regardless of vocation, place, or position, disciples of Jesus ask this: How can we use our gifts and resources to serve God's kingdom? Are we using our position and power to perpetuate inequality and self-advancement? Or are we using them to truly serve others? How does our vocation and calling help to serve kingdom priorities and honor its Lord?

12

Successful Failures

Triple Symbols

We've seen how Jesus steered an independent course from the existing religious parties in Palestine. He didn't endorse the "realistic" Sadducees' working hand-in-hand with the Romans. He spurned the rituals of conventional religion spearheaded by the progressive Pharisees. The serene life of an Essene commune didn't lure him either. And as we've noted, Jesus gave an emphatic no to the revolutionary violence of the patriotic rebels. These four responses to Rome's domination Jesus rejected. The kingdom he announced sidestepped these conventional options. But Jesus had a kingdom and his kingdom, like other kingdoms, had a flag.

Mere pieces of cloth, flags stir deep emotions and they spur us to action. Flags symbolize the sacred meanings and identity of a group or a nation. We care deeply about the meanings behind our flags. We explode in rage when someone stamps on them or burns them. The flags of the upside-down kingdom are upside-down indeed! They're not those which typically swirl around right-side-up kings. The flags of this kingdom are a manger, stable, donkey, basin, thorns, cross, and tomb. These aren't the signs of successful kings born in the V.I.P. suites of prominent hospitals. Conventional kings symbolize their power with armored limousines, security guards, and golden crowns. Imagine the surprise when Jesus said his kingdom was like a tiny mustard seed, a woman hunting for a coin, and sleazy shepherd searching for a sheep.

But don't be mistaken. Jesus is King. He doesn't walk into Jerusalem; he rides like a king. His mount, however, isn't the white stallion of a commander-in-chief, but the steed of a poor man—a donkey. Jewish prophecy envisioned the donkey as a royal mount for a gentle and peaceful king (Zech. 9:9-10). Jesus comes as a king, but a most unusual and surprising one. The donkey is but one of several kingdom symbols that emerge as Jesus moves toward Golgotha.

The *basin*, the *cross*, and the *tomb* become pivotal signs of the new kingdom. The cross has long served as the preeminent symbol—the flag—of the Christian church. Only looking at the cross, however, detracts us from its very reason for being. Three upside-down symbols flow together in the gospel story: the basin, the cross, and the tomb. The *basin* is actually the foremost Christian symbol. Jesus himself voluntarily selects a basin to capture the meaning of his ministry. The *cross* is a Roman symbol, a harsh sign of the state's power to execute criminals. The ruling powers used the cross, an instrument of death, to respond to Jesus' basin initiatives. But God had the last word with the *empty tomb*. It stands through the ages as a sign of God's reign over the forces of evil.

Although the crucifixion has captured Christian attention over the centuries, the Last Supper was the big moment for Jesus. In that dramatic meal he enacted the meaning of his life and ministry.[1] Jesus and his disciples arrived in Jerusalem during the annual pilgrim festival at Passover. This was the great ritual that celebrated the exodus of the Hebrews from slavery in Egypt. Later they were taken into exile again in Babylon. Although they eventually returned to Palestine, many Jews at the time of Jesus still considered their nation in exile under the Roman occupation. The Passover celebrations stirred memories of liberation from Egyptian slavery as well as hopes for freedom from Rome's oppression.

Apart from many festivities, the Passover centered on two rituals: (1) slaying a sacrificial lamb and sprinkling its blood on the mighty temple altar as atonement for sin, and (2) eating a special Passover meal consisting of roasted sacrificial lamb and wine. The meal, eaten in small groups inside the holy city, included liturgical reminders about the mighty exodus from Egypt and hopes for a messiah who would liberate the people from Roman control.

Jesus gathered his disciples for the ritual meal but it was no ordinary Passover supper. Jesus filled the dramatic moment with triple meanings. Indeed there are multiple layers of meaning to this special supper. First, this was a Passover meal that recalled all the rich historical meanings of liberation and exodus from slavery. This was a Jubilee meal! But it likely was an illegal one without the necessary sacrificial lamb.

Second, the celebration of the meal was a prophetic event that paralleled Jesus' dramatic purging of the temple a day or so before. As we saw in chapter eight, Jesus flipped over the money-changing tables to symbolize the end of the sacrificial system. Now in the upper room, in dramatic fashion, he introduces an alternative to the temple. He takes a loaf of bread, not a leg of lamb, and says in effect, "Consider this my body broken for you." Then he picks up a goblet of wine and says, "This wine is my blood poured out for your sins."

In these dramatic moments he overturns the entire sacrificial system—offering forgiveness without a lamb, without blood, far from the temple altar. Such pronouncements would be sheer blasphemy in the ears of the high priest. Such an illegal supper on a holy night in a back street alley would indeed be a last supper! Performing the improper Passover meal was likely one of the many reasons Jesus faced arrest.

Third, Jesus continues the drama. "The Kingdom of God is bursting in upon us as I speak. The moment of God's redemption and liberation is upon us." With words to this effect he announced that he was the long awaited Messiah and through his forthcoming death a new covenant would replace the blood on the sacrificial altar. Forgiveness—anytime anywhere—already offered in his ministry, would soon be available to everyone everywhere.

Liberation and forgiveness were Jubilee themes that rang with messianic hopes. Hearing these words in the upper-room, the disciples surely envisioned a military coup. They would be players in the over throw of the Romans and they would hold prominent seats in the new political kingdom.

But then Jesus shocked them again! After sharing the bread and the wine, he reached for a third symbol—a basin—and began to wash their feet. "He . . . took off his outer robe and tied a towel around himself. Then he poured water into a basin, and began to wash the disciples' feet, and to wipe them with the towel" (John

13:3-5). Peter was so surprised that at first he refused. In picking up the basin Jesus made it very clear that the disciples of his kingdom would not assault the temple with daggers. He was an upside down Messiah—one that carried a basin, not a dagger.

The Politics of the Basin

The towel and the basin are the tools of the slave.[2] This upside-down King uses the common tools of the servant—not the royal symbols of sword, chariot, and stallion. It was customary in Palestinian culture for a household slave to wash the feet of guests as they reclined on couches while eating a meal. As master of his disciples, Jesus has the customary right to expect them to wash his feet. But he forfeits these privileges. As Jesus kneels to wash, the disciple sits in the master's seat of power.

Foot washing isn't a pleasant task. It means bending over and facing dusty feet. The bending symbolizes obedient service, so foreign from the arrogant, "I'll serve you if you pay me well," attitude. The servant's hands touch feet splattered with filth and mud. Normally a master washed his own hands and face but not his crusty feet. That was the dirty work of slaves. The slave concentrated on his master's feet, ignoring his own hunger. Jesus bends over and does the dirty work. No one forces him. He chooses to serve. He's willing to take orders. The towel he uses is flexible. It gives personal care by adjusting to the size of the other's foot.

The towel and the basin have been called the tools and agents of *shalom*.[3] They're not mere decorative symbols hanging on a wall. They're the means by which something is actually done. These tools of the slave define our trade. They do the work a professional or a master would never do. These tools place us in the lower position, serving and raising the other to a superior one. In this one simple act, Jesus turns old social hierarchies upside down and replaces them with a new value: service. As we pick up the tools of servanthood and wash each other's feet, the distinction between master and servant fades. As we become servants to one another, we all become great ones in God's flat kingdom.

This wasn't the first time our King had touched bottom. King Jesus had been washing feet all his life. Towel and basin behavior characterized his entire mission. For three years, he had been using the basin. But not to exclude others like the Pharisees did with their cleansing rituals. Nor like Pilate, who used a basin to rid himself of responsibility for Jesus' death. Unlike for Pilate and the Pharisees, Jesus' basin was a sign of love and service. It took responsibility for others and welcomed them into the flat kingdom. But make no mistake—it was his basin work which set the stage for the cross. It was in fact the politics of his basin ministry that led to his death.

The cross didn't fall miraculously from the sky. Jesus could have avoided it by softening his message, by staying out of Jerusalem, or by not offering free forgiveness, but he didn't. He boldly announced and enacted the kingdom of God. The cross was the natural reaction of evil forces to the assertive presence of loving service without regard to sex, nation, religion, or ethnicity. The rugged tree was the violent tool of the powerful trying to crush his basin ministry. Without a basin there would likely have been no cross. In other words, we must distinguish between the cross and what led up to it.[4] Basin and cross, flags of two kingdoms, show the sharp difference in their values and methods.

We've already seen the basin in action. Jesus rankled the rich who oppressed the poor. He healed and shelled grain on the Sabbath. He ate with sinners and accepted tax collectors. He committed blasphemy, by calling God his *abba*, his daddy, and forgiving sins without a sacrifice. He violated and condemned the oral law. He welcomed a prostitute's anointing touch. He traveled with women in public. His parables stung religious leaders. He talked freely with Samaritans and Gentiles. He healed the sick. He blessed the helpless. He touched lepers. He entered pagan homes. He purged the sacred temple. He stirred up large crowds. This was the Jesus Movement in action. These acts, these politics of the basin, led directly to the cross. They were the outrageous acts that could only be silenced by a shameful public death to prove the authorities were still in charge.

In almost every instance Jesus challenged conventional understandings. He upset the bedrock assumptions of the pious. He actively used the basin and towel to serve the helpless irrespective of custom or position. He knew such deviant behavior might trigger a cross. But harassment from officials and the threat of death didn't stifle his crusade of love.

Such behavior threatened the entrenched powers. The chief priests and Pharisees said, "If we let him go on like this, everyone will believe in him, and the Romans will come and destroy both our holy place and our nation" (John 11:48). Many of the charges at his trial were false. But there can be no question that the leaders of the Sanhedrin thought his new teaching would break their fragile peace with Rome. Likewise Pilate was nervous that any religious turmoil might disturb his grip on Palestine. So, hand-in-hand, religious and political leaders joined to execute Jesus. He was more dangerous than Barabbas, the political rebel. In a warning to other would-be messiahs, his killers mocked him with a sign tacked on his cross— "King of the Jews." The warning was clear: Messiahs who disturb the peace will hang and bleed.

The Jesus Movement wasn't a one-person crusade. It was the inauguration of a kingdom with many disciple-citizens. So after washing the disciples' feet in the upper room, Jesus invited them to follow his example: "So if I, your Lord and Teacher, have washed your feet, you also ought to wash one another's feet. For I have set you an example, that you also should do as I have done to you" (John 13:14-15). He invites them to pick up their basins and join the movement.

Jesus also invites to us to join the basin trade. He invites us, however, to more than a periodic, ceremonial ritual. He invites us to follow him with lives of service and peacemaking. He calls us to be people of the basin, not saints who sit on rocking chairs pondering the mysteries of God's salvation. The word and event become one in Jesus Christ. The Word has become flesh and lives among us. The facticity of Jesus—God in human skin—reveals God's very nature. We incarnate the Word when we use the basin, when we act in Jesus' name. Words without acts are empty. Acts of basin ministry authenticate our words.

The Scriptures are clear. The greatest disciples in the kingdom are the ones who *do* and teach the commandments (Matt. 5:19). "Not every one who says to me, 'Lord, Lord,' will enter the kingdom of heaven, but only the one who *does* the will of my Father in heaven" (Matt. 7:21, emphasis added). The final judgment sorts people based on their clothing, feeding, visiting, and welcoming of others (Matt. 25:31-46). Members of the family of God are those who *do* his will (Mark 3:35).

Jesus compares the one who hears and *acts on* his words to a wise man. "Why" he asks, "do you call me 'Lord, Lord,' and not *do* what I tell you?" (Luke 6:46). Jesus tells the lawyer he will live if he *does* the Great Commandment (Luke 10:28). After telling the Good Samaritan story, Jesus instructs us to go and *do* likewise (Luke 10:37). In parabolic form Jesus tells us that the servant who knows his master's will, but doesn't *do* it, will receive a severe beating (Luke 12:47, emphasis added in above verses). This call to an active basin ministry permeates the Gospels. We're asked to sell, give, love, forgive, lend, teach, serve, and go. There is only one caution. Basin initiatives are costly.

Expensive Decisions

"If any want to become my followers, let them deny themselves and take up their cross daily and follow me. For those who want to save their life will lose it, and those who lose their life for my sake, will save it. For what does it profit them if they gain the whole world, but lose or forfeit themselves? Those who are ashamed of me and of my words, of them, the Son of man will be ashamed when he comes in his glory and the glory of the Father and of the holy angels." (Luke 9:23-26)

For many years I assumed that a cross was a symbol of suffering—personal suffering I needed to bear. I saw tragedy, accident, genetic disability, or physical disease as a cross. It was something I couldn't avoid; something, which, in God's divine providence, had fallen upon me. As a disciple of Jesus, bearing my cross meant accepting my tragedy—enduring my sufferings without complaint or bitterness.

Do not misunderstand. God does walk with us through personal tragedies. The God who counts each hair on our heads must certainly count each tear. Indeed Jesus' suffering is a key distinctive of the Christian faith because it demonstrates that God is more than a mystical force that transcends the pain of this world. God also suffers. God understands and walks with us through the valley of pain and suffering. The cross can be a symbol of God's participation in such suffering.

But to think we carry a cross primarily through personal pain distorts its meaning.[5] A cross is not something God puts on us. It's not an accident or tragedy beyond our control. A cross is something we deliberately choose. We can decide if we want to accept a cross or not. Jesus' use of the words, "If any one," implies a free, deliberate choice. The cross for Jesus wasn't something which God imposed on him. The cross was the natural, legal, and political result of his basin ministry.

Long before Gethsemane, Jesus realized that a cross would follow his basin ministry. He repeatedly warns his disciples that he will eventually suffer and die. Even in Gethsemane the plea to "take this cup from me" isn't about a struggle to accept a predetermined plan. It's a struggle about living the way of love even in the pending doom of destruction. It's a temptation to flee, to fight, and retaliate in the face of the ugly cross. Despite these temptations, Jesus *chooses* to stay in Jerusalem and face the harsh choruses of "crucify him, crucify him."

To view the cross as less than a choice makes a farce of Jesus' wilderness temptation. Moreover, it makes him into a thoughtless puppet and renders his entire life irrelevant. It also implies that an angry god kills a son just to satisfy the god's own need for sacrificial blood.[6] Ironically this is far from the image of the compassionate God portrayed by Jesus throughout the Gospels. Moreover, and doubly ironic, Jesus demolished the entire sacrificial system when he announced full forgiveness, direct from God—any time, any place without a bloody offering. The metaphor of sacrifice provides one way of viewing Jesus' death, yet it comes not from the lips of Jesus but from church leaders who years later used it to interpret his death—after the fact.

A cross is an expensive decision. It has costly social consequences. We might paraphrase Jesus by saying, "Take up your basin with the full awareness that it may bring suffering, rejection, punishment, and apparent failure." Jesus clarifies the social consequences of cross-bearing in three ways. First, we must be willing to deny personal ambition when we pick up a cross. The values of our society may applaud selfish gain, political power, and individual fortune. Denying ourself doesn't mean belittling or demeaning our self, however. But it does mean refusing to allow the values of the popular mainstream culture to mold our calling, our vocation, our ambition.

Second, Jesus says that if we follow his way it may look like we've "lost" our lives in this world. We may appear as social failures if we engage in significant basin ministries. Since the tools of our trade are the tools of a slave, and slaves are deemed failures, we may at times appear to have "lost" our lives by this world's standards. Jesus' words articulate the most fundamental inversion of the upside-down kingdom. He says, in essence, if we pick up a basin and towel for his sake, the world may write us off. On the other hand, if we play by the rules of this world's game and serve the idols of this world, we may lose our lives in the kingdom of God. Trying to save our life, we may lose it. Giving our life away in loving service, we may discover it.

Jesus hints at the third social consequence of cross bearing when he talks about shame. Shame is a social concept. He notes that we may be ashamed to engage in a basin ministry which bucks prevailing social currents. We may for a time use our towel and basin. But ridicule may tempt us to put them away and play by the old rules. And so Jesus concludes, if we're ashamed of him and of his words, so will God be ashamed of us when God comes in full glory (Luke 9:26). Matthew sums it up this way, "Whoever denies me before others, I also will deny before my Father in heaven" (Matt. 10:33). The rooster reminded Peter of this a few days later. And the rooster crows again and again whenever would-be disciples deny Jesus in word or deed.

These clues all point to the fact that Jesus wasn't talking primarily about an inner, spiritualized, or mystical cross. Nor was he talking about accidents or genetic disabilities. He was describing expensive decisions, decisions with real social consequences (Luke 9:23). He was talking about decisions to enter Jerusalem and to enact dramatic parables of judgment in the temple plaza under the nose of the high priest. Such decisions, such crosses, are costly because they bring political consequences.

Cost Analysis

The life of discipleship was for Jesus a serious commitment. It ruptured all other loyalties and ties. "So therefore, none of you can become my disciple, if you do not give up all your possessions" (Luke 14:33). He understood that the way of the basin was costly. He feared that enthusiastic joiners might discount the cost of following him. So one day, as enthusiasts were surging after him, he told two parables to underscore the cost (Luke 14:25-33).

A farmer builds a magnificent tower. He sits down and calculates the price of the materials before he starts building. But if after he starts, his funds run out, the neighbors will mock him and ridicule his stupidity. Likewise, disciples who don't carefully count the cost before saying, "yes" to Jesus will look like fools if they break their promise later on.

In the second story, a king prepares for battle with another king. He sits down and calculates the strength of the opposing forces to see if he has a reasonable chance of winning. If he miscalculates the opponent's strength and enters the battle with too few soldiers, his army will be crushed. Disciples should likewise calculate the real cost of following Jesus before beginning the journey.

Jesus in fact discouraged some fair weather followers. On one occasion a bright-eyed enthusiast ran up and asked to join the disciple crowd. Jesus reminded him that a disciple's life may bring insecurity and social ostracism because even "Jesus has nowhere to lay his head" (Luke 9:58). In another instance, Jesus invites someone to follow him. But the prospect wants to go home for a six-day mourning ceremony for his dead father. Jesus tells him to come immediately, proclaim the kingdom, and let the dead bury the dead (Luke 9:60).

Another potential recruit wanted to go home to say farewell. Jesus reminded him, "No one who puts a hand to the plow and looks back is fit for the kingdom of God" (Luke 9:62). One hand guides the light Palestinian plow.[7] The other hand, usually the right, carries a six-foot stick with a spike on the end to prod the oxen. The left hand regulates the depth of the plow, lifts it over the rocks, and keeps it upright. The farmer continually watches the legs of the oxen to keep the furrow in sight. A farmer who loses focus ends up meandering in circles around the field. Such confusion awaits the disciple who is not fully engrossed in basin ministries.

In all these instances Jesus is saying three things. First, following him will be socially expensive. When the disciples decided to follow Jesus they "left everything" (Luke 5:11, 28). Second, he expects prospective disciples to sit down and calculate the cost of following him before they decide. Otherwise they'll end up ridiculed, confused, and devastated. Third, kingdom living requires a singularity of focus and energy. It is full-time work that requires full-time devotion.

No hocus-pocus is involved here. Disciples follow Jesus' way fully aware they may face resistance. We deliberately love and serve even if it prompts ridicule. Picking up the cross means we engage in an active basin ministry knowing that it sometimes may bring rejection.

The nature of crosses and their consequences depends on the social and political setting. The same act of love in one political context may bring smiles—but in another country imprisonment, torture, or even death. Regardless of the response, disciples of the upside-down Jesus don't retaliate with violence. They search instead for third-way options that extend respect and love even to enemies.

Cross-bearing isn't a one-time decision. It's a daily assessment of our willingness to make expensive decisions for the sake of Christ. Again and again, day after day, the call comes, "Whoever does not carry the cross and follow me, cannot be my disciple" (Luke 14:27). "Whoever does not take up the cross and follow me is not worthy of me" (Matt. 10:38).

Following in the way of Jesus doesn't mean going barefoot, remaining celibate, shepherding sheep, or camping in rural areas. We are not talking about wearing sandals and fishing with nets. We follow him by engaging in basin ministries that embody kingdom values. We follow by making expensive decisions.

The *substance* of Christian faith lies in our willingness to walk in the way of Jesus. Costly discipleship is not a fluffy faith that worships the cultural gods of success. Just follow Jesus, we are told, and we'll be successful in almost everything. Just give our hearts to him, we hear, and we'll rise to the top of the ladder. Be "born again" and we'll win more beauty contests, hit more home runs, make more sales, and receive more awards. Such froth and fizz merely coats old social values with a sweet religious veneer.

By contrast, Jesus calls us to costly discipleship—to expensive decision-making. Following Jesus means not only turning over personal habits and practices, but turning to a new way of thinking. This new kingdom logic counters much of what we take for granted. Jesus calls for a reformation of values, behavior, and thinking. To follow Jesus, to be converted, means turning around, and joining a community anchored on kingdom norms and values.

This becomes clear when Jesus says his followers may *appear* to have lost their lives in this world. Our overriding temptation is to save our lives in both systems. We want to save our life in this world and in the kingdom of God. We want to succeed by secular standards *and* by kingdom values. Making it in the kingdoms of this world often requires accommodation and compromise. Jesus draws a hard line when he says that those who strive to save their lives may lose them—may find their lives evaporating. And that those who lose their lives in basin ministries may discover new joys and life eternal.

Amid such hard talk shines a big word of hope. The cross is *not* the last word. It's but the middle step in the threefold sequence of basin, cross, and tomb. Happily the cross isn't the symbol of defeat as it first appears to be. Apart from the Scripture we have few details of the resurrection story. What we do know is that the early church was empowered and energized by the empty tomb. In the Pauline letters and in other early church documents, it is the reality of the resurrection that fully persuades the apostolic church that Jesus indeed was Messiah. The resurrection assured them, beyond doubt, that the new age of God's kingdom had burst in upon them with its good news for Gentile and Jew alike.[8]

God's *final* word is the empty tomb. The cross unveils the nasty power of evil with all its brutality and violence. The resurrection reveals God's nonviolent victory over the principalities of darkness. With the vacant grave in view, Christians can live in hope, knowing God has trumped the powers of sin. With hope we now pick up basins which may bring crosses. Light shines at the end of the tunnel. Moreover, we have strength to suffer in the face of evil because the empty tomb signals God's steadfast love and care.

The Upside-Down Community

The power of the upside-down kingdom lies in the corporate life of its citizens.[9] Jesus' teachings on riches, power, and compassion assume that his people share a life together. Kingdom life means doing God's thing together. Jesus would have stirred little threat without a community of followers. A wandering vagabond dropping wise sayings doesn't threaten the established order.

Leaving personal ambitions behind, kingdom citizens use their gifts to embellish and enrich the body of Christ. An incarnational community, they embody the life-giving reign of God amid cultures bent on violence, destruction, and death. Jesus calls us to a community of discipleship, to a culture of discipleship as we give corporate witness to the love of God.

Congregational life wanes sometimes to little more than erratic attendance for an hour of worship. Many pressures compete for our time, loyalty, and money. Involvement in civic affairs, professions, hobbies, or leisure eclipses our commitment to church. Participation in congregational life becomes one of many options if, indeed, we have any "leftover" time. Jesus' call to discipleship elevates the corporate life of his people above other commitments. Regardless of the size or shape of our local body of Christ, it should not be the caboose of our commitments; it should propel and energize all our involvements.

The task of rebuilding the church is a new and urgent mandate for every generation. Creating a corporate life based on kingdom values is more critical than finding all the right answers to the pressing political and economic questions of our day. The creation of Christian community is a political act itself since it represents a distinct new social reality. As one scholar flatly declares, "This is the original revolution; the creation of a distinct community with its own deviant set of values."[10] This is the creation of a countercultural community, a new band that marches to a different drummer.

When it's faithful to its mission—being in the world, but not of it—the church is a prophetic minority, an alternate subculture. Jesus calls us to be salt and light in the world. As salt and light, the community of disciples that shares his name and bears his cross, enriches the larger culture. These images of Jesus symbolize a distinctive subculture, an alternative social reality. Citizens of the new kingdom have a different vision, a different set of values. They pledge allegiance to a different King. And at times that allegiance means they will sail against the prevailing social winds.

Participation in Christian community undergirds and supports our spiritual and emotional well-being. Following the beat of a different drummer requires a circle of spiritual siblings who provide mutual support and care. Different parts of the body serve each other in times of special need. As members of one another, we need each other's mutual care for our spiritual as well as social and material needs.

The community of disciples offers a corporate witness to God's love and grace. Without a community the lone disciple appears as just another "do-gooder." The witness of corporate love and care signals God's reign amid cultures filled with malice, threat, and fear. The Christian community embodies God's design for human integrity, wholeness, and shalom. It becomes our base for discerning the times, affirming our personal gifts, and empowering us for ministry.

The types of kingdom witness will vary. In some cases Christian communities may develop and operate their ministries. Many disciples will embody the values of the new kingdom through Christian ministry and service agencies. Other kingdom people will provide social and legal services to the needy under various institutional umbrellas.

Kingdom citizens will also participate in the worlds of politics, profession, and commerce as long as they can faithfully pursue upside-down agendas. Many disciples will witness to the upside down ways of Jesus in their daily work and family life. Other Christian siblings will engage in projects that witness against the abuse of human rights, militarism, economic injustice, racism, sexism, and other forms of oppression.

Regardless of time or venue, citizens in the upside-down kingdom will always pledge their allegiance to the flag of King Jesus.

And they will always be more concerned about doing justice for others than demanding it for themselves.

The critical issue doesn't involve finding the perfect strategy. The paramount question is this: Are we willing to embrace a basin ministry—willing to devote our energies to service of our King? More important than finely honed strategies is the compassionate service that flows from a vital experience of worship and prayer in Christian community. Finally, all forms of witness should point others not to ourselves or to the church. They should point ultimately to Jesus, our Savior and Lord.[11]

Habits of the Kingdom Community

As kingdom members we take our upside-down citizenship seriously. But we also know how to laugh. We've tasted God's grace. We know our eternal hope doesn't depend on sober-faced discipleship. We take our crosses seriously. Nevertheless, we also splurge. Since God's grace has touched our lives and warmed our hearts, we can laugh at ourselves and our feeble efforts. We understand that, as usual, the truth lies in the bosom of Grace—somewhere between the demands of discipleship and the joyful delight that flows from God's spirit of mercy.

The corporate life of the people of God will be visible and practical. We are the folks who engage in conspicuous sharing. We practice Jubilee. Generosity replaces consumption and accumulation. Our faith wags our pocketbooks. We give without expecting a return. We forgive liberally as God forgave us. We overlook the signs of stigma hanging on the unlovely. Genuine compassion for the poor and destitute moves us. We look and move down the ladder. We don't take our own religious structures too seriously because we know Jesus is Lord and Master of religious custom. We serve rather than dominate. We invite rather than coerce.

Love replaces hate among us. Shalom overcomes revenge. We love even enemies. Basins replace swords in our society. We share power, love assertively, and make peace. We flatten hierarchies and behave like children. Compassion replaces personal ambition among us. Equality overshadows competition and achievement. Obedience to Jesus blots out worldly charm. Servant structures replace rigid bureaucracies. We call each other by our first name, for we have one Master and one Lord, Jesus Christ. We join in a common life for worship and support. Here we discern the times and the issues. In the common life we discover the Spirit's direction for our individual and corporate ministries.

Generosity, Jubilee, mercy, and compassion—these are the marks of the new community. Freed from the grip of right-side-up kingdoms, we salute a new King and sing a new song. We transcend earthly borders, boundaries, and passports. We pledge allegiance to a new and already-present kingdom.

We pledge allegiance to the Lord
of the worldwide kingdom of God
and to the values
for which it stands—
one kingdom, under God,
with compassion and forgiveness
for *all*.

We live in a future already bursting upon us. We're the ones who turn the world upside down because we know there is another King named Jesus. As children of the Most High, we welcome the reign of God in our corporate lives each day. In the words of Jesus we proclaim, "Thy kingdom come. Thy will be done, on earth, as it is in heaven." For it is indeed God's kingdom, God's power, and God's glory, forever and ever. Amen.

Discussion Questions

Chapter One: Down Is Up

1. What do John the Baptist's and Mary's prophecies about the kingdom reveal about Jewish hopes and longings at the birth of Jesus?

2. In addition to the ladder, what other images might help to visualize the upside-down kingdom?

3. What difference does it make if we view the kingdom of God as an aggregate or a collectivity?

4. Which detour provides the greatest lure to bypass the message of Jesus? Why?

5. What other detour signs may prevent us from practicing biblical ethics today?

6. Provide examples of "spiritualizing" biblical stories that may weaken their concrete social meaning.

7. What was the most important idea in Chapter One?

8. What contemporary examples illustrate the reign of God's kingdom today?

Chapter Two: Mountain Politics

1. In what ways were the temptations of Jesus "real" temptations?

2. Did Jesus have the freedom to accept or reject the wilderness temptations?

3. What was the most significant aspect of Palestine's political history before Jesus' birth?

4. What contemporary situations resemble the oppression in Palestine at the time of Jesus?

5. What nationalistic movements today are comparable to the freedom fighters who wanted independence from Rome?

6. Why were the disciples so slow to understand Jesus' rejection of the use of force?

7. What does it mean to say that Jesus was a revolutionary? In what ways was he? In what ways not?

8. What sort of political temptations do we face today?

Chapter Three: Temple Piety

1. How does the description of the temple in this chapter compare with your previous knowledge of the temple?

2. What parallels, if any, exist between institutionalized religion in Jesus' time and organized religion today?

3. If you had been living in Jesus' time, which of the religious groups might you have joined? Why?

4. Does your religious tradition have an "oral law" today which serves as a commentary on biblical Scriptures?

5. Why was Jesus so cautious about his messianic identity?

6. If you had been Mary or Zechariah, what kind of Messiah might you have expected?

7. In what ways are churches tempted to engage in elaborate religious display?

8. Who are the heroes and the villains in society today?

Chapter Four: Wilderness Bread

1. In what ways do we encounter similar temptations to Jesus' three temptations?

2. Why is *bread* such a prominent symbol throughout the New Testament?

3. Do you think the bread temptation was larger than Jesus' personal hunger?

4. Does it "spiritualize" a serious problem like poverty to say that "Jesus is the bread of life"?

5. Which economic situations today are similar to those in Jesus' time?

6. How do our economic arrangements today contribute to poverty, to wealth?

7. How does Jesus' bread temptation speak to those of us in comfortable economic situations?

8. Might someone in poverty interpret the bread temptation differently than someone living in affluence? How? Why?

Chapter Five: Free Slaves

1. How do the principles of Jubilee mesh with capitalist economic systems, socialist systems?

2. In what ways might Jubilee principles apply to our financial involvements today?

3. List examples of spiritual and economic integration in your own life.

4. Identify ways our economic concerns control or wag our religious beliefs.

5. What differences should our faith make in our financial affairs?

6. What is the difference between ownership and stewardship?

7. How might the Jubilee principles apply to the economic life of your parish, congregation, or small group fellowship?

Chapter Six: Luxurious Poverty

1. Identify instances when the six warnings of Jesus might apply to material possessions in your life.

2. What aspect of wealth has been most troublesome in your experience? Why?

3. What economic practices today might produce a poor Lazarus?

4. What is the most surprising comparison between Zacchaeus and the rich young ruler?

5. Summarize the central message of Jesus' economic teachings.

6. How do Jesus' teachings about material possessions illustrate the Jubilee framework?

7. In what ways do typical inheritance practices help or hinder the Jubilee vision of Jesus?

8. Identify some persons and organizations which follow Jubilee principles today.

Chapter Seven: Right-Side-Up Detours

1. Which of the nine detours is most prevalent in your personal experience? Which in the life of your congregation?

2. Identify other detours that may circumvent the biblical teaching on wealth.

3. List some typical assumptions about economic life, which may clash with Christian faith.

4. Identify examples of financial practices that may be immoral even though they are legal.

5. Do you consider yourself rich? Why or Why not?

6. What ways have you discovered to limit your consumption?

7. How do you respond to the five signs of upside-down giving?

Chapter Eight: Impious Piety

1. Do we have equivalents of the oral law in the life of the church today?

2. How do you reconcile the "irreverence" of Jesus with his message of love?

3. Are any of Jesus' criticisms of religious leaders applicable to the church today?

4. In what sense might Christians today be Pharisees? Sadducees?

5. Can you distinguish between kingdom, church, culture, and structure in your local context?

6. Identify some brittle skins in your congregation, in your denomination.

7. In what ways are religious traditions helpful in the life of an individual or congregation?

8. What is your response to the proposal for institutional sabbaticals?

Chapter Nine: Lovable Enemies

1. What types of persons in our contemporary world might represent the Samaritan in the parable of the Good Samaritan?

2. Create contemporary parables based on the stories of the Foolish Father and the Good Samaritan.

3. What are the consequences of saying that love and compassion form the very nature of God?

4. What are the implications of saying that everyone is my neighbor?

5. Identify examples of persons or organizations that have exceeded the norm of reciprocity.

6. Is it possible to live the way of agape love in individualistic, competitive societies?

7. Does God ever "bless" the military actions of particular countries?

8. Given the teachings of Jesus, how can Christians justify participation in military efforts?

9. Are there conditions when it's appropriate for the disciples of Jesus to use force? Lethal violence?

Chapter Ten: Inside Outsiders

1. In what ways does the "birds of a common feather" principle operate in your own life?

2. Consider the persons you've invited to your home over the past year. How many of these came from boxes different than your own?

3. Identify some stigmatized people in your community. How might your church open new doors to these persons and groups?

4. How do stereotypes related to race, sex, and ethnicity oppress people today? In your local community? In the world?

5. What kinds of boxes exist inside your church fellowship? How can they be lessened?

6. What rules of social etiquette might citizens of the upside-down kingdom violate if they take social boxes less seriously?

7. Have you ever felt especially close to someone from a different cultural background because of your common faith in Jesus Christ?

8. What are ways the mission of the church can strike a delicate balance between sameness and difference?

Chapter Eleven: Low Is High

1. What ladders of social ranking are important in your community? In your congregation?

2. To what extent do salaries and hourly wages determine the value and importance of persons?

3. What kinds of power are prominent in the life of your congregation?

4. Identify both abuses and positive uses of power.

5. In what ways are Jesus' understanding of power and authority relevant to us today?

6. Identify specific ways your congregation embodies flat kingdom ideals? What more could it do to practice kingdom values?

7. How have the seven factors that shape our social rungs (p. 233) influenced your own position and place in life?

8. Propose specific ways that you and others can pursue flat kingdom principles in your work, congregation, and community.

Chapter Twelve: Successful Failures

1. What difference does it make when we view the cross as a response to Jesus' basin ministry?

2. Identify some crosses you are presently carrying or facing.

3. What are some of the factors that led to Jesus' death?

4. Discuss and compare the three symbols of Christian faith.

5. In your own words, what does Jesus mean by "saving" and "losing" one's life?

6. In what ways is the church a counterculture—an alternate social reality?

7. In what ways are you involved in an upside-down community?

8. Discuss some strategies for Christian service and ministry that you and/or your fellowship could engage in.

9. How can we maintain a healthy balance between radical discipleship and a joyful understanding of God's Grace?

Guide for Discussion Leaders

*T*his book is designed for use in small discussion groups and classes in a variety of educational settings. The Discussion Questions should help to stimulate vigorous dialogue. Encourage students to reflect on the questions in preparation for discussion. Many of the chapters include additional questions embedded in the text which you may also find helpful to stimulate conversation on the chapter.

A brief summary of the chapters may aid your preparation and organization. The first chapter introduces the concept of the kingdom of God as well as some of the issues surrounding its interpretation. Chapters 2, 3, and 4 deal with Jesus' temptations in the context of the political and historical setting. They focus respectively on politics, religion, and economics in first century Palestine. These three chapters provide an essential foundation for the rest of the book because they introduce the social context for Jesus' life and death.

Chapter 5 deals with the beginning of Jesus' ministry and situates it in the context of the Old Testament Jubilee. Chapter 6 investigates the teachings of Jesus related to economic issues. Chapter 7 focuses on excuses which often serve as contemporary detours around Jesus' teaching on wealth. Jesus' relationship to religious leaders and religious tradition is summarized in Chapter 8. The theme of agape love and nonretaliation form the bedrock of Chapter 9. Chapter 10 traces Jesus' acceptance of a wide range of diverse people and Chapter 11 grapples with his teaching on status, service, and power. The final chapter focuses on the meaning of the cross and discipleship.

Because the book usually provokes lively discussion, many groups have found it difficult to cover a chapter in a single, one-hour session. There are a variety of ways in which the chapters might be organized for discussion.

1. The ideal pattern would allot two sessions for each chapter (24 sessions). This permits time for reflection between discussions

and allows participants to read more carefully and grapple with issues in more depth. One session might be devoted to reviewing and discussing the content of the chapter and looking more carefully at the scriptural passages cited in the chapter. The second session could address the discussion questions.

2. Another option is to assign one chapter per session (12 sessions).

3. For a six-session sequence, the best combination of chapters would be 1 and 2; 3 and 8; 4 and 5; 6 and 7; 10 and 11; 9 and 12 (6 sessions).

4. A more abbreviated four-meeting sequence might cluster the chapters in this pattern: 1-4; 5-7; 8-9; 10-12 (4 sessions).

Let me offer several suggestions to enhance discussion.

(1) Distribute books to participants with a reading assignment *before* the first session.

(2) Encourage students to read key passages directly from the Gospels.

(3) Ask several students to be responsible for subsections of a chapter. They might prepare additional background material on a particular topic.

(4) Consider rotating discussion leaders for some sessions.

(5) Consider breaking large groups into smaller groups of three to five for at least some of the discussion.

(6) Encourage students to write down several questions that emerge as they read and bring the questions to the discussion group.

(7) Encourage all persons to participate; discourage one or two persons from dominating the conversation.

(8) Near the end of the series, encourage individuals and the group to commit themselves to several specific changes they will make as a result of the study.

(9) Consult other reference works such as Bible dictionaries and at least one other interpretation of the life of Jesus for the sake of comparison. I especially recommend N. T. Wright (1999) *The Challenge of Jesus*, Borg and Wright (1999) *The Meaning of Jesus*, and Yancey (1995) *The Jesus I Never Knew*.

NOTES

Chapter 1: Down Is Up

1. Jeremias (1971:97) points out that the terms *kingdom of God* and *kingdom of heaven* have an identical meaning. New Testament scholars generally agree on the centrality and salience of the kingdom theme in Jesus' teaching. See for example Borg and Wright (1999:33-36), Crossan (1992:265-266), Vermes (2001:215-224), and Wright (1999:34-35). Crossan (1992:457-60) provides a detailed inventory of kingdom sayings in the Gospels and other source documents. In a provocative study, Sheehan (1986) proposes that the essence of the kingdom was distorted as the early church transformed the kingdom into another religion—Christianity.

2. Verhey (1984) explores the "Great Reversal" theme in an excellent study of ethics and the New Testament. His interpretation of social inversion in the Gospels, although developed independent of my work, coincides in many ways with the perspective of this book. For other discussions of the reversal theme in the Gospels consult Herzog (1994), Neyrey (1991b:296-301), and Sanders (1995:196-204).

3. This is essentially the position taken and more fully developed in Yoder (1994:11). In his words, Jesus is "not only relevant but also normative for a contemporary Christian social ethic." For an analysis of Yoder's ethical views, see Carter (2001).

4. Jeremias (1971:98). Helpful discussions of the history of the scholarship dealing with the kingdom of God can be found in Chilton (1984:1-26), Chilton and McDonald (1987), Riches (1982:87-111), and Sanders (1985:123-244).

5. Verhey (1984:13).

6. In their book, *Excavating Jesus*, Crossan and Reed (2001) combine the findings of textual criticism and archaeology to unearth new evidence about Jesus from both fields.

7. The title of Vermes' (2001) book is *The Changing Faces of Jesus*. The Gospels include different layers or strata of historical material: the words of Jesus, the views of the redactors, oral traditions, and influences from the early Christian communities. The respective editors of the Gospels, of course, offer different slants, different views, of Jesus. While I am aware of the multitude of interests shaping the historical text, I am primarily interested in the synoptic face of Jesus as best we can see it. Focusing on his broad synoptic face is less sensitive to the nuances of the particular editors, but nonetheless captures the broad essence of his message.

8. The timing of the kingdom and its eschatological character has been addressed by numerous scholars. For samples see Chilton and McDonald

(1987), Hiers (1970, 1973), Ladd (1974a, 1974b), Pannenberg (1969), Perrin (1963, 1976), Sanders (1995:169-188), Vermes (2001:217-220), and Wright (1996:198-228).

9. Schweitzer (1922) in his now classic study, *The Quest of the Historical Jesus*, first published in 1906, argued that Jesus' apocalyptic view shaped his ethical instruction. Some advocates of Schweitzer's apocalyptic interpretation include Hiers (1970, 1973) and Sanders (1975). Herzog (1994:30-39) makes a distinction between anachronizing and modernizing Jesus in his critique of the earlier studies of the historical Jesus that considered him irrelevant for social ethics. For a thorough review of the scholarly search for the historical Jesus, see Allen's (1998) comprehensive study.

10. The British theologian, Dodd (1936), was an early proponent of this view, often called "realized eschatology." Crossan (1992:282-283, 287-288) emphasizes that the kingdom Jesus spoke of was "here and now."

11. Borg and Wright (1999:37). The scholarly consensus has clearly shifted toward multiple meanings of the kingdom's timing. See Bright (1953:216-217), Chilton (1984), Chilton and McDonald (1987), Crossan (1992:287-292, 1994:55-58), Kraus (1974:32), Perrin (1976), Sanders (1985:150-56), and Wright (1996:198-228).

12. Perrin (1976:29-35) offers this helpful distinction. In the interest of simplicity I have labeled Perrin's steno symbol "specific" and his tensive symbol "general." Borg and Wright (1999:74-75) discuss some of the multiple meanings of the kingdom.

13. I have borrowed this illustration directly from Wright (1996:198).

14. Crossan (1992:287)

15. Ladd (1974b).

16. Sanders (1975:31).

17. Ladd (1974b:303).

18. Sanders (1975:29).

19. John Howard Yoder (1994) in *The Politics of Jesus* developed this argument and stimulated my initial interest to write the first edition of *The Upside-Down Kingdom*. The growing tendency of scholars to link Christian social ethics with the kingdom of God and the teachings of Jesus is illustrated by Cassidy (1978), Hays (1996), Hauerwas (1983), Longenecker (1984), Mealand (1981), and Myers (1988). Chilton and McDonald (1987) and Perkins (1981) argue that the parables provide the best insights into the social ethics of the kingdom.

One of the difficulties in shaping modern social ethics from the synoptic Gospels is the fact that Jesus and his disciples were an itinerate band wandering through the rural countryside. They were the initial stage of a social movement of religious revitalization and showed little interest in the questions related to building and maintaining the social institutions that are necessary to support an enduring social order and stable society. In the Acts of the Apostles as well as in some of the New Testament letters, the questions of institution building and preservation assume a higher priority than in the Gospels. For a sociological treatment of the itinerate character of Jesus and his disciple band, see Theissen (1978). A discussion of the different social needs that correspond with the institutional stages of a social movement, as they apply to the role of wealth in Luke and Acts, can be found in Kraybill and Sweetland (1983).

Chapter 2: Mountain Politics

1. McVann (1991:346-348) discusses the importance of these symbols in biblical literature.

2. Hengel (1977:17-21) suggests that Jesus took a critical stance against all the political powers of his day. Hengel, however, does not relate this critical posture to the temptation.

3. A number of studies are helpful to reconstruct the political and social history of Palestine in the centuries surrounding the life of Jesus. For example, see Bruce (1971), Enslin (1956), Guignebert (1959), Horsley (1987), Horsley and Hanson (1985), Lohse (1976), Martin (1975), Metzger (1965), and Myers (1988).

4. Enslin (1956:8).

5. Lohse (1976:25).

6. Enslin (1956:13-14).

7. The material in this general section is adapted from Horsley (2002:2).

8. Jeremias (1975:124).

9. Enslin (1956:60).

10. Metzger (1965:24).

11. For a discussion of the uprising of 4 B.C.E., see Freyne (1980) and Horsley (1987:50-54). Freyne (1980, 1988) argues that for the most part, Jewish protest movements were rooted primarily in Judea rather than in Galilee.

12. See Crossan (1992:198-202), Hengel (1973:29), and Horsley (1987:113).

13. Hengel (1971:10).

14. I am indebted to Horsley and Hanson (1999), whose extensive research on bandits, prophets, and messiahs laid the foundation for understanding these protest movements. Building on Horsley and Hanson's work, Crossan (1992:451-452) provides a chronological listing of the various types of protesters as well as an extended discussion of each incident. My numbers come from Crossan. The actual numbers may be higher because these numbers are the ones recorded by the early Jewish historian Josephus, upon who most scholars rely. Hanson and Oakman (1998:86-95) in their discussion of bandit groups, identify 16 such groups between 47 B.C.E. and 195 C.E.

15. The Zealots did not emerge as an organized resistance movement until 67-68 C.E. according to Horsley (1987) and Crossan (1992). The Sicarii (dagger men) were likely urban terrorists and the Zealots may have been rural bandits who eventually organized and came into Jerusalem. Was the revolutionary Judas, son of Hezekiah (4 B.C.E.), the same person as Judas of Galilee (6 C.E.), founder of the Fourth Philosophy? Horsley (1987) and Horsley and Hanson (1999) contend that the historical evidence offers negative answers to all these questions. Freyne (1980:216-29) points out, however, that this Judas might have changed his mind over a ten-year period and

indeed be the same person. For additional background on the Zealots, see Hengel (1989).

16. Crossan (1992) and Horsley (2002).

17. Lohse (1976:42).

18. Kelber (1974:78) points out the symbolic significance of the mountain in Mark's Gospel.

19. In an influential book, Brandon (1968) argued that Jesus was a Zealot and supported the use of violence. Horsley (1987) and Crossan (1992) provide evidence that the Zealots did not form as a movement until after Jesus' death. Nevertheless, apart from the Zealot connection, one can argue that Jesus may have supported the use of violent force even if he wasn't violent himself.

20. This is the argument made by Harris (1975:179-203).

21. See Brandon (1968) and Cullmann (1970).

22. Cullmann (1970), Hays (1996:332-335), and Hengel (1971, 1973) refute the allegations that Jesus used or supported the use of violent means of force. The central argument of Yoder's (1994), *The Politics of Jesus,* is that Jesus taught and embodied nonviolence. Cassidy (1978) and Ford (1984), using Luke's Gospel, argue that Jesus advocated nonviolence. Myers (1988), in a political reading of Mark, contends that Jesus practiced not only nonviolence, but also nonviolent resistance—symbolic direct action. See also Wink (1992 and 1998) for a similar view. By contrast, Horsley (1987:318-26) in his lengthy study of Jesus and violence concludes that there is little evidence that Jesus advocated either nonviolence or violence. His conclusion rests, however, on a questionable reading of Jesus' command to "love enemies."

23. For overwhelming evidence that the Christian Church in the first two centuries endorsed pacifism see Fiensy (2002:558-561) and Wink (1992: 209-229).

Chapter 3: Temple Piety

1. Excellent descriptions of the architecture of the temple and its operation can be found in Crossan and Reed (2002:193-201), Jeremias (1975:200-205), and Hanson and Oakman (1998:139-156). See Elliot (1991:218-224) for a brief, but thorough examination of the temple purity system and ritual.

2. This is the estimate of Hanson and Oakman (1998:143).

3. Metzger (1965:55).

4. Jeremias (1975:75).

5. See Hanson and Oakman (1998:144) for more detail and scriptural injunctions that prescribe the various sacrifices.

6. Jeremias (1975:160-212).

7. My discussion of the Torah is based primarily on Guignebert (1959:62-67). For an introduction to the Torah, see Neusner (1979).

8. Jeremias (1975:233-245) and Saldarini (1988:241-276) are the basic references for this section on the scribes.

9. Jeremias (1975:243).

10. This oral commentary is called, "the tradition of the elders" in Mark

7:3. Saldarini (1988:298-307) provides an excellent overview of the sparse data available on the Sadducees. Although many scholars note that the Sadducees opposed the oral law of the Pharisees, Saldarini contends that it is possible the Sadducees had some of their own oral interpretations as well.

11. For extended discussions of the Pharisees, see Borg (1984), Jeremias (1975:246-67), Moxnes (1988), and Saldarini (1988).

12. See Crossan and Reed (2002:154-158) for an overview of the archaeological evidence on Qumran.

13. Martin (1975:109-16) and Ford (1984:13-36) summarize the revolutionary messianism in the Jewish tradition. See Crossan (1992:106-113, 198-206), Vermes (2001:29-54), and Wright (1999:74-125) for additional discussions of Messianic hopes and Jesus' self-understanding of his Messianic identity.

Chapter 4: Wilderness Bread

1. Yoder (1994) suggests this reading of the bread temptation.

2. There are numerous descriptions of social stratification in first-century Palestine. For an analysis of the Galilee region, see Freyne (1980, 1988). Consult Hanson and Oakman (1998:99-130), Herzog (1994), Mealand (1981), Moxnes (1988), Myers (1988), Saldarini (1988), and Stambaugh and Balch (1986) for thorough discussions of social classes and economic stratification at the time of Jesus. Oakman (1986) provides a detailed description of production and economic distribution in Palestine. Harland (2002) reviews the primary sources and secondary literature regarding the state of our knowledge about the Palestinian economy. Two key differences between the social organization of ancient Palestinian society and modern societies were patron-client relationships and a limited pool of material goods in a pre-capitalist economy. For thorough discussions of these issues see (Hanson and Oakman (1998), Malina (2001b), and Neyrey (1991a).

3. Certainly there was some trade and mercantile relations in Palestine, but scholars debate the extent of trade within Palestine and its contribution to the national economy (Harland, 2002:517-520).

4. Hoehner (1972:73).

5. Jeremias (1975:92-99) and Finkelstein (1962:11-16) describe the affluence of the Jerusalem aristocrats.

6. Crossan and Reed (2002:211-271).

7. Sanders (1985:174-211) argues persuasively that the "people of the land" should not be lumped together with "sinners" as is often done by New Testament scholars. Oakman (1991) provides a careful description of the culture and economy of rural peasants in Palestine.

8. Baron (1952:1:275).

9. Enslin (1956:127).

10. Hoehner (1972:70).

11. Hanson and Oakman (1998:113-115).

12. Trocme (1973:87-88). Freyne (1980, 1988) contends that despite the growth of large estates, some peasants, at least in Galilee, continued to farm their own plots.

13. Oakman (1986:72), in detailed calculations, estimates that on the low side, a farmer paid one half of his crop in taxes and rent, and on the high side, two thirds. More importantly, when seed and other costs are added to the taxes, Oakman estimates that at most 1/5—and possibly as low as 1/13—of the crop was actually available to the farmer for subsistence living. See Harland (2002) for an overview of the literature on taxes in Palestine.

14. Much of the tax information comes from Guignebert (1959:39), Hanson and Oakman (1998:113-116), and Jeremias (1971:110).

15. Neusner (1975:29).

16. Baron (1952:279).

17. This essentially is the thesis developed by Borg (1987). Others, who argue that Jesus had an economic vision that extended beyond a new understanding of holiness, have challenged it.

18. Oakman (1986:176-82) offers a detailed description of the role and work of a carpenter in first-century Palestine.

19. Jeremias (1971:221) and Bately (1972:5-9) argue that Jesus was of the poor class. Freyne (1988:241) demonstrates that Jesus and his followers were not landowners, but neither were they destitute beggars. They were likely among the more economically mobile of the peasant culture. Hengel (1974:27) contends that because of his occupation, Jesus came from a class of skilled workers.

Although Jesus grew up in a low-class family, it was an artisan family, likely in the upper ranks of the lower class. Second, the lifestyle of Jesus and his disciples may have been sparse during his ministry because they deliberately rejected their original family status. As Jesus called disciples to follow him, he urged them to leave their occupations. Thus while Jesus and at least some of his disciples had roots in the upper ranks of the lower class, their subsequent behavior during his ministry reflected an embrace of the lifestyle of the poorest of the poor—day-to-day itinerants, wandering about, living from hand to mouth. Theissen (1978:10-16) shows that after Jesus began teaching, he and his disciples were wandering itinerants who had few if any possessions.

20. Bately (1972:5-9).

21. This is essentially Theissen's (1978:10-16) argument in his sociological study.

Chapter 5: Free Slaves

1. Crossan and Reed (2001:27-41) provide a concise overview of Nazareth at the time of Jesus from both textual and archaeological evidence. They suggest that elements of this story may have been created by Luke and may more accurately reflect Luke's world than Jesus' setting in 30 C.E. Other scholars also think that Luke's story of Jesus' sermon at Nazareth is Luke's own amplified version of Mark's account of Jesus in Nazareth (Mark 6:1-6). See for example Meier (1994:491). Sanders (1995:98-101) describes the function of a synagogue and its relation to the temple. See Meier (1991) for an extensive study of the social context and origins of Jesus.

2. It is unclear if Jesus followed an assigned lectionary reading for the day

or selected the Isaiah passage himself. Ringe (1985:39) thinks the lectionary hypothesis is suspect.

3. A variety of scholars have provided extensive discussions of the Hebrew Jubilee: Blosser (1978), Ford (1984), Gnuse (1985), Gregorios (1975), North (1954), Sider (1999:65-67), Sloan (1977), Strobel (1972), Trocme, (1973, 2002), and Yoder (1994). Perhaps the best one which links the Jubilee image in Luke 4 to the rest of Jesus' teaching is the excellent work of Ringe (1985, 1995:65-71, 2002:70-78). An exception is Vaux (1965:1:176) who rejects the notion that Isaiah 61:1-2 refers to the Jubilee.

4. The key issue, which is summarized by Sloan (1977:166-94), is whether or not Jesus was invoking the Jubilee proclamation with its full socioeconomic ramifications, or merely using it in an eschatological mode to call for a response to the announcement of God's salvation. Yoder (1994) and Trocme (1973) argue for concrete social meanings of the Jubilee in Jesus' usage whereas Sloan (1977:171-73) opts for a more eschatological interpretation, contending that such a view does not deprive it of social meaning. Edwards (n.d.) rejects the hypothesis that Jesus was explicitly restoring the Jubilee program in Nazareth. Gregorios (1975) makes a clear case for a Jubilean interpretation of Luke 4:18-19. Wright (1996:294-295) raises good objections to the idea that Jesus was trying to persuade Israel to keep the Jubilee year. However, Wright argues Jesus very likely expected his followers to embrace Jubilee among themselves.

5. Apart from the question of the social specificity of Jesus' use of the Jubilee in the Nazareth context, the Jubilean themes of release, liberty, and forgiveness are important in Luke's rendition of Jesus' ministry. Blosser (1978), Sloan (1977), Yoder (1994), and especially Ringe (1985, 1995:65-71, 2002:70-78) demonstrate the centrality of the Jubilee motif in Luke's theology.

6. Neusner (1973:14-18).

7. Trocme (1973:39) calculates that Jesus preached in Nazareth in a sabbatical year.

8. Strobel (1972) argues that it was not only a sabbatical year—but was actually the Jubilee year itself when Jesus appeared in the Nazareth synagogue. I am indebted to Walton Z. Moyer for translating Strobel's article for me from the German.

9. Gregorios (1975:187).

10. Jeremias (1971:104).

11. The rejection of Jesus at Nazareth has two plausible scenarios: (1) the crowd shifted from applause to condemnation in the course of the sermon or (2) the audience was astonished with anger throughout the episode. The traditional interpretation has favored the crowd reversal thesis since they at first "spoke well of him, and wondered at the gracious words which proceeded out of his mouth," and later "were filled with wrath." Ford (1984:64), following Jeremias, shows that the crowd may have been angered throughout the incident, especially when Jesus dropped the reference to the Day of Vengeance toward the heathen. Thus it's possible that "they were astonished because he spoke of the mercy of God" (toward Gentiles).

12. Trocme (1973:42). Oakman (1986:153-56) argues persuasively for a material meaning of debts in the context of the Lord's Prayer.

13. This, of course, is an oversimplification of the classic idealist/materialist debate in both philosophy and the social sciences. Rather than a monocausal process, the intricate tie between ideas and their material context is a complicated, dialectical process of ongoing interaction.

14. Ringe (2002:70-78) shows the variety of ways the Jubilee theme appears in Jesus' teachings and ministry.

Chapter 6: Luxurious Poverty

1. Yoder (1994) follows Luke's narrative in *The Politics of Jesus* in developing his argument that the social ethics of Jesus are normative for today. Helpful social analyses and interpretations of Luke's story can be found in Cassidy and Scharper (1983), Neyrey (1991a), and Ringe (1995).

2. For extended discussions of Jesus' teaching on wealth and possessions, consult Hengel (1974), Herzog (1994), Johnson (1977), Kraybill and Sweetland (1983), Mealand (1981), Moxnes (1988), Myers (1988), Oakman (1986), Pilgrim (1981), Ringe (1985), and Wright (1999).

3. For an exegesis of Jesus' stories and parables that is rooted in the sociocultural context of Palestine, I especially recommend Bailey (1983). A concise overview of the issues related to scholarship on the parables is provided by Gowler (2000). See Herzog (1994), Hultgren (2000), Longenecker (2000), Scott (1989), and Wierzbicka (2001) for interpretations of the parables that are sensitive to the cultural and socio-economic context of Palestine.

4. As Ringe (1995:115-16) notes, the seed has a double meaning in the parable. It is both the Word of God and the persons who receive the Word. The double allegory is resolved with the distinction (verse 10) that listening and understanding do not always go together. It is possible that the interpretation of the parable (verses 11-15) is an editorial addition to the original story. For an excellent summary of the various scholarly interpretations of this parable, see Wierzbicka (2001:156-265).

5. Yoder (1994:61).

6. Jeremias (1972:183). Historically, many exegetes have separated this story into two parts suggesting that the last section (verses 27-31), perhaps added later, was a polemic against the request for Jesus to perform "signs" to persuade his hearers. I follow Herzog (1994:115-130) who argues for the unity of the story and situates it squarely in the economic context of class disparities in Palestine.

7. Jordan and Doulos (1976:65-66).

8. For an exegesis of Luke 16:1-13 situated in the cultural context of Palestine, see the work of Bailey (1983:86-118). Derrett's (1970:48-85) discussion of the story gives a detailed picture of the economic norms in Palestine and provides the foundation for my discussion. Building on Derrett's work, Moxnes (1988:139-142) provides a plausible interpretation of this story which has informed my analysis. One of the best and most thorough analyses of the story—one that solves most of its apparent inconsis-

tencies—is given by Herzog (1994:233-258). See also Wright (1999) who builds on Herzog.

9. Derrett (1970:62).

10. I am indebted to Herzog (1994:257) for seeing this contrast between the beginning and end of the story.

11. Luke or other editors may have added verses 10 to 16 to the original story. See Moxnes (1988) for a discussion of the relationship between the Pharisees and wealth, particularly in the context of Luke's Gospel.

12. Example stories like the rich fool and the Good Samaritan, unlike many parables, show how kingdom citizens should live and act.

13. For a thorough exegesis of the meaning of this story, see Wierzbicka (2001) to whom I am indebted for some key ideas. See also Wright (1999).

14. Ringe (1995) and Wierzbicka (2001) provide helpful interpretations of these verses.

15. Malina and Rohrbaugh (1992:324-25) clarify the biblical usage of the terms "rich" and "poor" and underscore the social power dimensions. The poor are vulnerable at the hands of the rich.

16. Jeremias (1971:112) suggests that the Lucan version is surely the original. Matthew's Gospel was formulated in a church fighting the temptation of Pharisaic self-righteousness. The "poor in spirit" emphasis was a needed corrective. Wierzbicka (2001:28-40) develops the convincing argument that with the Aramaic word *anawim*, Jesus likely meant both attitude and condition. He surely meant actual economic poverty when he spoke of the "hungry" in the beatitudes.

17. Wierzbicka (2001:32-38) shows how suffering is the key underlying theme that all impoverished people in the beatitudes share.

18. Myers (1988:274-75) and Ringe (1995:228) argue that this saying must be understood literally as meaning a camel and a needle.

19. Baron (1952:252).

20. Jeremias (1975:311-12).

Chapter 7: Right-Side-Up Detours

1. See Ringe (1995:233-335) and Wierzbicka (2001:404-413) for careful interpretations of this story. Herzog (1994:150-168) in a thorough and creative exegesis situated in the ancient economic context, argues that the third servant, contrary to typical interpretations was a hero, a "whistle-blower," who exposed the greed of the other two servants and the wealthy owner, all of whom were benefiting from outlandish interest charges.

2. Jordan and Doulos (1976:118).

3. Birch and Rasmussen (1976:179-182) cite the misinterpretation of this statement as a classic example of the misuse of Scripture in social ethics.

4. Derrett (1970:266-278).

5. Sider (1997) proposed this concept as a creative way to tithe expanding incomes.

6. Hengel (1974:29). For a biblical theology of material possessions, see Blomberg (1999).

7. David Meyers (2000) poses this question in his book, *The American*

Paradox: Spiritual Hunger in An Age of Plenty. See also Frank (2000) for a similar argument.

8. The estimates of global poverty and hunger vary by source; however, these numbers are typical. For additional and updated statistical estimates consult some of the organizations on the list of Website Resources at the back of this book. For starters, I recommend The Worldwatch Institute, Bread for the World, and UNICEF. The Worldwatch Institute publishes an annual State of the World book, which includes recent data and reports on many of these issues. Other helpful resources include Anderson and Cavanaugh's (2000) *Field Guide to The Global Economy* and Gardner and Halweils' (2000) *Underfed and Overfed*.

9. The term *status escalation* comes from Robert Frank's (2000) book, *Luxury Fever*.

10. For an in-depth study of these issues, see the book, *Our Ecological Footprint*, by Wackernagel and Rees (1996).

11. See the list of websites at the back of this book for organizations that are working to change global policies and structures that promote and protect economic injustice.

12. Ronald Sider (1999) in *Just Generosity* articulates a biblical vision for overcoming poverty in America and cites examples of Jubilee in action.

Chapter 8: Impious Piety

1. Adler (1963:40-41).

2. Danby (1933).

3. Strack (1969:26-28).

4. For an excellent analysis of the passion for holiness in the religious milieu in Jesus' time, especially as the Pharisees embodied it, consult Borg (1984, 1987). Wright (1992:181-203) provides a historical and theological introduction to the Pharisees that situates them in Jesus' context.

5. For a contrasting view, see Sanders (1985:245-80, 1995:205-223), who argues that Jesus did not violate the law except for one or two minor infractions. This view is based partly on little distinction between written and oral law, but mostly on the assumption that Jesus' confrontations with the law are the later creations of the early church and redactors who were writing polemics against the Pharisees. Wright (1999:56-58) refutes Sander's view and argues that it's unlikely that the redactors added all the criticism of the Pharisees to the text. Wright contends that Jesus was in fact breaking the law not to destroy it, but to show how the new kingdom would transform it and who was in charge of it.

6. Swartley (1983:70) makes this observation and uses the Sabbath for a fascinating case study in comparative biblical hermeneutics.

7. Danby (1933:106).

8. Danby (1933:110).

9. Danby (1933:123-127).

10. Jeremias (1971:271-380) laid the foundation for understanding racial and religious purity in Israel in his classic work, *Jerusalem in the Times of Jesus*. Two thorough studies of religious purity in ancient Palestine, which

reflect greater social science sophistication, are Malina (2001b:161-197) and Neyrey (1991b).

11. Borg (1984:78-96) offers an excellent analysis of the meaning of Jesus' table fellowship to which I am indebted.

12. Jeremias (1971:115-16).

13. For extended discussions of Jesus' provocation in the temple, consult Borg (1984:163-200, 1987:174-77), Horsley (1987:285-300), Myers (1988:297-306), and Sanders (1985:61-76).

14. Various outer courts surrounding the temple building itself were used for public worship and designated for particular groups, e.g., the Court of Women, and the Court of Israel. Borg (1987:174) contends that the "Court of the Gentiles," typically referred to by scholars, is a modern, not an ancient, designation.

15. Kelber (1974:97-102) expands the traditional interpretation that the temple cleansing was done primarily to open up the outer court to the Gentiles. He also suggests that the prohibition to carry vessels had more religious significance than stopping people who were taking a shortcut through the temple. Sanders (1985:61-91) contends that the temple incident was not merely chasing out money changers or "cleansing" the temple for the purpose of restoring it to routine operation. It was rather a defiant public act directed against the temple itself, and it was this provocative act that more than any other led to Jesus' death. Myers (1988:297-306) argues that the temple was fundamentally an economic institution and sees Jesus taking symbolic direct action against the temple operation. For additional discussions of the scholarly perspectives on the meaning of Jesus' actions in the temple, see Crossan and Reed (2001:218-222), Myers (1988:297-304), Sanders (1995:253-262), and Wright (1999:62-72).

16. Kelber (1974:101) makes a case that the purge was intended to shut down the temple operation at least in a symbolic, if not final sense.

17. We may not have an objective picture of what Jesus said about the Pharisees because Jewish-Christian conflicts raged as the Gospels were being written. The Gospel accounts reflect one side of the story. Written after Jews and Christians had become bitter enemies, the Gospels may exaggerate the conflict with the Pharisees. Wright (1999:56-57), however, contends that all of Jesus' conflict with the Pharisees cannot be attributed to the later controversies in the early church.

18. Jeremias (1975:253-55) points out that Matthew put scribes and Pharisees into the same category. Jesus denounced the Pharisees primarily for their emphasis on tithes and ritual washing while the scribes or lawyers were criticized for their attention to social status. See Luke 11:37-52.

19. See Borg (1987:157-60) for an excellent discussion on this point.

20. Jeremias (1972:139-44) provides helpful insight into this story. Elliot (1991:213-240) situates the story in a provocative analysis of the distinction between temple and household in Luke-Acts.

21. Jeremias (1972:132).

22. For a discussion of the relations between church and kingdom, consult Ladd (1974a:105-19) and Bright (1953), especially Bright's chapter 8, "Between Two Worlds: The Kingdom and the Church."

23. Kraus (1974:34).

24. Rodney Clapp (1996), in *A Peculiar People*, shows how the church can shape its own culture in post-Christian societies.

25. Klaassen (2001) shows how the irreverence toward sacred objects, places, and times was typical of the Anabaptists of the 16th century.

Chapter 9: Lovable Enemies

1. Various interpreters vouch for different themes as the primary one in Jesus' articulation of the kingdom. I have emphasized agape. Borg (1987) stresses the compassion of Jesus—or "wombishness," as he likes to call it. For Oakman (1986) the key theme is generosity.

2. Bailey (1983:158-206) and Jeremias (1972:128-32) provide helpful cultural background to this parable, for which I am indebted.

3. Wright (1996:125-131) argues that the parable in this deeper sense was telling the story of the arrival of the new kingdom.

4. See Bailey (1983:33-56) for details of the cultural context.

5. Jeremias (1975:352). For additional background on the Samaritans, consult Coggins (1975) and Ford (1984:79-95).

6. Jeremias (1975:357).

7. Jeremias (1975:358).

8. Crossan (1973:65).

9. Wierzbicka (2001:373-379) sketches some of the conflicting views of this story and offers a succinct summary of its meaning. Wright (1996:304-307) emphasizes that Jesus uses the story for redefining the boundaries of the covenant people governed by the Torah and thereby defines the inclusive mission and broad scope of his kingdom.

10. Moxnes (1988:129-34) offers an excellent discussion of this hospitality story in the context of reciprocal exchange patterns in Palestinian culture.

11. Moxnes (1988:157).

12. Walter Wink (1992:175-193) exegetes Matthew (5:38-42) in a compelling way within the cultural context of Jesus' time. He shows how turning the other cheek, giving the cloak, and going the second mile were all forms of nonviolent resistance that oppressed people could use to humiliate their oppressors. I am indebted to him for my interpretation of this passage.

13. See Wink (1992:177-184) for a detailed exegesis of these examples.

14. The definition of "enemies" in this biblical passage is crucial. If as Horsley (1987:255-272) contends, the enemies that Jesus had in mind were local and personal—not foreign and political—the teaching loses its political impact. Klassen's (1984) careful analysis of this teaching disagrees with Horsley. The examples of enemies which Jesus uses in parable and story suggest a broader definition than the one proposed by Horsley. Schwager (1987:171-80) in a creative analysis discusses enemy love in the context of social psychological theories of scapegoating. A variety of essays in Swartley (1992) explore *Love of Enemy and Nonretaliation in The New Testament*.

15. I am indebted to Tom Yoder Neufeld for seeing the complimentary themes of resistance and nonresistance in the message of Jesus and in the larger body of scripture. Neufeld presented this argument in a lecture at

Messiah College in April 2002, titled "Resistance and Nonresistance: Two Legs of a Biblical Peace Stance."

16. Walter Wink (1992:175-229, 1998:98-111), with careful biblical exegesis, describes Jesus' third way in contrast to the flight and fight options. I am indebted to him for these understandings.

17. Hays (1996:317-346) offers an excellent summary of the texts on nonviolence in the New Testament, as well as some six detours around nonviolence, all of which he refutes.

18. The literature on the various responses of the church to violence and militarism is voluminous. For a helpful introduction to the contradictory hermeneutical positions taken by various theological traditions, see Swartley (1983:96-149). Essays describing the peacemaking efforts of many churches have been compiled by Schlabach and Hughes (1997).

19. In his groundbreaking work, Glen Stassen (1992) identifies seven specific steps for just peacemaking that are applicable to international relations.

20. John Howard Yoder (1994:193-211) offers an incisive exegesis of Romans 13:1-7, which I recommend and to which I am indebted.

21. For a more in-depth discussion of some of these difficult questions, see Friesen (1986), Roth (2002), and Yoder (1983).

22. Wink (1992:13-31, 224-25) describes the myth of redemptive violence in a compelling manner that applies to violence in everyday life as well as war.

23. See Brueggemann (1982) for an exegesis of the biblical meaning of shalom. Perry Yoder (1987) provides one of the best introductions to the concept of shalom, especially as it relates to salvation and justice. A series of biblical essays edited by Yoder and Swartley (1992) provide helpful resources for understanding the biblical notions of shalom and peace.

24. See for example the many works of Gene Sharp, but especially his *Methods of Nonviolent Action* (1973). Ackerman and Duvall (2001) provide an excellent overview of nonviolent interventions in the 20th century. Although Walter Wink's work is primarily theological, he cites many examples of nonviolent interventions. See especially Wink (1992:243-257). Hays (1996:317-344) makes a strong theological case for nonviolence based on the teachings of Jesus and the moral vision of the New Testament.

25. For information on Christian Peacemaker Teams consult their web site in the Website Resources of this book. The writings of international peace builder, John Paul Lederach (1995, 1997, 1999), provide many examples of nonviolent means of conflict transformation and international peace building. See also the website for the Conflict Transformation and Peace-Building Program of Eastern Mennonite University in the Website Resources.

26. For introductions to restorative justice based on the way of Jesus and the New Testament, I especially recommend Marshall (2001), Strang and Braithwaite (2001), and Zehr (1990, 2003).

Chapter 10: Inside Outsiders

1. Jeremias (1975) devotes six chapters (12-17) to the maintenance of racial purity in the Hebrew community. My discussion is indebted to his careful research.

2. The extent to which Jesus himself welcomed Gentiles is somewhat ambiguous. Sanders (1985:212-21) contends that Jesus started a movement which "came to see the Gentile mission as a logical extension of itself." But Sanders doubts that Jesus himself welcomed Gentiles.

3. For an elaboration, see Tannehill (1972).

4. I am indebted to Willard M. Swartley, my former instructor, for solving the riddle of the symbols in these three chapters of Mark's Gospel. A comprehensive treatment can be found in Swartley (1973). For a popular treatment see Swartley (1981:94-130). Myers (1988:223-27) concurs with this interpretation.

5. Matthew generally takes a more negative view toward Gentiles than Mark or Luke. Perhaps because he is writing to a Jewish audience, Matthew often depicts Jesus with typical Jewish attitudes. Matthew is the only writer who reports Jesus saying that he is sent only to the lost sheep of the house of Israel (Matt. 10:6; 15:24). Jesus warns his followers not to pray like the Gentiles who heap up empty phrases (Matt. 6:7). In a derogatory manner, Jesus lumps tax collectors and Gentiles together as negative models for his disciples (Matt. 5:47; 18:17). The Gentiles seek anxiously after things (Matt. 6:32). And the Gentiles have hierarchies of authority (Matt. 20:25). The disciples can expect to be dragged before Gentiles (Matt. 10:18). Jesus himself expects to be mocked before Gentiles (Matt. 20:19). In all these instances, Gentiles are castigated in Matthew's gospel.

6. Yoder (1994) devotes chapter 11 to Paul's concept of justification as it relates to the reconciliation of Jew and Greek.

7. Jeremias (1975) has an excellent discussion on the role of women in Hebrew culture in chapter 18. It is the basic historical source for this section. For several introductory sources on the role of women in the New Testament, consider Evans (1983), Praeder (1988), Ruether (1981), Siddons (1980), and Swartley (1983).

8. Jeremias (1975:375).

9. Jeremias (1975:376).

10. Wahlberg (1975:94).

11. Jeremias (1975:305, 311).

12. Crossan (1994:54-74) says that Jesus' constant emphasis on radical egalitarianism and open commensality filled his kingdom with nuisances and nobodies.

13. Jeremias (1971:104).

14. Longenecker (1984) in several insightful essays argues that the mandate of the gospel as practiced by the early church envisioned a new community where social barriers crumbled between male and female, slave and free, Jew and Greek.

Chapter 11: Low Is High
1. This comment about the determinative significance of social class originates with Peter Berger. See Berger and Berger (1975:62).

2. Hatfield (1976:17).

3. Comparison and domination are considered two of the most basic social realities by many sociologists. These themes in the many works of the French sociologist Pierre Bourdieu have been summarized by Swartz (1997). Kerbo (2003) offers massive data and an analysis that confirms the extent of social stratification and inequality in several countries as well as in the global system. Walter Wink (1992) provides a thorough theological analysis of what he calls the "domination system."

4. Wright (1996:168-197) discusses Jesus' view and use of authority and his self-understanding as a prophet as he redefines the meaning of the kingdom of God.

5. Jeremias (1971:219).

6. Chilton and McDonald (1987:79-90) offer a penetrating analysis of the controversy over children with a special emphasis on its ethical implications.

7. The Aramaic and Greek words for child are somewhat ambiguous and in certain cases are also used for slave or servant. It's possible that the disciples were turning away slaves, but even so, the meaning of Jesus' action and teaching remains unchanged.

8. Minear (1976:21) in Chapter 1 provides an especially helpful discussion of Jesus' view of hierarchy.

9. This of course is what John Howard Yoder (1994) means by the title of his book, *The Politics of Jesus*.

10. Minear (1976:21) and Hengel (1977:18-20).

11. Hengel (1977:21).

12. N. T. Wright (1992 and 1996), in his massive study of Jesus, argues persuasively that the best way to understand Jesus and his kingdom is to focus on his acts, stories, and riddles. The meaning of Jesus is revealed in these actions and stories of action, more than in wordy ideas.

13. Redekop (1976:147) suggests this thesis. For a discussion of the use and abuse of power in Anabaptist communities, see the series of essays edited by Redekop and Redekop (2001).

Chapter 12: Successful Failures
1. My interpretation of the Last Supper is largely indebted to Wright's (1996:554-611, 1999:82-92) analysis of the symbolic meaning of the Passover meal in juxtaposition with Jesus' prophetic act in the temple days earlier. Wright also argues persuasively that Jesus, in ways that may seem strange to us in the modern world, likely understood himself to be a Jewish prophet who anticipated that he would die as part of the process of cleansing and restoring the temple in preparation for the new Kingdom. He likely saw his pending death as a sacrifice, as part of the messianic task that would inaugurate a new reality, a new kingdom that would eclipse the temple (Wright 1996: 604-605).

2. I am indebted to Brueggemann's (1982) excellent essay on the tools and trade of the Christian's basin ministry.

3. Brueggemann (1982).

4. Burkholder (1976:134) makes this point. The reasons for Jesus crucifixion are many and complicated. I certainly do not claim to have solved the politics and theological mysteries of his murder, but I do contend that his three-year ministry of teaching, caring, and acting is what produced the complicated mix of factors that led to his death. Unfortunately some interpretations of his death attribute it to a divine robotic plan. Such views, constructed by theologians over the centuries, largely over look his life in its real social context, and thus not only distort the basic Christian gospel, but also render Jesus irrelevant for social ethics. We must continually remind ourselves that the Pauline and early church's sacrificial interpretations of Jesus death were post-Easter interpretations. For a lively interchange between two scholars with different interpretations see Borg and Wright (1999:79-110). Other thoughtful discussions of the reasons for Jesus' death can be found in Crossan (1992:361-394), Myers (1988:354-411), Crossan and Reed (2001:222-229), Sanders (1995:249-274), Weaver (2001), and Wright (1996:540-611).

5. See Yoder (1994:129-133) for a critique of the way the term "cross" is typically used in Protestant pastoral care.

6. One of the best discussions of Jesus' death from a pacifist perspective in the context of classical theories of atonement is J. Denny Weaver's (2001) book, *The Nonviolent Atonement*.

7. Jeremias (1972:195).

8. For a thoughtful and provocative case for the reality of the resurrection that rests on the testimony of the early church see Wright (1999:126-149).

9. Hauerwas (1983) offers a creative vision for the peaceable community of the new kingdom.

10. Yoder (1971:28).

11. For resources on the centrality and primacy of the church as a local community of mutual support and witness consult Clapp (1996), Hauerwas (1991), Hauerwas and Willimon (1990), Hinton (1993), and Yoder (1992).

Select References

The select references include sources cited in the notes as well as other relevant items.

Ackerman, Peter and Jack Duvall
   2001   *A Force More Powerful: A Century of Nonviolent Conflict.*
           New York: St. Martin's Press.
Adler, Morris
   1963   *The World of the Talmud.* 2nd ed. New York: Schocken
           Books.
Allen, Charlotte
   1998   *The Human Christ: The Search for the Historical Jesus.* New
           York: Free Press.
Anderson, Sarah and John Cavanaugh
   2000   *Field Guide to the Global Economy.* New York: The New
           Press.
Bailey, Kenneth E.
   1983   *Poet & Peasant and Through Peasant Eyes: A Literary-
           Cultural Approach to the Parables of Luke.* Grand Rapids,
           Mich.: Eerdmans.
Bailie, Gil
   1995   *Violence Unveiled: Humanity at the Crossroads.* New York:
           Crossroad.
Baron, Salo Wittmayer
   1952   *A Social and Religious History of the Jews.* Vol. 1. New
           York: Columbia University Press.
Bately, Richard
   1972   *Jesus and the Poor.* New York: Harper & Row.
Berger, Peter L. and Brigitte Berger
   1975   *Sociology: A Biographical Approach.* 2nd ed. New York:
           Basic Books, Inc.
Birch, Bruce C., and Larry L. Rasmussen
   1976   *Bible and Ethics in the Christian Life.* Minneapolis:
           Augsburg.
Blomberg, Craig L.
   1999   *Neither Poverty Nor Riches: A Biblical Theology of Material
           Possessions.* Grand Rapids, Mich.: Eerdmans.

Blosser, Donald
    1978   "Jesus and the Jubilee, Luke 4:16-30: The Year of Jubilee and Its Significance in the Gospel of Luke." Ph.D. diss., Scotland: University of St. Andrews.

Borg, Marcus J.
    1984   *Conflict, Holiness & Politics in the Teachings of Jesus.* Studies in the Bible and Early Christianity, Vol. 5. New York: Edwin Mellen Press.
    1987   *Jesus: A New Vision: Spirit, Culture, and the Life of Discipleship.* San Francisco: Harper & Row.

Borg, Marcus J., and N.T. Wright
    1999   *The Meaning of Jesus: Two Visions.* New York: Harper Collins Publishers.

Brandon, S. G. F.
    1968   *Jesus and the Zealots.* New York: Scribners.

Bright, John
    1953   *The Kingdom of God.* Nashville: Abingdon.

Bruce, F. F.
    1971   *New Testament History.* New York: Doubleday.
    1983   *The Hard Sayings of Jesus.* The Jesus Library. Ed. Michael Green. Downers Grove, Ill.: InterVarsity Press.

Brueggemann, Walter
    1982   *Living Toward a Vision: Biblical Reflections on Shalom.* 2nd ed. New York: United Church Press.

Burkholder, J. Lawrence
    1976   "Nonresistance, Nonviolent Resistance, and Power." In *Kingdom, Cross, and Community.* Eds. Calvin Redekop and J. Richard Burkholder. Scottdale, Pa.: Herald Press.

Capon, Robert Farrar
    2002   *Kingdom, Grace, Judgement: Paradox, Outrage, and Vindication in the Parables of Jesus.* Grand Rapids, Mich.: Eerdmans Publishing Co.

Carter, Craig A.
    2001   *The Politics of the Cross.* Grand Rapids, Mich.: Brazos Press.

Cassidy, Richard J.
    1978   *Jesus, Politics, and Society: A Study of Luke's Gospel.* Reprint. Maryknoll, N.Y.: Orbis Books.
    1987   *Society and Politics in the Acts of the Apostles.* Maryknoll, N.Y.: Orbis Books.

Cassidy, Richard J., and Philip J. Scharper
    1983   Eds. *Political Issues in Luke-Acts.* Maryknoll, N.Y.: Orbis Books.

Chilton, Bruce
   1979   *God in Strength: Jesus' Announcement of the Kingdom.*
           Plochl: Freistadt.
   1984   Ed. *The Kingdom of God in the Teaching of Jesus.*
           Philadelphia: Fortress.
Chilton, Bruce, and J. I. H. McDonald
   1987   *Jesus and the Ethics of the Kingdom.* Grand Rapids, Mich.:
           Eerdmans.
Clapp Rodney
   1996   *A Peculiar People: The Church as Culture in a Post-
           Christian Society.* Downers Grove, Ill.: InterVarsity Press.
Coggins, R. J.
   1975   *Samaritans and Jews: The Origins of Samaritanism
           Reconsidered.* Atlanta: John Knox Press.
Crossan, John Dominic
   1973   *In Parables.* New York: Harper & Row.
   1992   *The Historical Jesus: The Life of a Mediterranean Jewish
           Peasant.* New York: Harper Collins Publishers.
   1994   *Jesus: A Revolutionary Biography.* New York: Harper
           Collins Publishers.
Crossan, John Dominic, and Jonathan L. Reed
   2001   *Excavating Jesus: Beneath the Stones, Behind the Texts.* New
           York: Harper Collins Publishers.
Cullmann, Oscar
   1970   *Jesus and the Revolutionaries.* New York: Harper.
Danby, Herbert
   1933   Trans. *The Mishnah.* London: Oxford University Press.
Derrett, J. Duncan M.
   1970   *Law in the New Testament.* London: Darton, Longman,
           and Todd.
Dodd, C. H.
   1936   *The Parables of the Kingdom.* London: Nisbet.
Edwards, George
   n.d.   "Biblical Interpretation and the Politics of Jesus" (unpub-
           lished manuscript).
Elliott, John H.
   1991   "Temple Versus Household in Luke-Acts: A Contrast in
           Social Institutions." In *The Social World of Luke-Acts:
           Models for Interpretation.* Jerome H. Neyrey, ed. Peabody,
           MA: Hendrickson Publishers.
Enslin, Norton Scott
   1956   *Christian Beginnings I and II.* New York: Harper.

Evans, Mary J.
  1983 *Women in the Bible: An Overview of All the Crucial Passages on Women's Roles.* Downers Grove, Ill.: InterVarsity Press.
Fiensy, David A.
  2002 "What Would You Do for a Living?" In *Handbook of Early Christianity: Social Science Approaches.* Anthony J. Blasi, Jean Duhaime, and Paul-Andre Turcotte, eds. New York: Altamira Press.
Finkelstein, Louis
  1962 *The Pharisees.* Philadelphia: Jewish Publication Society.
Ford, J. Massyngbaerde
  1984 *My Enemy Is My Guest: Jesus and Violence in Luke.* Maryknoll, N.Y.: Orbis Books.
Frank, Robert
  2000 *Luxury Fever: Money and Happiness in an Era of Success.* Princeton, N.J.: Princeton University Press.
Freyne, Sean
  1980 *Galilee from Alexander the Great to Hadrian, 323 B.C.E. to 135 C.E.: A Study of Second Temple Judaism.* Wilmington, Del.: Michael Glazier, Inc.
  1988 *Galilee, Jesus, and the Gospels: Literary Approaches and Historical Investigations.* Philadelphia: Fortress.
Friesen, Duane K.
  1986 *Christian Peacemaking and International Conflict: A Realist Pacifist Perspective.* Scottdale, Pa.: Herald Press.
Gager, John G.
  1975 *Kingdom and Community: The Social World of Early Christianity.* Englewood Cliffs, N.J.: Prentice-Hall.
Gardner, Gary and Brian Halweil
  2000 *Underfed and Overfed: The Global Epidemic of Malnutrition.* Washington, D.C.: Worldwatch Institute.
Glen, John Stanley
  1962 *The Parables of Conflict in Luke.* Philadelphia: Westminster.
Gnuse, Robert
  1985 *You Shall Not Steal: Community and Property in the Biblical Tradition.* Maryknoll, N.Y.: Orbis Books.
Gowler, David B.
  2000 *What Are They Saying about the Parables.* Mahwah, N.J.: Paulist Press.
Grant, F. C.
  1926 *The Economic Background of the Gospels.* Oxford: Oxford University Press.

Grant, Robert M.
1977   *Early Christianity and Society.* San Francisco: Harper &
        Row.
Gregorios, Paul
1975   "To Proclaim Liberation." In *To Set at Liberty the
        Oppressed.* Geneva: World Council of Churches.
Guignebert, Charles
1959   *The Jewish World in the Time of Jesus.* New York:
        University Books.
Hanson, K. C., and Douglas E. Oakman
1998   *Palestine in the Time of Jesus: Social Structures and Social
        Conflicts.* Minneapolis: Fortress Press.
Harland, Philip A.
2002   "The Economy of First-Century Palestine: State of the
        Scholarly Discussion." In *Handbook of Early Christianity:
        Social Science Approaches.* Anthony J. Blasi, Jean Duhaime,
        and Paul-Andre Turcotte, eds. New York: Altamira Press.
Harris, Marvin
1975   *Cows, Pigs, Wars, and Witches.* New York: Random
        House.
Hatfield, Mark
1976   *Between a Rock and a Hard Place.* Waco, Tex.: Word
        Books.
Hauerwas, Stanley
1983   *The Peaceable Kingdom: A Primer in Christian Ethics.*
        Notre Dame, Ind.: University of Notre Dame Press.
1991   *After Christendom.* Nashville: Abingdon.
Hauerwas, Stanley, Chris K. Huebner, Harry J. Huebner, and Mark
        Thiessen Nation
1999   *The Wisdom of the Cross: Essays in Honor of John Howard
        Yoder.* Grand Rapids, Mich.: Eerdmans.
Hauerwas, Stanley, and William Willimon
1990   *Resident Aliens: Life in the Christian Colony.* Nashville:
        Abingdon.
Hays, Richard B.
1996   *The Moral Vision of the New Testament.* New York: Harper
        Collins.
Hengel, Martin
1971   *Was Jesus a Revolutionist?* Philadelphia: Fortress.
1973   *Victory over Violence.* Philadelphia: Fortress.
1974   *Property and Riches in the Early Church: Aspects of a Social
        History of Early Christianity.* Philadelphia: Fortress.
1977   *Christ and Power.* Philadelphia: Fortress.

1989   *The Zealots*: London: T&T Clark.

Herzog, William R. II
1994   *Parables as Subversive Speech: Jesus as Pedagogue of the Oppressed*. Louisville, Ky.: Westminster/John Knox Press.

Hiers, Richard H.
1970   *The Kingdom in the Synoptic Tradition*. Gainesville: University of Florida Press.
1973   *The Historical Jesus and the Kingdom of God*. Gainesville: University of Florida Press.

Hinton, Jeanne
1993   *Communities: The Stories and Spirituality of Twelve European Communites*. Guilford, Surrey: Eagle.

Hoehner, Harold
1972   *Herod Antipas*. Cambridge: The University Press.

Hollenbach, Paul
1989   "The Historical Jesus Question in North America Today." *Biblical Theology Bulletin*. 19:11-22.

Horrell, David G.
2002   "Social Sciences Studying Formative Christian Phenomena: A Creative Movement." In *Handbook of Early Christianity: Social Science Approaches*. Anthony J. Blasi, Jean Duhaime, and Paul-Andre Turcotte, eds. New York: Altamira Press.

Horsley, Richard A.
1987   *Jesus and the Spiral of Violence: Popular Jewish Resistance in Roman Palestine*. San Francisco: Harper & Row.
2002   "The New World Order: The Historical Context of New Testament History and Literature." In *The New Testament: Introducing the Way of Discipleship*. Wes Howard-Brook and Sharon Ringe, eds. Maryknoll, N.Y.: Orbis Books.

Horsley, Richard A., and John S. Hanson
1999   *Bandits, Prophets, and Messiahs: Popular Movements in the Time of Jesus*. Harrisburg, Pa.: Trinity International. (First publication 1988 by Harper & Row).

Howard-Brook, Wes and Sharon H. Ringe
2002   Eds. *The New Testament: Introducing the Way of Discipleship*. Maryknoll, N.Y.: Orbis Books.

Hultgren, Arland J.
2000   *The Parables of Jesus: A Commentary*. Grand Rapids, Mich.: Eerdmans.

Interpreter's Dictionary of the Bible, The
1976   4 vols. Nashville: Abingdon.

Interpreter's Dictionary of the Bible, Supplementary Volume
    1976   Nashville: Abingdon.
Jeremias, Joachim
    1971   *New Testament Theology*. New York: Charles Scribner's
            Sons.
    1972   *The Parables of Jesus*. New York: Charles Scribner's Sons.
    1975   *Jerusalem in the Time of Jesus*. Philadelphia: Fortress.
Johnson, Luke T.
    1977   *The Literary Function of Possessions in Luke-Acts*. Society of
            Biblical Literature Dissertation Series, no. 39. Ph.D.
            diss., Missoula, Mont.: Scholars Press.
Jordan, Clarence, and Bill Lane Doulos
    1976   *Cotton Patch Parables of Liberation*. Scottdale, Pa.: Herald
            Press.
Kee, Howard Clark
    1980   *Christian Origins in Sociological Perspective: Methods and
            Resources*. Philadelphia: Westminster.
Kelber, Werner H.
    1974   *The Kingdom in Mark*. Philadelphia: Fortress.
    1979   *Mark's Story of Jesus*. Philadelphia: Fortress.
Kerbo, Harold R.
    2003   *Social Stratification and Inequality: Class Conflict in
            Historical, Comparative, and Global Perspective*. New York:
            McGraw Hill.
Klaassen, Walter
    2001   *Anabaptism: Neither Catholic Nor Protestant*. 3d ed.
            Waterloo, Ont.: Pandora Press.
Klassen, William
    1984   *Love of Enemies: The Way to Peace*. Philadelphia: Fortress.
Kraus, C. Norman
    1974   *The Community of the Spirit*. Grand Rapids, Mich.:
            Eerdmans.
Kraybill, Donald B., and Linda Gehman Peachey
    2002   *Where Was God on September 11?: Seeds of Faith and Hope*.
            Scottdale, Pa.: Herald Press.
Kraybill, Donald B., and Dennis M. Sweetland
    1983   "Possessions in Luke-Acts: A Sociological Perspective."
            Perspectives in Religious Studies. 10:3(Fall).
Kreider, Alan
    1987   *Journey Towards Holiness: A Way of Living for God's Nation*.
            Scottdale, Pa.: Herald Press.
Kreider, Carl
    1980   *The Christian Entrepreneur*. Scottdale, Pa.: Herald Press.

1987   *The Rich and the Poor: A Christian Perspective on Global
        Economics.* Scottdale, Pa.: Herald Press.
Kyrtatas, Dimitris J.
2002   "Modes and Relations of Production." In *Handbook of
        Early Christianity: Social Science Approaches.* Anthony J.
        Blasi, Jean Duhaime, and Paul-Andre Turcotte, eds. New
        York: Altamira Press.
Ladd, George E.
1974a   *A Theology of the New Testament.* Grand Rapids, Mich.:
        Eerdmans.
1974b   *The Presence of the Future.* Grand Rapids, Mich.:
        Eerdmans.
Lederach, John Paul
1999   *Journey Toward Reconciliation*: Scottdale, Pa.: Herald
        Press.
1997   *Building Peace: Sustainable Reconciliation in Divided
        Societies.* Washington D.C.: U.S. Institute of Peace Press.
1995   *Preparing for Peace: Conflict Transformation Across
        Cultures.* Syracuse, N.Y.: Syracuse University Press.
Lee, Bernard J.
1988   *The Galilean Jewishness of Jesus: Retrieving the Jewish
        Origins of Christianity.* New York: Paulist Press.
Lohse, Eduard
1976   *The New Testament Environment.* Nashville: Abingdon.
Longenecker, Richard N.
1984   *New Testament Social Ethics for Today.* Grand Rapids,
        Mich.: Eerdmans.
2000   Ed. *The Challenge of Jesus' Parables.* Grand Rapids, Mich.:
        Eerdmans.
Malina, Bruce J.
1996   *The Social World of Jesus and the Gospels.* London and New
        York: Routledge.
2001a   *The Social Gospel of Jesus: The Kingdom of God in
        Mediterranean Perspective.* Minneapolis: Fortress Press.
2001b   *The New Testament World: Insights from Cultural
        Anthropology.* 3rd edition. Louisville, Ky.:
        Westminster/John Knox Press.
Malina, Bruce J., and Richard L. Rohrbaugh
1992   *Social Science Commentary on the Synoptic Gospels.*
        Minneapolis: Fortress.
Marshall, Christopher D.
2001   *Beyond Retribution: A New Testament Vision for Justice,
        Crime, and Punishment.* Grand Rapids, Mich.: Eerdmans.

Martin, Ralph
1975   *New Testament Foundations*. Grand Rapids, Mich.:
        Eerdmans.
McClendon, James Wm., Jr.
1986   *Ethics: Systematic Theology*. Vol. 1. Nashville: Abingdon
        Press.
McVann, Mark
1991   "The Rituals of Status Transformation in Luke-Acts:
        The Case of Jesus the Prophet." In *The Social World of
        Luke-Acts: Models for Interpretation*. Jerome H. Neyrey,
        ed. Peabody, Mass.: Hendrickson Publishers, Inc.
Mealand, David L.
1981   *Poverty and Expectation in the Gospels*. Reprint. London:
        SPCK.
Meeks, Wayne A.
1983   *The First Urban Christians, The Social World of the Apostle
        Paul*. New Haven: Yale University Press.
1993   *The Origins of Christian Morality: The First Two Centuries*.
        New Haven: Yale University Press.
Meier, John P.
1991   *A Marginal Jew: Rethinking the Historical Jesus*. Vol. One.
        The Roots of the Problem and the Person. New York:
        Doubleday.
1994   *A Marginal Jew: Rethinking the Historical Jesus*. Vol. Two.
        Mentor, Message, and Miracles. New York: Doubleday.
Metzger, Bruce
1965   *The New Testament: Its Background, Growth, and Content*.
        Nashville: Abingdon.
Minear, Paul S.
1976   *To Heal and to Reveal*. New York: Seabury Press.
Moxnes, Halvor
1988   *The Economy of the Kingdom: Social Conflict and Economic
        Relations in Luke's Gospel*. Philadelphia: Fortress.
Myers, Ched
1988   *Binding the Strong Man: A Political Reading of Mark's
        Story of Jesus*. Maryknoll, N.Y.: Orbis Books.
2002   "Mark's Gospel: Invitation to Discipleship. In *The New
        Testament: Introducing the Way of Discipleship*. Wes
        Howard-Brook and Sharon Ringe, eds. Maryknoll, N.Y.:
        Orbis Books.
Myers, David G.
2000   *The American Paradox: Spiritual Hunger in an Age of
        Plenty*. New Haven and London: Yale University Press.

Neusner, Jacob
    1973   *From Politics to Piety: The Emergence of Pharisaic Judaism.*
            Englewood Cliffs, N.J.: Prentice Hall.
    1975   *First Century Judaism in Crisis.* Nashville: Abingdon.
    1979   *The Way of Torah: An Introduction to Judaism.* North
            Scituate, Mass.: Duxbury Press.

Neyrey, Jerome H.
    1991a   Ed. *The Social World of Luke-Acts: Models for
            Interpretation.* Peabody, Mass.: Hendrickson Publishers,
            Inc.
    1991b   "The Symbolic Universe of Luke-Acts: 'They Turn the
            World Upside Down.'" In *The Social World of Luke-Acts:
            Models for Interpretation.* Jerome H. Neyrey, ed. Peabody,
            Mass.: Hendrickson Publishers, Inc.
    1991c   "Ceremonies in Luke Acts: 'The Case of Meals and
            Table-Fellowship.'" In *The Social World of Luke-Acts:
            Models for Interpretation.* Jerome H. Neyrey, ed. Peabody,
            Mass.: Hendrickson Publishers, Inc.

North, Robert
    1954   *Sociology of the Biblical Jubilee.* Rome: Pontifico Instituto
            Biblico.

Oakman, Douglas E.
    1986   *Jesus and the Economic Questions of His Day.* New York:
            Edwin Mellen Press.
    1991   "The Countryside in Luke-Acts." In *The Social World of
            Luke-Acts: Models for Interpretation.* Jerome H. Neyrey,
            ed.. Peabody, Mass.: Hendrickson Publishers.

Pannenberg, Wolfhart
    1969   *Theology and the Kingdom of God.* Philadelphia:
            Westminster.

Perkins, Pheme
    1981   *Hearing the Parables of Jesus.* New York: Paulist Press.

Perrin, Norman
    1963   *The Kingdom of God in the Teaching of Jesus.* Philadelphia:
            Westminster.
    1976   *Jesus and the Language of the Kingdom.* Philadelphia:
            Fortress.

Pilgrim, Walter E.
    1981   *Good News to the Poor: Wealth and Poverty in Luke-Acts.*
            Minneapolis: Augsburg Publishing House.

Praeder, Susan Marie
    1988   *The Word in Women's Worlds: Four Parables.* Wilmington,
            Del.: Michael Glazier, Inc.

Redekop, Benjamin, and Calvin Redekop
  2001 *Power, Authority, and the Anabaptist Tradition.* Baltimore:
      The Johns Hopkins University Press.
Redekop, Calvin
  1976 "Institutions, Power, and the Gospel." In *Kingdom, Cross,*
      and Community. Calvin Redekop and J. Richard
      Burkholder, eds. Scottdale, Pa.: Herald Press.
Riches, John
  1982 *Jesus and the Transformation of Judaism.* New York:
      Seabury Press.
Richardson, Peter, and Douglas Edwards
  2002 "Jesus and Palestinian Social Protest: Archaeological and
      Literary Perspectives." In *Handbook of Early Christianity:*
      Social Science Approaches. Anthony J. Blasi, Jean Duhaime,
      and Paul-Andre Turcotte, eds. New York: Altamira Press.
Ringe, Sharon H.
  1985 *Jesus, Liberation, and the Biblical Jubilee: Images for Ethics*
      and Christology. Philadelphia: Fortress.
  1995 *Luke.* Louisville, Ky.: Westminster/John Knox Press.
  2002 "Luke's Gospel: Good News for the Poor and for the
      Non-Poor." In *The New Testament: Introducing the Way of*
      Discipleship. Wes Howard-Brook and Sharon Ringe, eds.
      Maryknoll, N.Y.: Orbis Books.
Roth, John D.
  2002 *Choosing Against War: A Christian View.* Intercourse, Pa.:
      Good Books.
Ruether, Rosemary Radford
  1981 *To Change the World: Christology and Cultural Criticism.*
      New York: Crossroad.
Saldarini, Anthony J.
  1988 *Pharisees, Scribes, and Sadducees in Palestinian Society: A*
      Sociological Approach. Wilmington, Del.: Michael Glazier,
      Inc.
Sanders, E. P.
  1985 *Jesus and Judaism.* Philadelphia: Fortress.
  1995 *The Historical Figure of Jesus.* New York: Penguin Books.
Sanders, Jack T.
  1975 *Ethics in the New Testament.* Philadelphia: Fortress.
Schlabach, Theron, and Richard Hughes
  1997 Eds. *Proclaim Peace: Christian Pacifism from Unexpected*
      Quarters. Chicago: University of Illinois Press.
Schottroff, Willy, and Wolfgang Stegemann
  1984 Eds. *God of the Lowly: Socio-Historical Interpretations of the*

Bible. Trans. Matthew J. O'Connell. Maryknoll, N.Y.: Orbis Books.

Schriven, Charles
1988   *The Transformation of Culture: Christian Social Ethics After H. Richard Niebuhr*. Scottdale, Pa.: Herald Press.

Schwager, Raymund
1987   *Must There Be Scapegoats? Violence and Redemption in the Bible*. Trans. Maria L. Assad. San Francisco: Harper & Row.

Schweitzer, Albert
1922   *The Quest of the Historical Jesus*. New York: Macmillan.

Scott, Bernard Brandon
1989   *Hear Then the Parable*. Minneapolis: Fortress Press.

Sharp, Gene
1973   *The Politics of Nonviolent Action*. Boston: Porter Sargent Publishers.
1997   *Nonviolent Action: A Research Guide:* New York: Garland Publishers.

Sheehan, Thomas
1986   *The First Coming: How the Kingdom of God Became Christianity*. New York: Random House.

Siddons, Philip
1980   *Speaking Out for Women: A Biblical View*. Valley Forge, Pa.: Judson Press.

Sider, Ronald J.
1996   *Living Like Jesus: Eleven Essentials for Growing a Genuine Faith*. Grand Rapids, Mich.: Baker Books.
1997   *Rich Christians in an Age of Hunger*. Rev. ed. Downers Grove, Ill.: InterVarsity Press.
1999   *Just Generosity: A New Vision for Overcoming Poverty in America*. Grand Rapids, Mich.: Baker Books.
2002   *Churches That Make a Difference*. Grand Rapids, Mich.: Baker Book House.

Sloan, Robert B., Jr.
1977   *The Favorable Year of the Lord: A Study of Jubilary Theology in the Gospel of Luke*. Ph.D. diss. Austin, Tex.: Schola Press.

Stambaugh, John E., and David L. Balch
1986   *The New Testament in Its Social Environment*. Philadelphia: Westminster.

Stassen, Glen H.
1992   *Just Peacemaking: Transforming Initiatives for Justice and Peace*. Louisville, Ky.: Westminister/John Knox Press.

Strack, Hermann L.
    1969   *Introduction to the Talmud and Mishnah*. New York:
            Atheneum.
Strang, Heather, and John Braithwaite
    2001   Eds. *Restorative Justice and Civil Society*. Cambridge:
            Cambridge University Press.
Strobel, August
    1972   *Jesus in Nazareth*. Berlin: Walter de Gruyter.
Swartley, Willard M.
    1973   "A Study in Markan Structure: The Influence of Israel's
            Holy History Upon the Structure of the Gospel of
            Mark." Ph.D. diss., Princeton Theological Seminary.
    1981   *Mark: The Way for All Nations*. Scottdale, Pa.: Herald
            Press.
    1983   *Slavery, Sabbath, War, and Women: Case Issues in Biblical
            Interpretation*. Scottdale, Pa.: Herald Press.
    1992   Ed. *The Love of Enemies and Nonretaliation in The New
            Testament*. Louisville, Ky.: Westminster/John Knox Press.
    2000   Ed. *Violence Renounced: René Girard, Biblical Studies, and
            Peacemaking*. Telford, Pa.: Pandora Press U.S.
Swartz, David
    1997   *Culture and Power: The Sociology of Pierre Bourdieu*.
            Chicago: University of Chicago Press.
Tannehill, Robert C.
    1972   "The Mission of Jesus According to Luke." In *Jesus of
            Nazareth*, Ed. Walther Eltester. Berlin: Walter de Gruyter.
Theissen, Gerd
    1978   *Sociology of Early Palestinian Christianity*. Trans. John
            Bowden. Philadelphia: Fortress.
Tidball, Derek
    1984   *The Social Context of the New Testament: A Sociological
            Analysis*. Grand Rapids, Mich.: Zondervan.
Trocme, Andre,
    1973   *Jesus and the Nonviolent Revolution*. Scottdale, Pa.: Herald
            Press.
    2002   *Jesus and the Nonviolent Revolution,* revised and updated.
            Farmington, Pa.: Plough Pubishing House.
Vaux, Roland de
    1965   *Ancient Israel: Social Institutions*. Vol. 1. New York:
            McGraw Hill.
Verhey, Allen
    1984   *The Grand Reversal: Ethics and the New Testament*. Grand
            Rapids, Mich.: Eerdmans.

Vermes, Geza
  1973   *Jesus the Jew: A Historian's Reading of the Gospels*. London: Collins.
  2001   *The Changing Faces of Jesus*. New York: Viking Compass.
Wackernagel, Mathis and William Rees
  1996   *Our Ecological Footprint: Reducing Human Impact on the Earth*. Stony Creek, Conn.: New Society Publishers.
Wahlberg, Rachel Conrad
  1975   *Jesus According to a Woman*. New York: Paulist Press.
Weaver, J. Denny
  2001   *The Nonviolent Atonement*. Grand Rapids, Mich.: Eerdmans.
Wierzbicka, Anna
  2001   *What Did Jesus Mean?: Explaining the Sermon on the Mount and the Parables in Simple and Universal Human Concepts*. New York: Oxford University Press.
Williams, James G.
  1996   Ed. *The Girard Reader.* New York: Crossroad Publishing Co.
Wink, Walter
  1986   *Unmasking the Powers: The Invisible Forces That Determine Human Existence*. Philadelphia: Fortress.
  1992   *Engaging the Powers: Discernment and Resistance in a World of Domination*. Minneapolis: Fortress Press.
  1998   *The Powers That Be: Theology for a New Millenium*. New York: Galilee Doubleday.
Wright, N.T.
  1992   *The New Testament and the People of God*. Philadelphia: Fortress Press.
  1996   *Jesus and the Victory of God*. Minneapolis: Fortress Press.
  1999   *The Challenge of Jesus: Rediscovering Who Jesus Was*. Downers Grove, Ill.: InterVarsity Press.
Yancey, Philip
  1995   *The Jesus I Never Knew*. Grand Rapids, Mich.: Zondervan Publishing House.
Yoder, John Howard
  1971   *The Original Revolution*. Scottdale, Pa.: Herald Press.
  1983   *What Would You Do?* Scottdale, Pa.: Herald Press.
  1984   *The Priestly Kingdom: Social Ethics as Gospel*. Notre Dame, Ind.: University of Notre Dame.
  1992   *Body Politics: Five Practices of the Christian Community Before the Watching World*. Nashville: Discipleship Resources.

1994   *The Politics of Jesus*. 2d ed. (First edition 1972), Grand Rapids, Mich.: Eerdmans.

1997   *For the Nations: Essays Public and Evangelical*. Grand Rapids, Mich.: Eerdmans.

Yoder, Perry B.

1987   *Shalom: The Bible's Word for Salvation, Justice, and Peace*. Newton, Kan.: Faith & Life Press.

Yoder, Perry B., and Willard Swartley

1992   *The Meaning of Peace: Biblical Studies*. Louisville, Ky.: Westminster/John Knox.

Young, Brad

1989   *Jesus and His Jewish Parables: Rediscovering the Roots of Jesus' Teaching*. New York: Paulist Press.

Zehr, Howard

1990   *Changing Lenses: A New Focus for Crime and Justice*. Scottdale, Pa.: Herald Press.

2003   *The Little Book of Restorative Justice*. Intercourse, Pa.: Good Books.

Zin, Howard

2002   *The Power of Nonviolence: Writings by Advocates of Peace*. Boston: Beacon Press.

Website Resources

The following organizations provide helpful information and resources for social justice, service, and peacemaking activities.

America's Second Harvest: Ending Hunger www.secondharvest.org

American Friends Service Committee 215-241-7000, www.afsc.org

Amnesty International 1-800-AMNESTY, www.amnestyusa.org

Bread for the World—Seeking Justice, Ending Hunger 1-800-82Bread, www.bread.org

Brethern Press www.brethrenpress.com

Cascadia Publishing House www.cascadiapublishinghouse.com

Christian Peacemaker Teams 773-277-0253, www.prairienet.org/cpt

Church of the Brethren www.brethren.org

Church World Service 212-870-2061, www.churchworldservice.org

Compassion International www.compassion.com

Eastern Mennonite University Conflict Transformation Program 1-800-710-7871, www.emu.edu/ctp

Educational Concerns for Hunger Organization 941-543-3246, www.echonet.org

Environmental Magazine www.emagazine.com

Freedom from Hunger 1-800-708-2555, www.freedomfromhunger.org

Friends of the Earth 877-843-8687, www.foe.org

Habitat for Humanity 1-800-422-4828, www.habitat.org

Herald Press www.heraldpress.com

Heifer Project International 1-800-422-0755, www.heifer.org

Hunger in America www.hungerinamerica.org

Hunger Site, The www.thehungersite.org

International Rescue Committee 1-877-Refuge, www.intrescom.org

Mennonite Central Committee 717-859-1151, www.mcc.org

Oxfam America www.oxfamamerica.org

Oxfam International www.oxfam.org

Pandora Press U.S. www.pandorapress.com

Project Care 1-800-422-7385, www.care.org

Sojourners Community of Faith, Culture and Politics www.sojo.net

U. N. International Children's Education Fund 1-800-For-kids,
www.unicefusa.org

UNICEF www.unicef.org

Witness for Peace www.witnessforpeace.org

World Bank Atlas www.worldbank.org/data/wdi2001/atlas.htm

World Economy Project www.villageorpillage.org/index.html

World Health Organization www.who.int/en

Worldwatch 202-452-1999, www.worldwatch.org

Index of Scripture Cited

General Index

The Author

Donald B. Kraybill holds a Ph.D. in sociology and serves in a joint appointment with Messiah College (Pa.) and Elizabethtown College (Pa.) where he is a Senior Fellow in the Young Center for Anabaptist and Pietist Studies. In addition to serving as a pastor, Kraybill has held a variety of leadership roles with Mennonite and Church of the Brethren organizations.

Widely recognized for his scholarship on Anabaptist communities, Kraybill is the author/editor of more than fifteen books on Anabaptist faith and life, including *The Riddle of Amish Culture* (Johns Hopkins University Press) and *Where Was God on September 11?* (Herald Press).

1153